Jan Kersting

Stability of cooperation in the international climate negotiations

An analysis using cooperative game theory

Stability of cooperation in the international climate negotiations

An analysis using cooperative game theory

by
Jan Kersting

KIT Scientific Publishing

Dissertation, Karlsruher Institut für Technologie
KIT-Fakultät für Wirtschaftswissenschaften

Tag der mündlichen Prüfung: 22. Juni 2017
Referenten: Prof. Dr. K.-M. Ehrhart, Prof. Dr. M. Uhrig-Homburg

Impressum

KIT Scientific Publishing

Karlsruher Institut für Technologie (KIT)
KIT Scientific Publishing
Straße am Forum 2
D-76131 Karlsruhe

KIT Scientific Publishing is a registered trademark
of Karlsruhe Institute of Technology.
Reprint using the book cover is not allowed.

www.ksp.kit.edu

Print on Demand 2017 – Gedruckt auf FSC-zertifiziertem Papier

ISBN 978-3-7315-0700-0
DOI 10.5445/KSP/1000072088

Stability of cooperation in the international climate negotiations

An analysis using cooperative game theory

Zur Erlangung des akademischen Grades eines
Doktors der Wirtschaftswissenschaften

(Dr. rer. pol.)

von der Fakultät für Wirtschaftswissenschaften
des Karlsruher Instituts für Technologie (KIT)

genehmigte
Dissertation
von

Jan Kersting, M.Sc. Wirt.-Math.

Tag der mündlichen Prüfung:	22. Juni 2017
Referent:	Prof. Dr. K.-M. Ehrhart
Korreferentin:	Prof. Dr. M. Uhrig-Homburg

Abstract

Global greenhouse gas emissions need to be substantially reduced to avoid dangerous climate change. As emission reductions in one country also benefit all other countries, international cooperation is needed for effective emission mitigation. It is not immediately clear if stable global climate cooperation is achievable, as each country has the right to reject an agreement.

Game theory is a commonly used tool for a formal analysis of this situation. The concept of core stability nicely reproduces the requirement of consensus for decisions in the international climate negotiations and has been applied in some theoretical and numerical analyses in the literature. However, these analyses miss several important real-world properties.

This thesis introduces five such properties into the model of international climate cooperation based on core stability: international economic effects, different pathways of future technological development, the influence of technological uncertainty on decision making, the influence of uncertainty about climate damages on decision making, and cooperation in non-global groups. To study the impact of the first two properties, a numerical model of emission levels and utility of each country for each possible coalition of countries is constructed. The influence of uncertainty is examined with a theoretical model, applying several concepts from the game-theoretical literature. Finally, a theoretical analysis is performed to determine the stability of cooperation in non-global groups, with a numerical application to the Group of Twenty.

The analyses show that the introduction of real-world properties into the core stability model substantially changes the results, compared to the original model. Global climate cooperation is found to be unstable in certain scenarios after the introduction of international economic effects, mainly caused by fossil-fuel market effects. Further, uncertainty about the future development of low-carbon technologies and of climate damages can present an obstacle to stable global cooperation, if risk preferences between countries vary substantially. Non-global groups also do not necessarily offer a way to stable cooperation, as outsiders exploit cooperation in the group.

This thesis is based on four papers prepared at the Fraunhofer Institute for Systems and Innovation Research (ISI) in Karlsruhe under the supervision of Professor K.-M. Ehrhart at the Karlsruhe Institute of Technology (KIT) and is written in English.

Kurzfassung

Der globale Ausstoß von Treibhausgasen muss substanziell reduziert werden, um schädlichen Klimawandel zu verhindern. Effektive Emissionsminderung benötigt internationale Kooperation, da sich Emissionsreduktionen eines Landes global auswirken. Die Erreichbarkeit stabiler globaler Klimakooperation ist ungewiss, da ein Abkommen durch jedes Land abgelehnt werden kann.

Die Anwendung von Spieltheorie erlaubt eine formale Analyse dieser Situation. Das Konzept der Kernstabilität reproduziert zentrale Eigenschaften der internationalen Klimaverhandlungen und wurde bereits in einigen theoretischen und numerischen Analysen verwendet. Dabei wurden allerdings einige wichtige Eigenschaften der realen Klimaverhandlungen nicht berücksichtigt.

Diese Dissertation integriert fünf dieser Eigenschaften in das Modell der internationalen Klimaverhandlungen basierend auf Kernstabilität: internationale ökonomische Effekte, unterschiedliche Pfade der zukünftigen technologischen Entwicklung, den Einfluss von technologischer Unsicherheit auf Entscheidungen, den Einfluss von Unsicherheit über den Klimawandel auf Entscheidungen und Kooperation in nicht-globalen Gruppen. Für die Analyse der ersten beiden Eigenschaften wird ein numerisches Modell von Emissionen und Nutzen jedes Landes für jede mögliche Koalition von Ländern erstellt. Der Einfluss von Unsicherheit wird mit einem theoretischen Modell untersucht, welches mehrere Konzepte der spieltheoretischen Literatur anwendet. Schließlich wird eine theoretische

Analyse der Stabilität von Kooperation in nicht-globalen Gruppen durchgeführt, welche am Beispiel der Gruppe der zwanzig wichtigsten Industrie- und Schwellenländer (G20) quantifiziert wird.

Die Analysen zeigen, dass die Integration von weiteren Eigenschaften der realen Klimaverhandlungen in das Modell der Kernstabilität substanziellen Einfluss auf die Ergebnisse hat. Globale Klimakooperation ist nicht stabil in bestimmten Szenarien unter Berücksichtigung internationaler ökonomischer Effekte. Unsicherheit über die zukünftige Entwicklung von klimafreundlichen Technologien und des Klimawandels kann ebenfalls ein Hindernis für stabile globale Kooperation darstellen, falls sich die Risikopräferenzen verschiedener Länder substanziell unterscheiden. Weiterhin bieten nicht-globale Gruppen nicht zwangsläufig einen Weg zu stabiler Kooperation, da Kooperation in der Gruppe durch Außenstehende ausgenutzt wird.

Diese Dissertation basiert auf vier Papieren, welche am Fraunhofer-Institut für System- und Innovationsforschung (ISI) in Karlsruhe unter der Betreuung von Professor K.-M. Ehrhart am Karlsruher Institut für Technologie (KIT) erstellt wurden. Sie ist in englischer Sprache verfasst.

Contents

List of Figures

List of Tables

List of Abbreviations

CO_2	Carbon Dioxide
°C	Degree Celsius
ANZ	Australia / New Zealand
AS	All Singletons
BAU	Business As Usual
BC	Best Coalition
CA	Copenhagen Accord
CCS	Carbon Capture and Storage
CGE	Computable General Equilibrium
CHN	China
CNRS	Centre National de la Recherche Scientifique
COP	Conference of the Parties
CT	Chander and Tulkens
CWS	ClimNeg World Simulation model
DART	Dynamic Applied Regional Trade model
EU	European Union
EUR	Europe
EXP	Fossil Fuel Exporters region
G20	Group of Twenty
GC	Global Cooperation
GDP	Gross Domestic Product

GHG	Greenhouse Gas
GTAP	Global Trade Analysis Project
IEA	International Energy Agency
IND	India
INDC	Intended Nationally Determined Contribution
IPCC	Intergovernmental Panel on Climate Change
JPN	Japan
JRC-IPTS	European Commission Joint Research Center - Institute for Prospective Technological Studies
KP	Kyoto Protocol
LMDC	Like-Minded Developing Country Group
mean	Mean technology scenario
MEF	Major Economies Forum On Energy And Climate
NAM	North America
NDC	Nationally Determined Contribution
NPV	Net Present Value
NTU-game	Cooperative Game with Nontransferable Utility
OECD	Organisation for Economic Cooperation and Development
opt	Optimistic technology scenario
PA	Paris Agreement
PANE	Partial Agreement Nash Equilibrium
pess	Pessimistic technology scenario
POLES	Prospective Outlook on Long-term Energy Systems model
PV	Photovoltaic
RCP	Representative Concentration Pathway
REDD	Reducing Emissions from Deforestation and Forest Degradation

RICE	Regional Integrated model of Climate and the Economy
ROW	Rest of the World
STACO	Stability of Coalitions model
t	Tonnes
tn	Trillion
TU-game	Cooperative Game with Transferable Utility
UN	United Nations
UNFCCC	United Nations Framework Convention on Climate Change
US	United States of America
Wh	Watt-hour
WIM	Warsaw International Mechanism on Loss and Damage
WITCH	World Induced Technical Change Hybrid model
WTO	World Trade Organization

List of Functions and Variables

α_i	Level of risk aversion of a country
γ_i	Mitigation cost of a country
$\tilde{\gamma}_W$	Mitigation cost of player W in the $\sim$ game in the proof of Proposition 6
δ	Balanced map
δ^{Singl}	Balanced map corresponding to *All Singletons* case
$\hat{\delta}$	Balanced map with weight shifted from singleton coalitions to joint coalition
θ	Amount of technological uncertainty
κ_i	Amount of uncertainty about climate damages of a country
$\tilde{\kappa}_W$	Amount of uncertainty of player W in the $\sim$ game in the proof of Proposition 6
λ_i	Inverse of mitigation cost of a country
μ	Mean of normal distribution
π_i	Damage cost of a country
π_S	Damage cost of a coalition
$\bar{\pi}_j(.)$	Boundary value of π_j for a (non-)empty core in the climate club game
$\bar{\pi}_j^{ul}$	Upper boundary value of π_j for a (non-)empty core in the climate club game
$\bar{\pi}_j^{ll}$	Lower boundary value of π_j for a (non-)empty core in the climate club game

$\hat{\pi}_i$	Country i's share of total damage cost of a climate club
$\tilde{\pi}$	Modified damage cost in Proposition 10
$\tilde{\pi}_W$	Damage cost of player W in the $\sim$ game in the proof of Proposition 6
σ^2	Variance of normal distribution
τ_i	Combination of damage cost and uncertainty from climate damages of a country, defined in (C.16)
$\chi(.)$	Reduction factor of global emissions under technological uncertainty, if a coalition has formed
$\psi(.)$	Reduction factor of global emissions under uncertainty about climate damages, if a coalition has formed
$a(.)$	Condition for non-emptiness of the core of the climate club game, see (6.4) and (6.18)
a_3, a_2, a_1	Constants of polynomial form of A
A	Numerator of fraction used in the proof of Proposition 3, defined in (C.8)
b_3, b_2, b_1	Constants of polynomial form of B
B	Denominator of fraction used in the proof of Proposition 3, defined in (C.8)
$ce_i(.)$	Certainty equivalent of a payoff for country i
$C_i(.)$	Consumption of a country
C_i^0	Baseline consumption of a country
C_S^0	Baseline consumption of a coalition
$\tilde{C}_W^0$	Baseline consumption of player W in the $\sim$ game in the proof of Proposition 6
d	Allocation of the expected value of a payoff for each country under expectation and risk allocation
$D_i(.)$	Damages of a country

$e(.)$	Excess of an allocation
$erf(.)$	Error function
E	Vector of emissions of all countries
E_i	Emissions of a country
$E_i(.)$	Emissions of a country, if a coalition has formed
E_S	Emissions of a coalition
E_i^0	Baseline emissions of a country
E_S^0	Baseline emissions of a coalition
$\tilde{E}_W^0$	Baseline emissions of player W in the $\sim$ game in the proof of Proposition 6
$F(.)$	Function used in the proof of Proposition 10
$F^{total}(.)$	Function used in the proof of Proposition 10
$g(.)$	Fraction used in the proof of Proposition 6, defined in (C.17)
h	Allocation shares of a payoff for each country under pure payoff allocation
i	Member country of a coalition
j	Outsider country of a coalition
m	Number of coalitions in a partition
n	Number of players (countries) of the cooperative game
N	Grand coalition of all players (countries) of the cooperative game
$\tilde{N}$	Set of players in the $\sim$ game in the proof of Proposition 6
P	Partition of the set of countries
$\mathscr{P}$	Set of parameter combinations that lead to a non-empty core in the climate club game
$\mathscr{P}_s$	Set of parameter combinations that fulfill the conditions for a non-empty core in the climate club game for coalitions with s members

$\tilde{\mathscr{P}}$	Set of parameter combinations that do not fulfill condition (6.16)
$q_{\alpha_i}(.)$	α_i-quantile of a random variable
r	Allocation shares of the risk of a payoff for each country under expectation and risk allocation
R	Set of countries outside of a climate club
s	Number of countries in a coalition
S	Coalition of countries
t	Number of countries in a climate club
T	Set of countries in a climate club
$u_i(.)$	Utility of a country
$U_i(.)$	Utility of a country as a stochastic variable
$v(.)$	Value of a coalition
$v^T(.)$	Value of a coalition in the subgame of a climate club
$V(.)$	Value of a coalition as a stochastic variable
W	New player replacing two singleton players in $\sim$ game in the proof of Proposition 6
x	Allocation of the value of a coalition
X	Variable used in the proof of Proposition 10
y	Symmetric allocation of a subgame
Y	Variable used in the proof of Proposition 10
$z(.)$	Probit function
$z_{max}(.)$	Maximum of probit function for all values of α of a coalition
$\tilde{z}_W$	Probit value of player W in the $\sim$ game in the proof of Proposition 6
Z	Variable used in the proof of Proposition 10

1 Introduction

The Earth's surface temperature has increased by almost 1°C above the pre-industrial level, due to the emission of greenhouse gases (GHGs), mainly carbon dioxide (CO_2) (Intergovernmental Panel on Climate Change (IPCC), 2013). If global GHG emissions continue to rise according to the historical precedent, surface temperature will increase by a further 2°C to 4°C by 2100. This climate change poses risks in several areas, including coastal protection, food security and human health (IPCC, 2014a). Even if the temperature increase is held to 2°C above the pre-industrial level, global economic losses from climate change will amount to 0.2%-2.0% of income, with losses "more likely than not to be greater, rather than smaller, than this range" (IPCC, 2014a).

In order to prevent the worst impacts of climate change, global GHG emissions need to be reduced. However, this is complicated by the fact that GHG emission reductions in one country are a *public good*, as other countries cannot be excluded from receiving the benefit of emission reductions (in the form of reduced climate change impacts). Consequently, the amount of emission reductions is less than the globally optimal level, because each country only accounts for the benefits occurring in its sovereign territory. This situation is sometimes referred to as the "tragedy of the commons" (Hardin, 1968). To solve this tragedy, countries can enter into international agreements, or treaties. As countries cannot be forced into an agreement, it has to be in the self-interest of all countries to participate in the agreement. Such an agreement is called *stable*.

All countries would prefer if other countries reduced their emissions, while not having to reduce emissions themselves. On the other hand, global cooperation leads to an optimal amount of emission reductions on a global level and therefore creates a net benefit, which can be distributed among countries. Consequently, it is not immediately clear whether a stable agreement is achievable. So far, international negotiations have had limited success at restricting global GHG emissions.

1.1 Background

1.1.1 International climate negotiations

For the particular problem of climate change, negotiations about an agreement on GHG emission reductions are held under the United Nations Framework Convention on Climate Change (UNFCCC). The UNFCCC was adopted at the Rio Earth Summit in 1992 and entered into force in 1994. Its objective is "to achieve [...] stabilization of greenhouse gas concentrations in the atmosphere at a level that would prevent dangerous anthropogenic interference with the climate system" (United Nations, 1992). Membership in the UNFCCC is almost universal, as 197 countries have ratified the Convention (UNFCCC, 2016c). To achieve its goal, the UNFCCC hosts annual Conferences of the Parties (COPs), at which countries negotiate and adopt climate agreements.

The first agreement adopted under the UNFCCC is the Kyoto Protocol (KP), which was negotiated at COP3 in 1997 (UNFCCC, 1998). It includes binding GHG emission targets for developed countries (so-called Annex I countries), but no such targets for developing countries. While the KP was initially signed by all major emitters, the United States (US) never ratified it and new president George W. Bush announced in 2001 that he opposed the KP, because large developing countries like China and India did not have to reduce their emissions under the KP (Dessai, 2001). The KP still entered into force without the US in 2005. However, the emission targets in the KP, running from 2008 to 2012, turned out to be rather unambitious, due to the global economic crisis of 2007, the issue of "hot air" emission reductions[1] in economies in transition (Morel and Shishlov, 2014) and the absence of the US.

The negotiation process for further emission reductions after the end of the KP period in 2012 was started in 2007, at COP13 on Bali. Under the *Bali Action Plan* (UNFCCC, 2007), a long-term solution was to be agreed at COP15 in 2009. However, COP15 in Copenhagen failed to reach a global agreement, despite the presence of over 100 heads of state and government. Instead, several countries made non-binding emission reduction pledges in the Copenhagen Accord (CA) (UNFCCC, 2009).

After the failure of Copenhagen, a new negotiation process was started at COP17 in Durban. This process aimed to develop an agreement "applicable to all Parties" by COP21, which was held in Paris in 2015 (UNFCCC, 2011). In the run-up to the Paris conference, countries were requested to submit "intended nationally determined contributions" (INDCs), outlining their national climate strategy. To date, submitted INDCs cover 190 countries[2] (UNFCCC, 2016a). At COP21, the Paris Agreement (PA) was adopted (UNFCCC, 2015a), under which the formal process of submission of "nationally determined contributions" (NDCs) will be repeated every five years. However, the PA does not include binding emission reduction targets beyond each country's NDC. The PA also includes a target to hold the temperature increase to "well below 2°C" and intends to "pursu[e] efforts to limit the temperature increase to 1.5°C" (UNFCCC, 2015a, Art. 2). Mitigation efforts outlined in the currently submitted INDCs are not in line with least-cost 2°C scenarios (UNFCCC, 2016b, Figure 2).

[1] "Hot Air" refers to emission targets set above the business-as-usual emission level. This created a surplus of emission credits in some countries.

[2] The European Union submitted a joint INDC for all its member states.

The rules of decision making under the UNFCCC are not clearly defined, as countries failed to agree on rules of procedure prior to the first COP. Since then, the UNFCCC operates under draft rules of procedure (UNFCCC, 1996). As these draft rules include varying proposals for voting rules, all decisions have to be made by "consensus". In practice, consensus has usually been interpreted as the absence of a stated objection, i.e. a unanimity requirement (Vihma, 2015). Some recent COP decisions have however been adopted despite opposition by a few countries, sparking protests and delays at subsequent meetings (King, 07/06/2013; Vihma, 2015).

1.1.2 Modeling of international climate cooperation

The question of whether international cooperation on climate change among rational countries is actually possible has attracted much attention in the economic literature since the inception of the UNFCCC.
Game theory is a commonly used tool for a formal analysis of this situation. Each country is represented by a player in a game of international negotiation over emission levels. Players can cooperate with each other in a coalition, meaning that the wishes of all coalition members are taken into account when choosing emission levels. The analysis then centers on whether a coalition is *stable*, which is the case if no player has an incentive to change their behaviour. A particular case is the *grand coalition* of all players, whose stability is also described as the *stability of global cooperation*.
The analysis of the stability of a coalition requires assumptions about the behaviour and the decision making of players. Consequently, different stability concepts exist in the literature, which lead to vastly contrasting results[3]. The *core stability* concept replicates the requirement of consensus in the UNFCCC negotiations and focuses on the distribution of the benefit created by global cooperation. It predicts stable global cooperation (Chander and

[3] A more detailed discussion of the different models, stability concepts and the relevant literature is provided in Chapter 2.

Tulkens, 1995, 1997; Helm, 2001). *Internal and external stability* considers the incentives of individual countries to join or exit different coalitions. Under this concept, only coalitions with very few members can be stable (Carraro and Siniscalco, 1993; Barrett, 1994; Diamantoudi and Sartzetakis, 2006). *Farsighted stability* builds on internal and external stability by allowing individual countries to consider a sequence of coalition membership changes, instead of only one change. Global cooperation under this concept can be stable or unstable, depending on the specific model setup (Ray and Vohra, 2001; de Zeeuw, 2008).

Most of the literature on international climate cooperation is based on internal and external stability, while some studies also apply farsighted stability. Core stability, on the other hand, has only been utilized in very few studies beyond the initial analysis by Chander and Tulkens (1995, 1997) and its numerical applications.

1.2 Objective

The lack of development of core stability is surprising, given that the concept highlights two important features of the international climate negotiations, which are either ignored or reduced to minor points of interest in the other two stability concepts. First, core stability is based on a global unanimity requirement for stable climate agreements, in line with the consensus rule of the UNFCCC negotiations. Second, core stability focuses on the distribution of emission reduction cost and benefit between countries in a global agreement, a major point of friction in the international negotiations. Therefore, core stability nicely complements the focus on individual country incentives of the other two stability concepts. Further, an analysis of a particular issue with different concepts allows one to distill robust effects from model-specific effects, making core stability analyses also relevant for scholars preferring another stability concept.

The main objective of this thesis is the advancement of the theoretical model of international climate cooperation using core stability. In its original form, the model is characterized by a high level of abstraction. Countries' incentives are described by simple functions, which miss several key factors influencing the international climate negotiations. However, so far no attempt has been made to include important real-world properties into the core stability model. A reason for this lack of development might be the high complexity of the model, both theoretically and numerically, due to the large number of possible coalitions. Nevertheless, several real-world properties could reasonably influence the stability of global climate cooperation, so their inclusion in the model might provide additional insight.

In this thesis, I extend the core stability analysis by introducing five real-world properties into the model of climate cooperation. For each property, it is determined whether the result of stable global cooperation from the original model still holds up. Further, it is checked whether key parameters, in particular the extent of mitigation cost and damage cost, influence stability of cooperation.

First, I include international economic effects, such as technological spillovers and changes in fossil fuel prices. This is realised via a generalization of the cost of emission reductions, which is assumed to depend purely on domestic emissions in the original model and therefore misses international effects.

Second, I investigate the impact of different pathways of future technological development. In the original model, the cost of mitigation measures is fixed, masking large uncertainties in the future development of key low-carbon technologies.

Third, I integrate uncertainty about future technology development in the decision making process of countries. Depending on the risk preference, this inclusion can lead to higher or lower emission levels and influence the stability of cooperation. However, the original model only allows for decisions under certainty.

Fourth, I also include uncertainties about the extent of future damages from climate change. Similar to technological uncertainty, the original model does not allow countries to incorporate this lack of knowledge in their decision making.
Fifth, I modify the original model to study the stability of cooperation in non-global groups. The slow progress of negotiations under the UNFCCC has inspired the idea of negotiations in other fora, so-called *climate clubs*. Frequently mentioned as potential climate clubs are the Group of Twenty (G20) and the Major Economies Forum On Energy And Climate (MEF) (Hjerpe and Nasiritousi, 2015). The decision making in such groups is similar to the UNFCCC, as decisions are made by consensus of all members. Therefore, the core stability concept is a natural candidate for the analysis of stability of climate cooperation in such clubs. However, the model of core stability has so far only been used to study global cooperation.

1.3 Approach

Chapter 2 starts by giving an overview of the original model of core stability and of other stability concepts. The chapter further discusses the literature for all concepts and compares assumptions and results.
For the inclusion of international economic effects in Chapter 3, the consumption function in the original model of core stability is extended to incorporate consequences of emission mitigation in multiple countries. To assess the effects on stability of global cooperation, a numerical model of the extended setup is implemented, which allows for the calculation of the emission level and utility of each country for each possible coalition of countries. The model is applied using consumption functions from a computable general equilibrium (CGE) model and damage functions from the literature. The calculation is performed for three scenarios, depicting a range of possible damages from climate change. The chapter also discusses policy implications of the results.

In Chapter 4, the numerical model is used to determine the influence of future pathways for key low-carbon technologies, namely wind energy, solar photovoltaic, and carbon capture and storage. To this end, the model is applied to two additional sets of consumption functions from the CGE model, representing an optimistic and a pessimistic outlook on the development of these technologies. In addition, the incentives of key countries are analysed using detailed economic outputs from the CGE model. The additional consumption functions are again combined with three scenarios for climate damages, resulting in a total of nine specifications.

Chapter 5 considers the effect of uncertainty on the decision making of countries, and the subsequent impact on the stability of climate cooperation. The analysis in this chapter is based on the original theoretical setup without international economic effects, so as to avoid overlapping effects. The setup is extended, using concepts from the game-theoretical literature, to include uncertain utility and payoffs, as well as individual risk preferences for each country. This basic model is applied to both technological uncertainty and uncertainty in climate damages, as well as to two different concepts of an uncertain allocation present in the game-theoretical literature. For each specification, either an example of a game in which global cooperation is unstable is presented, or it is shown that global cooperation is stable for all parameters.

Finally, in Chapter 6 the original model of global cooperation is adapted to study the stability of cooperation in climate clubs. First, it is assumed that countries in a club are symmetric and the influence of key parameters on stability is analysed. Afterwards, the assumption of symmetry is dropped and the impact of heterogeneity is studied. Further, mitigation cost and climate damage parameters are estimated for the case of the G20, allowing for an assessment of its potential as a climate club.

Each chapter also provides a short literature overview on the corresponding topic and compares the results with relevant analyses from other stability concepts. The thesis concludes in Chapter 7, which also provides overarching conclusions and implications drawn from the results of the analyses, as well as a critical reflection of the applied methods and an outlook for further research.

Chapters 3 to 6 are based on four papers, which have been slightly edited for consistency and coherence in this thesis. Table 1.1 shows the authors, title and reference for each paper.

Chapter	Authors	Title	Reference
3	Jan Kersting, Vicki Duscha, Matthias Weitzel	Cooperation on climate change under economic linkages - How the inclusion of macro-economic effects affects stability of a global climate coalition	Kersting et al. (2017)
4	Vicki Duscha, Jan Kersting, Sonja Peterson, Joachim Schleich, Matthias Weitzel	Technological development of low-carbon power technology and the stability of international climate cooperation	Duscha et al. (2016)
5	Jan Kersting	Stability of global climate cooperation under uncertainty	Kersting (Forthcoming)
6	Jan Kersting	Cooperation of climate clubs	Kersting (2015)

Table 1.1: Overview of the papers prepared for this thesis.

2 Models of international climate cooperation

This chapter first describes the game-theoretical model of international climate negotiations based on core stability by Chander and Tulkens (1995, 1997), hereafter CT model. The model provides the basis for the analyses in this thesis. As the model is rooted in cooperative game theory, a brief introduction into the topic and its relevant concepts is given, followed by the specific setup of the CT model. Further, this chapter describes other stability concepts present in the literature and their results. Finally, the different concepts are compared and their applicability to the UNFCCC negotiations is discussed.

2.1 Cooperative game theory and the core

Peleg and Sudhölter (2007) provide the following definitions. Let $N = \{1,..,n\}$ be the set of players. Then a *cooperative game with transferable utility*, or TU-game, is described by the *value function* $v : \mathbb{R}^{2^n} \to \mathbb{R}$. We say that $v(S)$ gives the *value* for each possible *coalition* $S \subset N$ of players. As a normalization, $v(\emptyset) = 0$ for all cooperative games.

Then, the question for each cooperative game is how to divide the value of the grand coalition, $v(N)$. An *allocation* of the value of a coalition S is a vector $x \in \mathbb{R}^{|S|}$ with

$$\sum_{i \in S} x_i \leq v(S). \tag{2.1}$$

An allocation can be interpreted as a proposed agreement among S. For the grand coalition N, an allocation of its value is also called a *payoff vector*. This assumes that the value of the grand coalition can be freely distributed between the players, as indicated by the *transferable utility* label of the TU-game.

A *solution* of a cooperative game is a function assigning a set of allocations to each game. Different solution concepts exist. The focus in this thesis is on the concept of the *core*. An allocation lies in the core if the value of no coalition S is higher than its total allocated amount:

$$\sum_{i \in S} x_i \geq v(S) \; \forall S \subsetneq N \tag{2.2}$$

The condition ensures that no coalition has an incentive to deviate from the proposed agreement. The core fulfills several desirable properties for solution concepts, such as Pareto optimality and individual rationality (Peleg and Sudhölter, 2007, Chapter 2.3). Non-emptiness of the core can be checked by comparing the value of the grand coalition to the joint value of all partitions of N, where a partition of N is a set of pairwise disjoint coalitions containing all members of N. This idea is formalized and generalized in the Bondareva-Shapley Theorem:

Theorem 1 (Bondareva 1962; Shapley 1967)**.** *The core of a cooperative game is not empty if and only if*

$$v(N) \geq \sum_{S \subset N} \delta_S v(S) \tag{2.3}$$

for all balanced maps δ satisfying

$$\sum_{S \subset N} \delta_S \mathbb{1}_{i \in S} = 1 \; \forall i \in N. \tag{2.4}$$

For the purposes of this thesis, an allocation is called *stable* if it lies in the core. I also say that stable global cooperation is possible, if the core of the corresponding game is non-empty. Note that the core only assesses stability of cooperation among all players, not among certain sub-coalitions.
Other well-known solution concepts for TU-games are the ε-core, the kernel, the nucleolus and the Shapley value. As they have no further relevance for this thesis, the reader is referred to Peleg and Sudhölter (2007) and Rogna (2016) for a detailed discussion of these concepts.
Further, the transferability of utility in cooperation games may also be restricted. Such games are called *cooperative games with nontransferable utility*, or NTU-games. Many solution concepts, like the core or the Shapley value, have been adapted to NTU-games (see Peleg and Sudhölter, 2007, for details). As this thesis only considers TU-games, the upcoming chapters will refer generally to *cooperative games* when analysing TU-games.

2.2 The game of international climate cooperation

In the CT model each country is represented by one player. Let $N = \{1,..,n\}$ be the set of countries. The model then consists of the following components for all countries $i \in N$:

- emissions $E_i \in \mathbb{R}$.
- consumption function $C_i(E_i) : \mathbb{R} \to \mathbb{R}$, depending on a country's own emissions. It is assumed to be monotonically increasing up to a baseline emission level E_i^0, differentiable and concave.
- damage function $D_i(E_N) : \mathbb{R} \to \mathbb{R}$, depending on global emissions $E_N = \sum_{i \in N} E_i$. It describes the damages incurred by environmental pollution, climate change in this case. The function is assumed to be monotonically increasing, differentiable and convex.

Each country's utility is determined by the difference of consumption and damages,

$$u_i(E_i, E_N) = C_i(E_i) - D_i(E_N). \tag{2.5}$$

Therefore, utility depends on the emissions of all other players, through the damage function. In order to determine the value function v of the game, assume that a coalition $S \subseteq N$ forms. Members of the coalition maximize the joint utility of all coalition members. As utility also depends on the emissions of non-members, so-called *outsiders*, an assumption about their behaviour is needed. This assumption is the essential difference between different stability concepts. In the CT model, using core stability, it is assumed that outsiders split up into singletons and maximize individual utility. This so-called γ-assumption was first devised by Hart and Kurz (1983) for a general coalition formation game. It leads to the following parallel optimization problems:

$$\max_{(E_i)_{i \in S}} \sum_{i \in S} [C_i(E_i) - D_i(E_N)] \tag{2.6a}$$

$$\max_{E_j} C_j(E_j) - D_j(E_N) \;\; \forall j \notin S \tag{2.6b}$$

The resulting emission levels are sometimes referred to as a Partial Agreement Nash Equilibrium (PANE). Denote by $E_i(S)$ and $E_j(S)$ the PANE emission levels of coalition members and outsiders, assuming coalition S has formed. Assigning the result of (2.6a) to $v(S)$ defines the value function of the cooperative game, allowing for the calculation of the core. Helm (2001) showed that the core of the game is not empty for all functions fulfilling the assumptions mentioned above[1].
This result is a direct consequence of the γ-assumption. When a coalition of countries decides on whether to deviate from the grand coalition, it takes into account the reaction of the other countries, namely the dissolution of

[1] Specifically, these are monotonicity, differentiability and convexity / concavity.

any cooperation. Consequently, potentially deviating countries would face higher emission levels, and the associated higher damages, if the deviation was carried out. Therefore, an agreement can be designed to make global cooperation stable.

It is important to note that the result of core non-emptiness also relies on the possibility of monetary transfers. As shown in Equations (2.6), emission levels of members of a coalition are determined to the benefit of all coalition members. This is the cost-effective solution for the whole coalition, but requires countries with low mitigation costs to emit less than would be individually rational. In a stable global agreement, such countries need to be compensated for their high mitigation efforts to incentivise them not to deviate from the grand coalition.

Germain et al. (2003) analyse core stability of the dynamic game, i.e. the game in which GHG emissions build up over several time steps and cooperation is negotiated for each period. They show that the result of core non-emptiness from the static game still holds, by providing a core-stable transfer scheme for each time period. This dynamic analysis forms the basis for the application of numerical models (Eyckmans and Tulkens, 2003; Bréchet et al., 2011; Dellink, 2011). The result of core non-emptiness is found to be robust to varying slopes of the damage functions and to an economic update of the numerical model (Bréchet et al., 2011). It also holds for a disaggregation into six world regions (Eyckmans and Tulkens, 2003; Bréchet et al., 2011, using the ClimNeg World Simulation (CWS) model) and 12 world regions (Dellink, 2011, using the Stability of Coalitions (STACO) model). All studies also confirm the crucial role of transfers, as the allocation based on globally cost-effective emission levels is not core-stable, but transfers can construct a core-stable agreement. This result has also inspired an extension of the core stability concept to a situation without transferable utility, but with transferability of some other good (Kornek et al., 2014).

Currarini and Marini (2003) modify the core stability concept by allowing for a "first-mover advantage" of a deviating coalition. In this setup, emission levels of different countries are no longer set simultaneously. Rather, the deviating coalition sets its emission level first and all outsiders determine their emission level afterwards, by optimizing individual utility. In this setup, the deviating coalition is also called the *Stackelberg leader*. The leader position allows the deviating coalition to choose a relatively high emission level. The outsider countries then react to the high global emission level and find it in their best interest to choose a relatively low emission level. Therefore, the first-mover advantage leads to a higher value for the deviating coalition. Currarini and Marini (2003) show that, depending on the parameters of the game, this can cause the core of the game to be empty.

2.3 Other stability concepts

2.3.1 Internal and external stability

The concept of *internal and external stability* is the most often used stability concept for the analysis of international climate cooperation. It was originally introduced by D'Aspremont et al. (1983), who used it to study the formation of a cartel of competing firms.

Assume that a coalition S has formed and a member $i \in S$ evaluates the possibility of leaving the coalition. This player then assumes that after its deviation, the rest of the coalition stays intact. Therefore, the player compares its utility as a member of S to its utility as an outsider to the coalition of the remaining members of S. If all members of S prefer to stay inside the coalition, it is called *internally stable*:

$$u_i(E_i(S), E_N(S)) \geq u_i(E_i(S\backslash\{i\}), E_N(S\backslash\{i\})) \;\; \forall i \in S. \tag{2.7}$$

The right hand side in Equation (2.7), i.e. the utility a player would receive outside of a coalition, is also called the *outside option*. In contrast to the core stability concept, internal and external stability evaluates not just the stability of the grand coalition, but of all possible coalitions. For non-global coalitions, stability also needs to be assessed against deviations by outsiders, who might be better off after joining the coalition. A coalition S is called *externally stable*, if no outsider has an incentive to join the coalition:

$$u_j(E_j(S), E_N(S)) \geq u_j(E_j(S \cup \{j\}), E_N(S \cup \{j\})) \;\; \forall j \notin S. \tag{2.8}$$

The conditions for internal and for external stability also show that the concept only considers deviations from individual players, not from larger sets of players, as was the case for core stability.
The main feature of the internal and external stability concept is the presence of *free-rider* incentives. A player deviating from a coalition assumes that the rest of the coalition stays intact. While this remaining coalition adjusts their mitigation efforts to reflect the deviation, the new mitigation effort is still larger than in the situation of all players acting as singletons. The additional mitigation effort benefits all players, including the deviating player. However, the deviating player scales down its own mitigation effort after the deviation, because it considers only its own utility. Consequently, the deviating player *free-rides* on the mitigation effort of the remaining coalition members.
The application of the internal and external stability concept to international environmental agreements shows that a stable agreement can either have many signatories with small mitigation effort, or few signatories with higher mitigation effort, depending on the ratio of mitigation costs and benefits (Carraro and Siniscalco, 1993; Barrett, 1994). This is a direct result from the presence of free-rider incentives, which are highest for a large coalition with high mitigation effort. Diamantoudi and Sartzetakis (2006) provide an analytical solution of the model and show that the "many signatories" case resulted from a situation where countries abate more than they emit. If a country's emissions are required to be non-negative, the number of signatories in a model with symmetric countries is 2, 3 or 4 (Diamantoudi and Sartzetakis, 2006).

In its original formulation, internal and external stability does not allow for transfers between coalition members. This was remedied by the concept of *potential internal stability* (Eyckmans and Finus, 2004; Carraro et al., 2006), which is given if the total utility of all coalition members is larger than the sum of the outside options of all members:

$$\sum_{i \in S} u_i(E_i(S), E_N(S)) \geq \sum_{i \in S} u_i(E_i(S \setminus \{i\}), E_N(S \setminus \{i\})). \tag{2.9}$$

Under potential internal stability, the set of stable coalitions is slightly extended and includes some medium-sized coalitions (Carraro et al., 2006; Bréchet et al., 2011; Bosetti et al., 2013). However, it does not influence the stability of the grand coalition, which remains unstable.
Several numerical models have been applied to the internal and external stability setup (Bosello et al., 2003; Finus et al., 2005; Nagashima et al., 2009; Bréchet et al., 2011; Dellink, 2011; Bosetti et al., 2013; Lessmann et al., 2015). All studies confirm the result that only small coalitions are internally and externally stable, while some larger coalitions can be potentially internally stable.
Dellink (2011) quantifies the size of the free-rider incentives. He finds that the grand coalition would be stable if all countries would accept a loss from cooperation of roughly 1% of GDP or larger. For the usual setup without an acceptable loss from cooperation, Dellink (2011) also studies the impact of several model parameters, including amount of climate damages, regional damage distribution, mitigation costs, time horizon and discount rate. He finds that the (lack of) stability of coalitions is quite robust to changes in all parameters. For one parameter, the discount rate, Bosetti et al. (2013) arrive at a different result. While they confirm that large coalitions are not stable under a low discount rate, they find the grand coalition to satisfy potential internal stability for a high discount rate. However, as a high discount rate also implies rather low mitigation effort, the gain from cooperation in the grand coalition is rather low. Lessmann et al. (2015) compare the exis-

tence of stable coalitions under five different numerical models. While the theoretical results are largely confirmed, the share of potentially internally stable coalitions varies between 11% and 97% of all possible coalitions for the different models. The differences are found to mainly result from varying assumptions about climate damages in different regions.

Modifications

The largely grim results of the internal and external stability concept have inspired various studies, which try to make larger coalitions stable by modifying or extending the basic model. For example, different shapes of the functions underlying the model have been analysed. Karp and Simon (2013) study the effect of the form of the mitigation cost function. First, they confirm the result of only small stable coalitions for convex marginal mitigation costs. However, they also find that, if marginal mitigation costs are locally concave, coalitions of all sizes may be stable, including the grand coalition. Finus and Rübbelke (2013) account for additional private benefits of mitigation measures, also called co-benefits. They find that, while these benefits increase mitigation efforts irrespective of cooperation status, they actually have a neutral or negative impact on the size of stable coalitions.
Several studies assert that countries outside of a coalition incur an additional cost, for example via trade penalties. Hoel and Schneider (1997) conclude that the grand coalition can be stable if this cost is high enough. Barrett (1997); Lessmann et al. (2009) and Nordhaus (2015) study the specific case of trade penalties against outsiders of an agreement and find that this can induce large stable coalitions. Helm and Schmidt (2015) combine this setup with endogenous investments in research on low-carbon technologies. They find that early investments make free-riding more attractive and that subsequent stable coalitions are therefore often inefficient. This conclusion is supported by Lessmann and Edenhofer (2011), who find that the combination of a climate agreement with an agreement on mitigation technology research

is less effective than a separate agreement on technology standards. Eichner and Pethig (2015) also include international trade in the model and restrict the policy instrument to emission taxes, not the usual emission caps. They find that under this combination the grand coalition can be stable, due to the presence of leakage effects under emission taxes. The presence of both international trade and emission taxes, as well as relatively low climate damages, are necessary conditions for this result.

Further, some aspects of the design of a potential international climate agreement have been analysed. Finus et al. (2005) study different membership rules and voting schemes of an agreement, using a numerical model. They find that exclusive membership, i.e. members of an agreement having to approve the accession of a new member, produces additional stable coalitions, compared to the usual setup of open membership. Further, unanimity voting on the accession of an outsider leads to more stable coalitions than majority voting. Altamirano-Cabrera et al. (2008) analyse an agreement of uniform mitigation quotas for all members, instead of the usual cost-effective distribution of mitigation effort. They find that this design supports larger stable coalitions than the cost-effective mitigation distribution, although the grand coalition remains unstable under all designs. Gerber and Wichardt (2009) and McEvoy (2013) study deposit-refund systems as a mechanism for enforcement of agreements. Under such a system, all participants of an agreement deposit an agreed amount of money to a neutral financial institution, which returns the funds upon compliance with the set emission target. This can lead to a stable grand coalition, if the deposit is high enough to encourage compliance. Asheim et al. (2006); Finus and Rundshagen (2009) and Hagen and Eisenack (2015) allow for multiple parallel agreements and find that this can improve the number of cooperating countries and total mitigation efforts. Dellink (2011) designates some countries as "essential players", without which no agreement is enacted by assumption. This moves the internal and external stability concept closer to core stability, where all countries are "es-

sential". Dellink (2011) shows that appropriately chosen essential players and transfers can make the grand coalition stable in this setup.
Finally, some studies considers a "threshold game", in which catastrophic climate damages occur abruptly at a certain level of emissions. Barrett (2013) finds that, in this situation, no country has an incentive to leave an agreement, if this would cause emissions to rise above the threshold and the triggered damages are high. Consequently, large stable coalitions are possible in this setup. Schmidt (2015) studies the threshold game in a dynamic setting. He finds that this setup allows for further gains from cooperation, as cooperating countries can allocate their mitigation effort more efficiently over time.
For a more detailed overview of the literature on internal and external stability, see Finus (2001, 2003); Barrett (2005) and Hovi et al. (2015).

2.3.2 Farsighted stability

The previous two stability concepts, core stability and internal and external stability, differ mainly in the assumption a potentially deviating player makes about the reaction by the other coalition members. While the internal and external stability concept assumes no change in coalition membership, the core stability concept assumes the abandonment of cooperation. The concept of farsightedness, introduced by Chwe (1994), proposes another assumption. Here, the potentially deviating player assumes that its deviation would trigger a sequence of moves by other players. If the new coalition created by the deviation is not stable, further members would leave this coalition, or new players would join. This process would continue until another stable coalition is reached, and the utility of the originally deviating player in this new coalition is his outside option. All players are assumed to be able to rationally predict the emerging stable coalition and their outside option.
The farsightedness concept also enables the presence of multiple competing coalitions. Therefore it defines stable coalition structures, not just coali-

tions. As a player considering a deviation compares the status quo to the end-result of the emerging sequence of moves by the other players, the stability of a coalition structure depends on the stability of other coalition structures. Chwe (1994) therefore considers the "largest consistent set" of stable coalition structures.

Ray and Vohra (2001) apply the concept to international environmental agreements. In a model of symmetric countries, they show that for certain numbers of players (n = 2, 3, 5, 8, 13, 20, ...) the grand coalition is a stable coalition structure. Diamantoudi and Sartzetakis (2002) extend the model by allowing groups of countries to leave or join an agreement, not just individual countries. They find that this stabilizes larger agreements. In particular, they show that the grand coalition is farsightedly stable, if coordinated moves by groups of countries are allowed.

Eyckmans (2001) and Osmani and Tol (2009) apply numerical models to the concept and thereby drop the assumption of symmetric countries. Eyckmans (2001) investigates the case of the Kyoto Protocol and finds that, under a specific transfer rule, only few countries would benefit from leaving the Protocol. Osmani and Tol (2009) calculate all farsightedly stable coalitions in model of 16 world regions and also find that these coalitions substantially improve global mitigation efforts and welfare, compared to the situation without any agreement.

de Zeeuw (2008) combines farsighted stability with a dynamic model in which countries choose their mitigation effort at several time steps. It might then take some time for other countries to detect low mitigation efforts by a deviating country. Under this modification, large stable coalitions in the one-step model are no longer stable if damage costs are too high. However, if damage costs are very low, compared to mitigation costs, large coalition can be sustained.

Finally, Benchekroun and Ray Chaudhuri (2014) use farsighted stability to study the effect of a sudden availability of cleaner technologies on the stability of an agreement. They find that a small change in the emission intensity of an economy can result in a discrete change of the largest stable coalition. Therefore, the availability of clean technologies may destabilize an otherwise stable agreement, leading to lower global mitigation effort and welfare.

Overall, all studies find that farsighted stability supports larger coalitions with higher total mitigation efforts and higher welfare, compared to stable coalitions in the internal and external stability sense. The outside option for a potentially deviating country is usually worse under farsighted stability than under internal and external stability, because a deviation by one country is met with further deviations by other countries, reducing total mitigation efforts and thereby reducing welfare for the initial deviator. Consequently, the free-rider incentive is reduced and a potential deviator might prefer to instead stay in the agreement, making the agreement stable.

2.4 Comparison of stability concepts

This section briefly compares the different stability concepts. I start with a short clarification. In the discussion on the merits of the different stability concepts, core stability is often referred to as the approach of cooperative game theory, while internal and external stability is referred to as the approach of non-cooperative game theory. This characterization is slightly misleading. For the analysis of the stability of the grand coalition, the game using internal and external stability can also be written as a cooperative game, by computing the outside option of the deviating countries, assuming the non-deviating countries remain in a coalition (Tulkens, 1998; Breton et al., 2006). A similar argument applies to farsighted stability, using the outside option ultimately resulting from the sequence of moves triggered by a deviation. In addition, it can be shown that, if an internally stable global agreement exists, it is also core-stable (Tulkens, 2014). A further reconciliation of the approaches is performed by Chander and Wooders (2010), who introduce the "γ-core of an extensive game", as is typically used in non-cooperative game theory.

Rather than the type of game theory, the key difference between the three concepts lies in the assumed reaction of countries facing a deviation from an agreement: no further change of cooperation (internal and external stability), breakup into singletons (core stability) or consideration of own deviation based on utility (farsighted stability). The core stability assumption has been criticised, see e.g. Finus (2001). In particular, Finus takes issue with the fact that core stability assumes a reaction of countries to a deviation, but remains a static concept, i.e. the game occurs in only one time step. However, the consideration of potential reactions is firmly in the tradition of the Nash Equilibrium, which results from all players looking for a *best reply*. Finus also points out that the threat of countries to breakup into singletons is not renegotiation-proof and therefore considers the assumption to be "not very plausible".

However, I argue that for the analysis of climate cooperation under the UNFCCC, core stability best reflects the negotiation and decision making process. As pointed out in Chapter 1, decisions under the UNFCCC require "consensus", meaning the support of all countries. Of the introduced stability concepts, this unanimity requirement is best represented by the core stability assumption.

From a theoretical point of view, the γ-assumption is further justified in Chander (2007), where it is shown that the assumption corresponds to the behaviour in an equilibrium of the infinitely repeated game of international pollution. Further, a similar assumption is also used in studies focused on the bargaining process of international climate negotiations (Harstad, 2012; Caparrós and Péreau, 2015).

Therefore, the core stability concept clearly merits more attention than it has received in the literature so far. Its focus on unanimity and the distribution of benefits of global cooperation is not found in internal and external stability or in farsighted stability. Thereby, studies using core stability can complement the analyses based on the other two stability concepts.

Consequently, core stability forms the basis for all analyses in this thesis. Some comparisons to results from the other stability concepts are incorporated where appropriate. It is also pointed out when selected questions should be further analysed with a different stability concept.

3 Cooperation on climate change under economic linkages - How the inclusion of macroeconomic effects affects stability of a global climate coalition

This chapter investigates the reliance of the high degree of cooperation under the core stability concept on the underlying assumptions of the consumption function. More specifically, we generalize the modeling of consumption losses to incorporate international consumption effects of emission reduction measures. Current models are based on the assumption that a country's consumption loss due to emission mitigation measures only depends on the country's domestic emissions. This approach neglects the fact that in a globalized world action in one country affects utility in other parts of the world. An example: the introduction of extensive energy efficiency measures in one country results in (i) a demand reduction for fossil fuels and (ii) cost reductions for the energy efficiency measures applied. Hence, other countries can be affected by changes in fossil fuel prices and technology cost changes. Further, competitiveness of firms is affected and hence changes in world trade arise.

The aspect of a less domestically oriented consumption function is particularly relevant in cases where global mitigation activities are high, because such action causes fundamental technological and economic change on a global level. We therefore argue that the approach of taking purely domestic consumption functions might be appropriate for the calculation of the non-cooperative equilibrium, when mitigation activities in all countries are rather small. When calculating the value of coalitions applying (ambitious) mitigation targets, however, those international macroeconomic effects should be taken into account – an extension of the purely domestically oriented consumption functions used by Chander and Tulkens (1995, 1997) and Helm (2001).

Therefore, we modify the CT model by changing the definition of the consumption function to include consequences of emission mitigation in multiple countries. In a second step, we apply the global computable general equilibrium (CGE) model DART to quantify the consumption functions for regions and countries. Bringing together these consumption functions with damage functions taken from the RICE model (Nordhaus, 2010) allows us to provide the value function of the game. Subsequently, we calculate the core and the best partition of the game to check the stability of the grand coalition. To our knowledge no attempt has been made so far to include the international macroeconomic effects mentioned above into analyses applying the core-stability concept. While, for example, the WITCH model (Bosetti et al., 2013) includes macroeconomic effects, it has only been applied using the internal and external stability concept. The previous numerical analyses applying core stability were based on models that did not include macroeconomic effects. Moreover, the incorporation of macroeconomic effects means that the utility functions may violate the assumptions used in the theoretical proof of a non-empty core in the CT model by Helm (2001). This chapter may therefore also be seen as an attempt at a counter-example to this result, if assumptions about the form and dependence of functions are further relaxed.

Section 3.1 describes in detail our modifications of the CT model and the numerical models used for our calculations. Section 3.2 presents the results of the simulations. Section 3.3 discusses policy implications of our results. Section 3.4 concludes and offers an outlook for future work.

3.1 The model

The analyses in this chapter are based on the CT model, which is extended to allow for international macroeconomic effects. These extensions are presented in Section 3.1.1. Our approach on the quantification of the value function used within the theoretical framework is presented in Section 3.1.2. Several steps are necessary to derive the value function, including the application of the global CGE model DART to calculate countries' consumption functions and of the RICE model (Nordhaus, 2010) to calculate global damages.

3.1.1 Game-theoretical model

We adapt the consumption function of the CT model to be able to include the international macroeconomic effects mentioned at the beginning of this chapter. In the extended CT model, the function no longer just depends on a player's own emissions, but rather on the vector of emissions of all players.

$$C_i = C_i(E), \quad E = (E_1, .., E_n) \tag{3.1}$$

This formulation ensures that emission mitigation measures by one or multiple players can influence consumption of third players. The interaction occurs if the third player reduces emissions itself, as well as if it does not. The optimization problems that determine the emission level of each player are adjusted accordingly.

$$\max_{(E_i)_{i \in S}} \sum_{i \in S} [C_i(E) - D_i(E_N)] \tag{3.2a}$$

$$\max_{E_j} C_j(E) - D_j(E_N) \;\; \forall j \notin S \tag{3.2b}$$

In the formulation of the consumption function in the original CT model, the joint consumption function of a coalition was given by the sum of the

consumption functions of the single players (singleton coalitions). In the new modified model, there is no direct link between the consumption functions of singletons and the joint consumption functions of larger coalitions, who control the emission levels of all players within the coalition and include international effects. Therefore, a fundamental assumption for the theoretical result of a non-empty core by Helm (2001), namely the direct additivity of consumption functions in a coalition, is violated in the new modified model. To check whether the core of the modified game remains non-empty in all cases is the main aim of the remainder of this chapter.
Due to the high complexity of international macroeconomic effects, a detailed theoretical analysis of the modified model does not seem to be appropriate. Instead, we quantify the consumption functions with a numerical model, as outlined in the next section, without making prior assumptions about function form. Therefore, the assumptions about function form made by Helm (2001), namely monotonicity and concavity, might be violated by some consumption functions, as briefly highlighted in Section 3.2.1.

3.1.2 Quantification of the game

Quantification of the value function

As outlined in Section 3.1.1, we calculate the utility of each region as the difference between consumption and damages. Data on consumption and damages are taken from two different models. For the calculation of the consumption function we use the global CGE model DART. The application of DART specifically allows covering the international macroeconomic effects described above and included in the modified CT model. For the calculation of the damage function we follow the approach by Nordhaus (2010).
As most impacts of climate change only become relevant over a longer time frame (IPCC, 2013), we apply a time period from 2013 to 2300 for our calculation of the value function. Note that due to using two separate models

instead of an integrated model, feedback effects from changes in the climate on the economic system are not included.

CGE model DART

The DART (Dynamic Applied Regional Trade) model[1] is a recursive dynamic CGE model of the world economy, covering multiple sectors and regions. Producers in each region minimize cost of production while one representative agent per region maximizes its consumption. The model covers all important market-based repercussions resulting from climate policies, such as changes in the terms of trade due to a reduced demand of fossil fuels. DART is calibrated to the GTAP dataset 8.1 (Narayanan et al., 2012) with the base year 2007 and is aggregated to 12 sectors. The electricity sector is further disaggregated into conventional (fossil based, thermal) generation and generation from nuclear, hydro, wind, solar and biomass; carbon capture and storage (CCS) is available as an option for electricity generation from gas and coal (Weitzel, 2010). The costs of technologies are endogenous in the model and change over time. For our game-theoretic analysis, we use eight world regions based on countries' similarities (see Table 3.1).
For this application the model is run up to 2050. In a baseline scenario that assumes no climate policy, the model is calibrated to follow emission projections of the World Energy Outlook (International Energy Agency, 2013) and GDP projections of the OECD Environmental Outlook (OECD, 2012). Consumption functions are generated for all single regions (so-called singleton coalitions), for the grand coalition of all regions, and for all possible combinations of regions in between, resulting in a total of 255 coalitions. The functions are produced by implementing different emission reduction targets, ranging from 22% to 66% below the baseline in 2050, and observing the change in consumption over the time period 2013 - 2050. Emission reductions in the coalition region are achieved via a harmonized carbon tax, i.e. the

[1] For a more detailed description of the DART model, see the appendix of Weitzel et al. (2012) or `https://www.ifw-kiel.de/academy/data-bases/dart_e`.

target of the coalition region is achieved cost-efficiently. In this step it is assumed that no climate targets are enacted in regions outside of the coalition.

Regions used in game-theoretical analysis	**Countries or regions included**
North America (NAM)	Canada, US
Europe (EUR)	Europe
Australia / New Zealand (ANZ)	Australia, New Zealand
Japan (JPN)	Japan
Fossil Fuel Exporters (EXP)	Middle East, North Africa, Former Soviet Union
China (CHN)	China
India (IND)	India
Rest of the World (ROW)	Latin America, Africa, Pacific Asia

Table 3.1: Regions in the game-theoretical model.

It should be noted that, as highlighted before, due to the incorporation of international macroeconomic effects as in Equation (3.1), the consumption functions for coalitions of more than one member do not directly result from the consumption functions of single regions.

MATLAB's pchip function is used to interpolate between the calculated emission reduction targets. It produces a piecewise cubic polynomial with continuous first derivative and preserves extrema and monotonicity of the data. The algorithm is based on Fritsch and Carlson (1980).

The DART model calculates consumption and emissions up to 2050. We use a simple procedure to extend the calculations to 2300. For baseline emissions, we extrapolate per capita emissions for each region to 2100 based on the linear trend of per capita emissions from 2030 to 2050. Population values are based on the scenario for medium fertility of the UN World Population Prospects (United Nations, 2012). This procedure leads to an emissions path similar to the Representative Concentration Pathway RCP8.5, which was used in the IPCC's Fifth Assessment Report (Collins et al., 2013). We then use the simple extension rule for RCP8.5 (Meinshausen et al., 2011) to extend the baseline emissions path to 2300. This means constant emissions from 2100 to 2150, followed by a linear reduction of annual emissions to values consistent with stabilized atmospheric concentration in 2250, and constant emissions afterwards. For emission reduction targets, we linearly extend the trend in the relative reduction amount below baseline from the period up to 2050. In subsequent years, absolute emissions are given by baseline emissions multiplied by the extrapolated relative reduction amount. The coalition is considered jointly, while the emissions of outsider regions are calculated individually. The reduction of annual emissions is stopped when a region or coalition reaches net-zero emissions.

The procedure for consumption is similar. Baseline consumption is extrapolated based on per capita consumption. Annual data from 2013 to 2300 is discounted and aggregated, resulting in the net present value (NPV) of baseline consumption.

To reflect the intergenerational nature of climate change, the discount rate is determined based on the Ramsey formula (Arrow et al., 2012). Accordingly, the discount rate applied to a specific year is calculated as the sum of the rate of pure time preference and the product of the elasticity of the marginal utility of consumption and the per capita growth rate of consumption up to the specific year. For the rate of pure time preference and the elasticity of the marginal utility of consumption, we use the median values from a recent survey of economists (Drupp et al., 2015), which are 0.5% and 1, respectively. The per capita growth rate of consumption up to a specific year is calculated from the baseline consumption extension procedure described above. The resulting discount rate starts at 3.3% and declines to 1.5% in 2300. This is in line with the discount rate path advocated by Gollier and Hammitt (2014).

The implementation of emission reduction targets results in a consumption loss. This loss is simulated with the DART model for the period 2013 to 2050. For later years, we assume that the consumption loss relative to the baseline stays constant at the value for 2050 for all years after 2050. This assumption balances increasing consumption loss due to more expensive mitigation technologies needed to reach low emission levels, with decreasing consumption loss due to the development and cost reduction of low-carbon technologies over time. However, it can be seen as a rather conservative assumption on consumption losses. For coalitions, the joint relative consumption loss of all members is taken. Population values beyond 2100 are based on the UN World Population to 2300 report (United Nations, 2004).

Damage function

For the regional damage functions, we use the Regional Integrated model of Climate and the Economy (RICE)[2]. We use the baseline of the RICE-2010 version of the model, as described in Nordhaus (2010). Calculation of the damages in each region for each year is a two-step process. In the first step, the temperature change caused by a given level of cumulative CO_2 emissions up to the specific year is taken from RICE. The resulting temperature changes range from 0.83°C to 6.61°C over the pre-industrial level. This does not include a time component, i.e. the temperature change is the same if the same level of cumulative CO_2 emissions is reached in two different years[3] . In the second step, the temperature change is used to calculate the damages in each region. For regions that differ between our model and RICE, the values from the RICE model are disaggregated using 2013 GDP values from the World Bank indicator database (World Bank, 2014). The RICE model gives damages as a fraction of gross output. We convert these fractions to absolute numbers using baseline consumption levels. RICE includes

[2] `http://www.econ.yale.edu/~nordhaus/homepage/RICEmodels.htm`

[3] According to Collins et al. (2013, p. 1108), the amount of cumulative CO_2 emissions is a good indicator for the global temperature increase.

two types of damages: those caused by sea level rise and other damages. We include both types. This procedure generates absolute damages for each region and year up to 2300. The cumulative NPV of damages is then calculated using again the discount rate determined by the Ramsey formula, as in the method for consumption.

Damage Scenarios

We implement three sets of damage scenarios. The damages given by the RICE model form the basis for the *default damages scenario*. These estimates are at the upper end of the range given by the IPCC (IPCC, 2014a)[4]. In addition, we analyse two more damage scenarios: one scenario with damages only 50% as high as in the default damages scenario (*low damages scenario*), which is still significantly above the lower range given by the IPCC, and one scenario with damages twice as high as in the default damages scenario (*high damages scenario*)[5].

Game evaluation

The coalition and outsider regions choose their optimal emission level via the control variable of 2050 emission reduction targets below baseline. We find the equilibrium of emission reduction targets by successively calculating the best response of each region, starting with targets of one (meaning no reduction below baseline) for all regions. In this procedure, the coalition is treated as one entity, which controls a single joint emission reduction target. Best responses are calculated using the multi-level single linkage algorithm with low-discrepancy sequences by Kucherenko and Sytsko (2005). This is a global optimization algorithm, which uses multiple starting points for local optimizations. For the local optimization, we use the BOBYQA

[4] See Section 3.2.1 for details.

[5] As we consider only one decision based on future discounted values and damages tend to occur later in time than consumption losses due to emission reduction measures, the reduction (increase) in damages in the low (high) damages scenario could also be viewed as an increase (decrease) in the discount rate.

algorithm by Powell (2009). Both algorithms are supplied in the NLopt package (Johnson, 2014).
Due to runtime constraints with the DART model, we could not calculate consumption functions of outsider regions given a reduction target of a coalition. These functions are needed when calculating the best response of an outsider region. Instead, we use the consumption functions of the singleton coalitions, in which each region assumes that no other region introduces a reduction target, to calculate the best response emission reduction targets of outsider regions. Morris et al. (2012) show that this does not have a major impact on the optimal level of emission reductions. Rather, the consumption function reacts with parallel shifts up or down if another region reduces emissions. Therefore, this simplification does not have a considerable effect on optimal emission reduction targets in equilibrium. As the value function is determined by the sum of utility of coalition members, with no regard to the utility of outsiders, the value function is only slightly affected. Also, financial transfers between coalition members do not need to be explicitly considered, because the value of a coalition is defined over the sum of its members' utility.
The analysis of the resulting game focuses on the existence of a stable payoff vector, or, in other words, on the (non-)emptiness of the core of the game. Therefore, we calculate the **best partition** of the game. A **partition**

$$P = \{S_1, .., S_m\} \tag{3.3}$$

$$S_l \subseteq N, \ \bigcup_{l=1}^{m} S_l = N, \ S_k \cap S_l = \emptyset \ \forall k, l \leq m \tag{3.4}$$

is a set of coalitions, in which each player is a member of exactly one coalition. That is, a partition combines distinct cases (i.e. coalitions) for different regions. The value of the partition is calculated as the sum of the values of the coalitions. Consequently, the best partition of the game is the partition with the highest value of all partitions. If the partition which only contains the grand coalition is not a best partition[6], then the core of the game is empty, as the value of the grand coalition is not high enough to satisfy each coalition in the best partition[7]. In this case, we also calculate all other partitions with a higher value than the grand coalition. These are called **blocking partitions**[8].

3.2 Results

Results of the model are presented in two steps. In the first step, selected consumption functions from the DART model and the damage functions from the RICE model are presented, which serve as input for the game-theoretical model. The second step focuses on the results of the core stability analysis. As benchmarks we briefly present the cases of no cooperation and full cooperation. All monetary values are provided as NPV, cumulated over the entire model time period, 2013 - 2300.

3.2.1 Consumption and damage functions

The application of the DART model (see Section 3.1.2) produces functions showing the change in consumption of each coalition for different 2050 emission reduction targets. Figure 3.1 shows these functions for all singleton coalitions. To allow for better comparability across regions, consumption changes are shown relative to each region's baseline consumption. Note that, while the emission target is based on a specific year, 2050, consumption uses cumulative NPV. Table A.1 in Appendix A gives absolute baseline consumption for each region.

---

[6] It is possible for a game to have multiple best partitions with identical value.

[7] In the language of cooperative game theory, the game is not *cohesive*.

[8] Note that per the definition of the core of a cooperative game, there is no "stability" requirement for coalitions in blocking partitions. Such a requirement would assume "farsighted" players (Chwe, 1994; Diamantoudi and Sartzetakis, 2002), as outlined in Section 2.3.2. In our model, the existence of one or multiple blocking partitions is merely used as a sufficient condition for the emptiness of the core and does not make a statement on the outcome of the game.

Most regions only experience a relatively small decline in consumption between 0 and 0.6% of GDP for reduction targets between 0 and 30% below baseline. The Fossil Fuel Exporters region EXP is an exception, as it experiences the highest consumption loss of all regions.

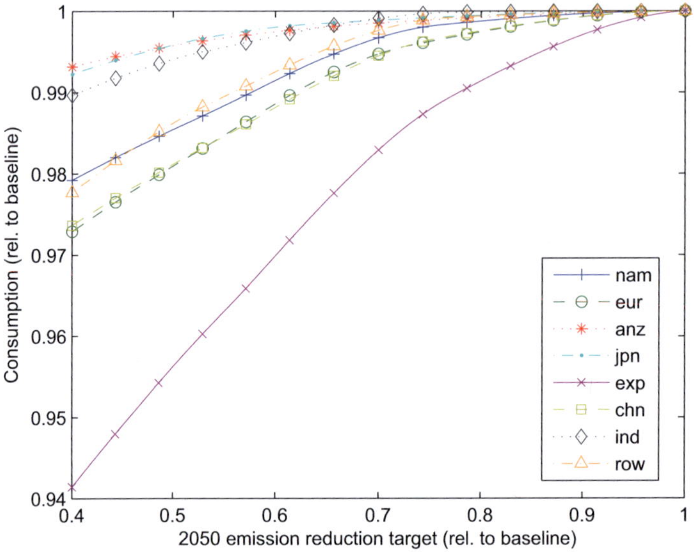

Figure 3.1: Consumption functions for singleton coalitions (NPV of consumption, relative to baseline).

The consumption functions for almost all coalitions are monotonically increasing and concave. An exception for monotonicity is the coalition {JPN, IND}, which experiences a slight increase in consumption when reducing emissions by up to around 20%. Also, several coalitions including CHN are not concave for ambitious emission reduction targets. Hence, the two assumptions of the form of the consumption functions by Helm (2001) do no longer hold in these cases.

Figure 3.2 shows regional damages for a given temperature increase over the pre-industrial level, relative to baseline consumption, in the default damages scenario. According to the projections, the lowest relative damages are expected to occur in the regions Australia / New Zealand, Japan and North America. The highest damages are projected for the regions Rest of the World, Fossil Fuel Exporters and China.

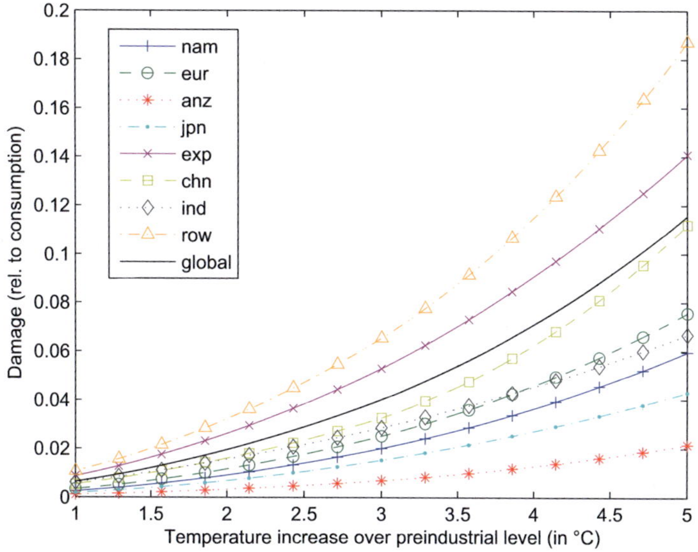

Figure 3.2: Regional damages depending on temperature change in the default damages scenario, relative to baseline consumption.

The figure also shows global relative damages, calculated as the average across all regions, weighted by regional consumption. For a temperature increase of 2°C, damages are 2.0% of consumption on a global level in the default damages scenario. This is at the upper end of the range given by the IPCC (IPCC, 2014a).

3.2.2 The gains of cooperation

In all damage scenarios, global cooperation leads to a substantial reduction in cumulative CO_2 emissions. Figure 3.3 shows the development of global emissions over time in the "All Singletons" case, where each region optimizes only its own utility, and in the case of global cooperation, where global utility is optimized. Emissions are shown for all damage scenarios. The baseline case without emission reduction measures in any region is shown for comparison[9]. The baseline case leads to a temperature increase of approximately 5.9°C in 2300 over the pre-industrial level.

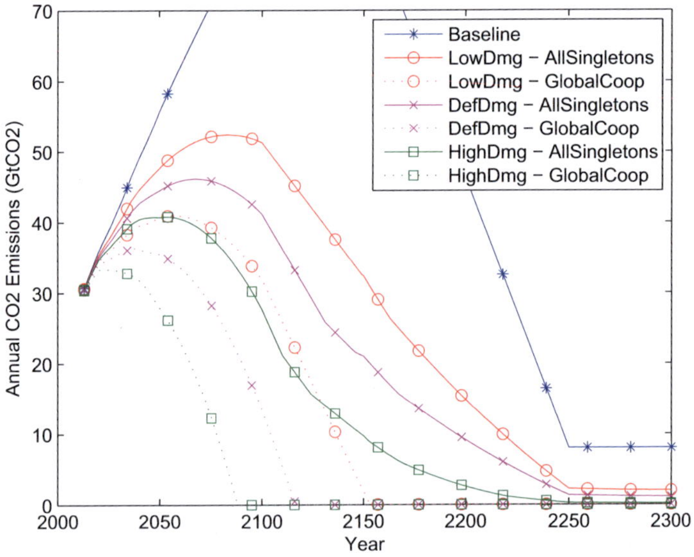

Figure 3.3: Global CO_2 emissions in the "All Singletons" and "Global Cooperation" cases, for all damage scenarios.

[9] The baseline case can be interpreted as a scenario in which regions do not acknowledge the existence of damages caused by climate change.

In the default damages scenario, the “All Singletons” case results in a global temperature increase in 2300 of 3.9°C with annual emissions peaking in 2068. For global cooperation, the emission peak is reached in 2037 and the emissions level is zero from 2117 onward, with a global temperature increase of 2.5°C in 2300.

In the low damages scenario, the “All Singletons” case produces a significantly higher temperature increase of 4.4°C in 2300. In case of global cooperation with low damages, annual emissions peak in 2057 and the emission level reaches zero in 2154. The result is a temperature increase of 3.1°C in 2300.

In the high damages scenario, the emission path in the “All Singletons” case is similar to the “Global Cooperation” case with low damages. Annual emissions peak in 2053 and the temperature increase in 2300 is 3.2°C. Global cooperation with high damages produces the most ambitious emission path, with a peak in 2023, an emission level of zero from 2089 onward, and a temperature increase of 2.0°C.

The differences in global and regional emission levels influence consumption, damages and total utility. Table 3.2 shows these values, in addition to CO_2 emissions and the resulting temperature increase at the end of the time period, as well as in 2100. For better readability, consumption and utility are shown as consumption loss and utility loss, compared to baseline consumption. All values are global, i.e. the sum of the values for all regions, and aggregated over the whole time period.

In all damage scenarios, damages are reduced by moving from the “All Singletons” case to global cooperation: from \$343tn to \$298tn (-13%) in the default damages scenario, from \$202tn to \$189tn (-6%) in the low damages scenario and from \$548tn to \$453tn (-17%) in the high damages scenario. Consumption losses due to emission reduction measures are small relative to absolute consumption (as shown in Figure 3.1). Global cooperation reduces consumption by \$96.78tn in the default damages scenario, by \$55.53tn in the low damages scenario and by \$148.61tn in the high damages scenario.

Damage Scenario		Cumulative CO_2 emissions ($GtCO_2$)	Temperature increase in 2100 (°C)	Temperature increase in 2300 (°C)	Consump-tion loss (NPV)	Damages (NPV)	Utility loss (NPV)
	Baseline	14,420	3.6	5.9	0	315.75	315.75
Low	All Singletons	7,807	3.1	4.4	5.86	196.16	202.03
	Global Cooperation	4,145	2.8	3.1	61.39	127.65	189.04
	Baseline	14,420	3.6	5.9	0	631.50	631.50
Default	All Singletons	6,205	3.0	3.9	13.60	329.63	343.23
	Global Cooperation	2,765	2.4	2.5	110.38	187.98	298.36
	Baseline	14,420	3.6	5.9	0	1,263.00	1,263.00
High	All Singletons	4,401	2.7	3.2	31.88	516.56	548.44
	Global Cooperation	1,804	2.0	2.0	180.49	272.60	453.09

Table 3.2: Key global results in the Baseline, “All Singletons“ and “Global Cooperation“ cases, for all damage scenarios (monetary values in trillion 2007 US$).

The results of the optimization for the “All Singletons” and “Global Cooperation” cases are shown in Table 3.3. It displays the 2050 emission reduction target of the given coalition and its utility loss in equilibrium for all damage scenarios. The game-theoretic value of each coalition corresponds to the baseline consumption of each coalition member, minus the displayed utility loss. In the “All Singletons” case, the sum of the utility loss of the coalitions gives the utility loss of the partition.

We find that global cooperation in the default damages scenario increases utility by $44.87tn compared to the “All Singletons” case, an increase of 0.6% of the absolute utility value. This corresponds to a net-avoidance of 14% of damages compared to the “All Singletons” case.

We also find that there is a large difference in the ambition level in the “All Singletons” case between different regions. In particular, China, India and Rest of the World realize relatively ambitious targets, even without cooperation. For India, this is the result of modest emission reduction costs, as seen in Figure 3.1. Rest of the World is the region with the highest relative damages of all regions and therefore reduces emissions in the “All Singletons” case by 32%, 28% and 39% in the default, low and high damages scenarios, respectively. China has the third highest relative damages and consequently also reduces emissions substantially, despite having the second highest emission reduction costs.

Damage Scenario	**Low**		**Default**		**High**	
	2050 emission target (rel. to baseline)	Utility loss (NPV)	2050 emission target (rel. to baseline)	Utility loss (NPV)	2050 emission target (rel. to baseline)	Utility loss (NPV)
Partition "Global Cooperation"	**72.57%**	**189.04**	**63.46%**	**298.36**	**50.05%**	**453.09**
N	72.57%	189.04	63.46%	298.36	50.05%	453.09
Partition "All Singletons"	**85.60%**	**202.03**	**79.95%**	**343.23**	**73.16%**	**548.44**
{NAM}	93.78%	16.99	85.93%	28.97	75.74%	45.86
{EUR}	97.45%	14.77	94.62%	24.89	88.34%	39.52
{ANZ}	100.00%	0.24	100.00%	0.40	100.00%	0.64
{JPN}	99.74%	1.25	99.42%	2.13	98.79%	3.35
{EXP}	98.48%	27.45	94.34%	47.41	81.76%	79.85
{CHN}	85.70%	19.58	75.53%	32.67	72.90%	48.27
{IND}	74.83%	10.98	71.57%	19.20	66.18%	31.83
{ROW}	72.32%	110.77	68.07%	187.56	61.22%	299.13

Table 3.3: Utility of the "Global Cooperation" and "All Singletons" cases in all damage scenarios (utility loss in trillion 2007 US$).

3.2.3 The cooperative game

The extreme cases "Global Cooperation" and "All Singletons" presented in the last subsection provide a standard against which we can compare other coalitions and partitions. As best partitions differ between scenarios, we discuss each damage scenario separately.

Default damages scenario

Table 3.4 shows selected partitions, including the best partition, and the respective targets and values of the member coalitions in the default damages scenario.

	2050 emission target (rel. to baseline)	**Utility loss (NPV, tn$2007)**
Partition "Global Cooperation"	**63.46%**	**298.36**
N	63.46%	298.36
Partition "All except ANZ"	**63.59%**	**297.50**
N\{ANZ}	63.25%	297.10
{ANZ}	100.00%	0.40
Partition "All except ANZ, JPN"	**64.95%**	**297.30**
N\{ANZ, JPN}	64.23%	294.77
{ANZ}	100.00%	0.40
{JPN}	99.42%	2.13

Table 3.4: Selected partitions in the default damages scenario.

We find that the "Global Cooperation" partition is not a best partition of the game in the default damages scenario, as we find partitions with lower utility losses than the grand coalition. That is, we find the core of the game to be empty, contrary to the original CT model. In this scenario, a partition has the highest utility if it consists of the coalition of all regions except Australia / New Zealand (ANZ) and Japan (JPN), and ANZ and JPN as singleton coalitions. In total, utility loss of the best partition is \$297.30tn, compared to \$298.36tn in the grand coalition.

Our result arises, because a stable global agreement would have to cover against two cases simultaneously: the "All Singletons" case and the case of partial cooperation by a group of regions with high benefits from emission reductions, a *coalition of the willing*.

Consider first the region ANZ, a large exporter of fossil fuels, mainly coal. To illustrate its motivations, it is useful to look at the partition "All except ANZ", which is worse than the best partition, but still better than the "Global Cooperation" partition. When global utility is optimized in the grand coalition, global emissions in 2050 are 63.46% of baseline emissions. In the "All Singletons" case, the regionally optimized targets lead to a global average emission level of 79.95% of 2050 baseline emissions. Consequently, negative consumption effects for ANZ occur when moving from the "All Singletons" case to global cooperation, due to lower global fossil fuel demand and prices. The driver behind this finding is the assumption that regions expect an "All Singletons" outcome if they do not participate in the grand coalition. Consequently, ANZ would need to be compensated for its consumption loss to be motivated to join the grand coalition. This compensation would have to come from the coalition of the willing, in this partition consisting of all other regions. However, when this coalition optimizes its emission level, it does not need to incorporate the wishes of ANZ. This leads to a more ambitious emission reduction target of 63.25% in the coalition of the willing. While global emissions in the case of the coalition of the willing are still larger than in the grand coalition (global average target of 63.59%, compared to 63.46% in the grand coalition), the difference is rather small, because ANZ only has relatively few domestic emissions, compared to the coalition of the willing. Therefore, the coalition of the willing only experiences very small gains from moving to global cooperation. These additional gains are not large enough to offset the consumption loss of ANZ.

The motivation for JPN is different and stems from the fact that it experiences the second lowest damages from climate change, after ANZ. As the economic situation of ANZ causes global cooperation to be unstable, JPN now faces the choice between the "All Singletons" case and joining the coalition of the willing described above. Due to the low damages experienced by JPN, the cost of the additional emission reduction effort required by a coalition of the willing outweighs the reduction in damages. Consequently, JPN also blocks global cooperation and the best partition is "All except ANZ, JPN".

It should be noted that the economic effects described above for ANZ also apply to the Fossil Fuel Exporters region EXP. However, this region also experiences the second highest damages from climate change. Therefore, the damage reduction caused by global cooperation outweighs the loss of fossil fuel export revenue for EXP.

The blocking partitions shown in Table 3.4 are not all blocking partitions that exist in the default damages scenario. In total, four such partitions exist, all consisting of ANZ and/or JPN as blocking regions, in addition to a coalition of the willing of the remaining regions.

In this default damages scenario, the difference in utility loss between global cooperation and the best partition is quite small. This is further underscored by the small number of blocking partitions. The next section shows that a reduction of damages increases both the utility deficit of global cooperation and the number of blocking partitions.

Low damages scenario

Table 3.5 shows selected partitions, including the best partition, in the low damages scenario.

	2050 emission target (rel. to baseline)	**Utility loss (NPV, tn$2007)**
Partition "Global Cooperation"	**72.57%**	**189.04**
N	72.57%	189.04
Partition "All except ANZ"	**72.73%**	**187.44**
N\{ANZ}	72.48%	187.20
{ANZ}	100.00%	0.24
Partition "All except ANZ, JPN"	**73.30%**	**184.18**
N\{ANZ, JPN}	72.75%	182.69
{ANZ}	100.00%	0.24
{JPN}	99.74%	1.25
Partition "All except ANZ, JPN, CHN"	**75.41%**	**183.95**
N\{ANZ, JPN, CHN}	72.62%	163.00
{ANZ}	100.00%	0.24
{JPN, CHN}	83.41%	20.71

Table 3.5: Selected partitions in the low damages scenario.

We find that "Global Cooperation" is not the best partition of the game and hence again the core of the game is empty. The best partition comprises ANZ as a singleton, a coalition of JPN and CHN, and a coalition of the willing of the remaining regions. Utility loss in the best partition is \$183.95tn, compared to \$189.04tn in the case of global cooperation. This difference is substantially larger than in the default damages scenario.
The behaviour of ANZ is caused by the same effects described in the default damages scenario. JPN again sees no benefit in joining the coalition of the willing, due to its low damages, compared to other regions. CHN's behaviour can be explained by the consumption loss due to emission reductions. For CHN, this is the third-highest of all regions (see Figure 3.1). Therefore, CHN also does not benefit from joining the coalition of the willing. However, as CHN does already reduce its emissions by roughly 15% in the "All Singletons" case, it can cooperate with JPN to better distribute these emission reductions. This reduces the joint consumption loss of CHN and JPN, as JPN has low emission reduction costs.
In total, we find 80 blocking partitions in the low damages scenario, a substantial increase over the four blocking partitions in the default damages scenario.

High damages scenario

Table 3.6 shows selected partitions, including the best partition, in the high damages scenario.
We find that – in contrast to the other two damage scenarios - "Global Cooperation" is the best partition of the game in the high damages scenario and that the core of the game is not empty, in line with the original CT model. Table A.2 in Appendix A shows one core-stable payoff vector.
The different outcome in this high damages scenario is driven by high gains from cooperation, which are induced by the relatively high damages. Both the inclusion of JPN and the inclusion of ANZ into the coalition of the willing

	2050 emission target (rel. to baseline)	**Utility loss (NPV, tn$2007)**
Partition "Global Cooperation"	**50.05%**	**453.09**
N	50.05%	453.09
Partition "All except ANZ"	**50.39%**	**454.24**
N\{ANZ}	49.93%	453.60
{ANZ}	100.00%	0.64
Partition "All except ANZ, JPN"	**51.58%**	**458.68**
N\{ANZ, JPN}	50.59%	454.69
{ANZ}	100.00%	0.64
{JPN}	98.79%	3.35
Partition "All except ANZ, JPN, CHN"	**59.34%**	**484.84**
N\{ANZ, JPN, CHN}	54.71%	432.91
{ANZ}	100.00%	0.64
{JPN, CHN}	72.57%	51.29

Table 3.6: Selected partitions in the high damages scenario.

without those two regions lead to a gain in utility. While both regions have only low damages compared to other regions, their damages in this scenario are high enough that even they benefit from a move from "All Singletons" to "Global Cooperation".

However, the economic effects which drove the results in the low and default damages scenarios are still apparent in the emission targets of the high damages scenario. The target in the case of "Global Cooperation" (50.05%) is still less ambitious than the preferred targets of the remaining coalition, when ANZ is excluded (49.93%). This means that, while ANZ prefers "Global Cooperation" to "All Singletons", it still favours a less ambitious target than the other regions. Therefore, to include ANZ in the joint target, the target becomes less ambitious. Nevertheless, these economic effects are outweighed by the high gains from cooperation in the high damages scenario.

Basic model without international effects

The previous subsections showed that our model can produce a game with empty core in some circumstances. This is in contrast to the original CT model, which always produces games with non-empty core. To show that this is not an artefact of the specific set up of the numerical model, we also analyse the core of the game if we do not take international effects of emission reductions into account. For that, an alternative version of the model is constructed, based only on the singleton consumption functions. The resulting model thus replicates the assumption of the original CT model that the joint consumption function of a coalition is given by the sum of the domestic consumption functions. Table 3.7 shows the results for the "All Singletons" case, the grand coalition and the selected partitions shown in prior sections. Consistent with the theoretical result by Helm (2001) and previous numerical applications of the core stability concept (Eyckmans and Tulkens, 2003; Bréchet et al., 2011; Dellink, 2011), we find that the core of this game is non-empty in all damage scenarios. Consequently, we conclude that our deviating results in the model with modified consumption functions are driven by this modification.

Damage Scenario	Low		Default		High	
	2050 emission target (rel. to baseline)	Utility loss (NPV, tn$2007)	2050 emission target (rel. to baseline)	Utility loss (NPV, tn$2007)	2050 emission target (rel. to baseline)	Utility loss (NPV, tn$2007)
Partition “Global Cooperation”	**69.35%**	**152.87**	**62.38%**	**253.91**	**50.65%**	**410.90**
N	69.35%	152.87	62.38%	253.91	50.65%	410.90
Partition “All except ANZ”	**69.69%**	**154.03**	**62.77%**	**256.43**	**51.11%**	**416.10**
N\{ANZ}	69.41%	153.79	62.43%	256.03	50.65%	415.47
{ANZ}	100.00%	0.24	100.00%	0.40	100.00%	0.64
Partition “All except ANZ, JPN”	**70.20%**	**155.30**	**63.49%**	**259.12**	**51.99%**	**421.31**
N\{ANZ, JPN}	69.59%	153.80	62.75%	256.59	51.01%	417.32
{ANZ}	100.00%	0.24	100.00%	0.40	100.00%	0.64
{JPN}	99.74%	1.25	99.42%	2.13	98.79%	3.35
Partition “All except ANZ, JPN, CHN”	**73.92%**	**176.68**	**67.36%**	**288.03**	**58.50%**	**468.18**
N\{ANZ, JPN, CHN}	70.31%	155.65	64.49%	252.96	53.66%	416.11
{ANZ}	100.00%	0.24	100.00%	0.40	100.00%	0.64
{JPN, CHN}	84.45%	20.79	75.28%	34.67	72.38%	51.43
Partition "All Singletons"	**85.60%**	**202.03**	**79.95%**	**343.23**	**73.16%**	**548.44**

Table 3.7: Selected partitions in the basic model without international effects (utility loss in trillion 2007 US$).

Note: Values for the individual regions under the “All Singletons” partition are identical to those presented in Table 3.3.

3.3 Policy Implications

Our results imply that, under the assumption that damages from climate change are not higher than the range given by the IPCC, it is not possible to design a straightforward global climate agreement, based on emission reduction targets and including all countries, under the UNFCCC. This is true even if all countries assume that there will be no coalition without them as a member, i.e. they neglect the existence of free-riding incentives. In our model, a global agreement is blocked by the consumption loss of a major fossil fuel exporter, who would experience revenue losses due to lower fossil fuel prices in a world with ambitious global GHG mitigation. All blocking countries assume that without their agreement no cooperation will take place at all, leaving them better off when not joining the coalition.
For the set of remaining countries, which we refer to as *coalition of the willing*, this situation presents two options. The first option is to stick to the idea of a global agreement under the UNFCCC and provide incentives for all countries to join. This would mean compensating the fossil fuel exporters for their consumption losses. Such compensation for the impacts of "response measures" is an essential demand by oil exporting countries, represented in the group of Like-Minded Developing Countries (LMDC), in the UNFCCC negotiations (LMDC, 2014). However, the results of our model indicate that such compensation measures would not be rational from the perspective of the coalition of the willing, as the additional avoided damages are not enough to make up for the consumption loss. As compensatory measures are not rational from an economic perspective, the incentive to compensate and incentivize blocking countries to join the coalition would have to come from other political reasoning. Fairness principles often discussed in the context of burden sharing, such as historic responsibility for the climate problem and the ability to pay for the solution, are one example. Countries could also be motivated by the aspiration to avoid a large temperature increase and the accompanying risk and regionally differentiated impacts. In addition, the

required compensation amount is small compared to total consumption (see Table A.1 in Appendix A). Therefore, if the decision is not based purely on a benefit-cost analysis of GHG mitigation but other arguments are taken into account, the coalition of the willing, or parts of it, could reasonably incentivize blocking countries to join the global climate agreement.

The second option for the coalition of the willing is to abandon the UNFCCC process and try to consummate an agreement among this coalition. This option would not be as environmentally effective as a global agreement, but could be close to it, depending on the exact specification of the coalition. Non-global *climate clubs* have been proposed as a solution for the climate problem in the literature (e.g. Eckersley, 2012; Weischer et al., 2012; Nordhaus, 2015) and initiatives exist for certain sectors and/or gases[10]. The idea of climate clubs will be further evaluated in Chapter 6.

Although our pessimistic result might seem to be caused solely by the ANZ region, the effects driving the result might be more impactful than the model is able to depict. Take the Fossil Fuel Exporters region, which also experiences large economic effects from global emission reductions. However, it does not cause a blocking partition, because it has the second highest damages of all regions and therefore benefits from global cooperation. However, the high damage estimate for this region is largely driven by the Middle East and North Africa and might not apply to Russia and other Former Soviet Union countries. These countries with high economic losses from global emission reduction measures and low climate damages might cause further blocking partitions in a model with higher regional disaggregation.

Nevertheless, our model implies that high gains from cooperation reduce blocking incentives and make a stable global agreement seem possible. Therefore, the promotion of the positive effects of emission reduction

[10] For example, the REDD+ Partnership supports measures to reduce emissions from deforestation, and the Climate and Clean Air Coalition is focused on short-lived GHGs. See Weischer et al. (2012) for an overview of climate clubs.

measures and further re-search in this area might improve the prospects of a global agreement.

3.4 Conclusion

We argue that a main weakness of earlier analyses on coalition stability stems from the fact that consumption functions are usually assumed to depend on domestic reductions only, while this is clearly not the case in a globalized world. Therefore, we extend the model by Chander and Tulkens (1995, 1997) to include international macroeconomic effects of emission reduction measures in multiple regions and quantify the new value function by applying two models, the DART model and the RICE model.

Contrary to the original theoretical paper and previous numerical applications, we find that, under the assumption that climate damages are in the IPCC range, the grand coalition in this setting is not stable. In the best partition of our default damages scenario, Japan and the fossil fuel exporting region Australia / New Zealand act as singletons, while a *coalition of the willing* of the remaining regions agrees on a joint emission reduction target. Australia / New Zealand stands to lose a substantial part of its fossil fuel export revenue, if global emission reduction measures are implemented and fossil fuel prices fall as a result. Therefore, as long as the region believes that it can block international cooperation by not signing off on a global agreement, it has no incentive to join an agreement, which does not include adequate compensation. This effect is amplified in a scenario with lower damages.

In contrast, under higher damages, no blocking partition exists and a stable global agreement is possible. While the economic effects mentioned above are still apparent, the high gains from cooperation, due to higher damages, outweigh all other effects in this scenario.

Our results point to alternative ways forward, if blocking partitions exist. The coalition of the willing of non-blocking countries can make the decision to compensate the blocking regions for their loss of consumption in the case of global cooperation. Such a decision would not be rational from the perspective of a pure benefit-cost analysis based on climate damages avoided and consumption loss, but might be reasonable if other factors such as historic responsibility or risk aversion are included. Alternatively, the coalition of the willing could terminate the quest for a global agreement and form a climate club outside of the UNFCCC. If designed properly, such an agreement might include very broad participation (Hovi et al., 2015).

Our model could be improved in a number of ways. It does not include a full feedback of the optimization of emission levels to the consumption side, in the way that integrated assessment models do (Leimbach et al., 2010; Nordhaus, 2010; Bosetti et al., 2013). Also, the model is static, meaning that the decision on the optimal emission level is only taken once. A dynamic version of the model could include decisions each year or every few years (de Zeeuw, 2008). In addition, a higher number of world regions is needed for a detailed analysis of countries' blocking incentives. Furthermore, despite the long time frame, the model does not include uncertainty about the future values of the consumption and damage functions (Dellink and Finus, 2012; Barrett, 2013; Finus and Pintassilgo, 2013). These issues are left for further research.

4 Technological development of low-carbon power technology and the stability of international climate cooperation

To achieve ambitious emission reduction targets, techno-economic analyses typically advocate investments in a mix of low- and no-carbon technologies, along with carbon dioxide removal technologies for the energy sector, which currently accounts for roughly two-thirds of global greenhouse gas emissions (e.g. International Energy Agency (IEA), 2015). Most of the extant literature assumes that the potential and costs of future technologies are known with certainty. Yet, estimations of the technological progress of a low-carbon technology, the development of its costs and its actual diffusion are highly uncertain. For example, carbon capture and storage (CCS) technology was expected to become one of the key bridging technologies for decarbonizing the energy system. In its 2008 World Energy Outlook, the IEA estimated that CCS would be applied to 9% of global fossil fuel based power generation capacity in 2030, in a 2°C target scenario (IEA, 2008). Six years later this figure had dropped to about 5% (IEA, 2014b). In many countries, CCS suffers from a lack of social acceptance and the necessary regulatory framework (e.g. for sequestration). Thus, investors in CCS currently face substantial market, policy, and technology uncertainties (e.g. von Hirschhausen et al., 2012; IEA, 2007). In comparison, the deployment of solar photovoltaic (PV) technology turned out to be much more dynamic than expected. The

80% drop in the costs of modules in mature markets between 2008 and 2012 (IEA, 2014a) was startling.

Some studies employing techno-economic models have explored the impact of technological uncertainty on global and regional mitigation costs (Clarke et al., 2015). CCS availability is typically found to significantly affect overall mitigation costs (e.g. Krey and Riahi, 2009; Kriegler et al., 2014). Yet these studies tend to be rather aggregate and assume a benevolent dictator to determine the burden-sharing of mitigation costs among countries. In reality, countries' mitigation efforts are more likely to be the outcome of political decision making and are driven by regional costs and benefits. While, according to Weitzel (2015), the fossil fuel market effects cancel out at the global level, the regional mitigation costs are more sensitive to technological uncertainty. Lüken et al. (2011) and Weitzel (2015, 2016) analyse the effects of technological uncertainty on regional mitigation costs and on the distribution of costs across countries. Assuming cooperation of countries, these studies find that the main source of uncertainty in mitigation costs is uncertainty about technology deployment in specific regions and the ramifications of this on the international fossil fuel markets. These impacts include changes to the world market price of fuels in response to carbon pricing.

Only few game-theoretical studies have allowed for uncertainty about mitigation costs in analyses of the stability of climate cooperation (e.g. Hong and Karp, 2014; Kolstad and Ulph, 2011; Finus and Pintassilgo, 2013; Dellink and Finus, 2012). These studies focus on the effects of uncertainty and risk aversion on the decision-making of countries, aspects that are further analysed in Chapter 5 of this thesis. However, the studies do not consider whether different technological pathways can themselves influence the stability of climate coalitions. Also, technological uncertainty in these studies is based on the mitigation cost function for a generic technology and not for specific technologies. In addition, these studies do not account for the general equilibrium effects of emission reduction measures (e.g. fossil fuel market effects). However, the findings of Chapter 3 suggest that these effects can substantially change the conclusions about the stability of climate coalitions. To the best of our knowledge, so far no study has included indirect cost effects and technological uncertainty when analyzing the stability of climate coalitions.

In this chapter, we simulate the impact that different technological assumptions about key low-carbon power technologies have on the stability of global climate cooperation and analyse the resulting burden sharing. We specifically take into account that assumptions about mitigation costs as well as the benefits of climate protection may differ across regions. Our conceptual framework builds on the model constructed in Chapter 3. Again, the numerical application uses sets of consumption functions from the CGE model DART, which has been augmented by technology-specific information on wind, PV and CCS plants for this purpose. These technologies typically account for a significant share of the electricity mix in climate protection scenarios[1].

We first explore the stability of global cooperation under different technological assumptions, similar to Chapter 3. Then, we derive scenarios to analyse the global and regional effects that influence the stability results. Finally, we discuss the outcomes of the different scenarios in depth for key regions.

The remainder of the chapter is structured as follows: Section 4.1 describes the integration of technological uncertainty into the DART model and the derived scenarios. Section 4.2 presents the results, focusing on the effects of the varying assumptions about the development of key mitigation technologies on cooperation and burden sharing. Section 4.3 concludes.

4.1 Methodology and Technology Scenarios

In this chapter, the analysis of Chapter 3 is extended by two additional technology scenarios and the associated cooperation cases. This section

[1] For example, in the 2°C target scenario of the 2014 World Energy Outlook (IEA, 2014b), wind, PV and CCS account for 17%, 13% and 7% of global electricity capacity in 2040, respectively.

describes the modeling approach for the integration of technological uncertainty into the DART model and the derived scenarios for the game-theoretical analysis.

4.1.1 Technological uncertainty in the power sector

To integrate technological uncertainty into the DART model, three in depth studies were undertaken for on-shore wind power (Capelli, 2014), solar PV (Renz, 2012) and CCS (Lämmle, 2012). An extensive review of the literature provided information on the ranges of the key parameters describing the future development of each technology including capital costs, learning rates, energy output and lifetime of the technology. The core findings for the three technologies are:

- The market for on-shore wind power is dominated by a single design, the three-bladed horizontal axis turbine. The future costs of generating electricity from on-shore wind power primarily depend on the learning rate, which captures the reduction in per unit electricity generation costs for a doubling of global capacity. The literature review shows values between 12% and 18% for the learning rate.

- Solar PV technologies vary by scale and where they are mounted (roof, facade, ground) and scale of the plant, giving rise to differences in installation costs and power output. However, the cost structure for all PV technologies is quite similar, as the major cost factor is the PV module (Renz, 2012). Therefore, the future cost development of all PV technologies can be captured using the same learning rate, which varies between 15% and 23% in the literature.

- The future development of CCS is more complex than wind or PV. Adding CCS to any process increases the capital costs required to capture, compress, transport, and store the CO_2. Operating costs also increase, because CCS implies a loss in production efficiency. Therefore, the best approach to modeling the future electricity generation costs of CCS is to apply a region- and technology-specific (gas and coal) *markup*, i.e. the additional cost of a unit of electricity produced in a CCS plant, compared to a reference non-CCS plant. This markup captures learning rates for individual components and efficiency penalties. The markup ranges between 31% and 53% for a gas-fired plant, and between 51% and 96% for a coal-fired plant. CCS can be applied in other industry sectors, e.g. cement or iron and steel, but this chapter focuses on its application in the power sector.

Based on these findings, the future cost development of PV and wind power is modeled via a learning-curve approach with an uncertain learning rate, while for CCS, technological uncertainty is modeled as a deviation from the expected markup (see Weitzel, 2015, for more details). The resulting parameter means and standard deviations are summarized in Table 4.1. Based on this we derive an optimistic and a pessimistic technology scenario, where the relevant parameters for all technologies mark the 99% confidence interval of the implemented distribution. These values are also shown in Table 4.1.

	LR-Wind	LR-PV	Markup CCS-Gas	Markup CCS-Coal
Mean	15.0%	19.0%	42.0%	74.0%
Standard deviation	1.4%	1.6%	5.0%	10.0%
Pessimistic scenario	11.7%	15.2%	53.0%	96.0%
Optimistic scenario	18.3%	22.8%	31.0%	51.0%

Table 4.1: Uncertainty and scenario parameters in DART.

The use of the DART model in this chapter is twofold: First, we employ DART to generate the sets of consumption functions that are used in the game-theoretical model to examine the stability of a global climate coalition, as described in Section 3.1. Since our focus is on the implications of technological uncertainty, consumption functions of all possible coalitions were created for the pessimistic, mean and optimistic technology scenario, thus extending the results of Chapter 3, in which functions from the mean scenario were used. Second, DART is used to analyse the global and regional effects of technological uncertainty in key scenarios in more detail.

4.1.2 Scenarios

In total, there are three different technology scenarios: *mean*, optimistic (*opt*) and pessimistic (*pess*) (see Table 4.1). For each scenario, several cooperation cases can be distinguished, which result in different emission targets for each region.
The baseline case - or business-as-usual (BAU) case - without emission reductions is used as the reference. We then use the game-theoretical model to calculate emission reductions for different cooperation cases for each of the three technology scenarios. These are the case of global cooperation (GC) of all regions and the "All Singletons" (AS) case, where each region individually maximizes its utility. As in Chapter 3, we also calculate the best partition to determine the stability of global cooperation for each scenario. For simplicity, this chapter presents the best coalition (BC), which we define as the coalition that causes the highest global value. The global value caused by a coalition is the value of the partition consisting of this coalition and the remaining regions as singletons. Results show that this special case corresponds to the best partition in each scenario. In addition, we call each coalition that causes a global value higher than GC a blocking coalition. Blocking regions are regions that appear as outsiders to a blocking coalition. All four cooperation cases (BAU, AS, BC, GC) are analysed in detail with the DART model by taking the emission reductions from the game-theoretical model and combining them with the underlying technology scenario. Emission reductions are implemented via a uniform tax in GC or BC that is en-

dogenously calculated to reach the specified reductions. Reductions of singleton regions in AS or potentially of outsider regions in BC are achieved via unilateral taxes.
Further, as a sensitivity analysis, we also vary the level of damages due to climate change, as in Chapter 3. The focus of this chapter is on the default damages scenario, in which damages are taken directly from the RICE model. We also run the game-theoretical model for the low damages scenario, in which damages are half those in the default damages scenario, and the high damages scenario, in which damages are twice as high as in the default damages scenario. In total, we calculate the combinations of three technology scenarios, three damages scenarios and four cooperation cases, for a total of 36 scenarios, of which the 12 default damages scenarios are analysed in more detail in this chapter.

4.2 The influence of technological uncertainty on cooperation and burden sharing

This section analyses the effects of different technological assumptions on the stability of a global climate coalition and the feasible burden sharing. As described in Section 4.1, consumption functions were generated for the *mean*, *pess* and *opt* technology scenarios, which were then used in the game-theoretical model to determine the stability of global cooperation. The default damages scenario is applied, unless otherwise indicated.

4.2.1 Cooperation in the different scenarios

Table 4.2 shows the emission levels for the "All Singletons" case, the grand coalition and selected other cooperation cases resulting from the game theoretical model. Percentage changes provided in brackets show emission changes compared to BAU with the same technology assumptions.

Generally, more optimistic technology assumptions lead to lower emission levels, even in the BAU scenario, while relative reductions do not show a clear trend. As expected, global emissions under "All Singletons" are much higher than under a grand coalition. These reductions are mainly driven by regions with relatively high damages, namely CHN, IND and ROW, while the other regions reduce their emissions only marginally. Global cooperation in contrast reduces emissions by roughly 36% below BAU.

Scenario	*pess*	*mean*	*opt*
BAU	56.3	55.6	53.9
All Singletons	44.8 (-20.4%)	44.5 (-20.0%)	42.4 (-21.3%)
Grand Coalition N	35.5 (-36.9%)	35.3 (-36.5%)	34.4 (-36.2%)
$N\backslash\{$ANZ$\}$	35.7 (-36.5%)	35.4 (-36.3%)	34.5 (-36.0%)
$N\backslash\{$ANZ, JPN$\}$	35.9 (-36.2%)	36.1 (-35.1%)	34.0 (-36.9%)

Table 4.2: Global emission levels (in GtCO_2) and % changes to the BAU with the same technology assumptions in 2050 caused by selected cooperation cases in different technology scenarios under default damages.

While the differences in emission levels across technology scenarios are not large on a global level, there are differences in cooperation among countries. We find that, for default damages, the grand coalition N is not stable for any technology scenario. Instead, other possible coalitions result in a higher global value (the global values for all relevant coalitions are provided in Table B.1 in Appendix B). In the *opt* scenario and the *mean* scenario, the best coalition consists of all countries except ANZ and JPN. While ANZ and JPN are the only blocking regions in the *mean* scenario, two more blocking regions exist in the *opt* scenario, namely EUR and EXP. In particular, the coalitions $N\backslash\{$ANZ, JPN, EXP$\}$, $N\backslash\{$EUR, ANZ, JPN$\}$ and $N\backslash\{$EUR, JPN$\}$ also result in a global value higher than the grand coalition, although this is still lower than the best coalition $N\backslash\{$ANZ, JPN$\}$.

In the *pess* scenario, we find a different best coalition, consisting of all regions except ANZ. This is the only blocking coalition in this scenario, indicating that global cooperation is "closer" to being stable than in the *mean* and *opt* scenarios. In particular, JPN is not among the blocking countries, in contrast to the other two scenarios.

The resulting emission levels of the best coalition are very close to those of global cooperation (see Table 4.2) For the coalitions without ANZ and JPN, the emission levels remain slightly higher, because the mitigation benefit of ANZ and JPN is not accounted for by the remaining regions, and vice versa. An exception here is the $N\backslash\{\text{ANZ, JPN}\}$ coalition in the *opt* scenario, which shows the lowest global emission levels of all scenarios. This is caused by low marginal mitigation costs for $N\backslash\{\text{ANZ, JPN}\}$ in the emission range implied by default damages. Marginal mitigation costs for N are higher, leading to higher optimal emissions.

Results for the other damages scenarios are summarized in Table 4.3. This shows the best coalition for all scenarios, the global emission level caused by the best coalition, the total number of blocking coalitions in each scenario, and all the regions that act as singletons in any of the blocking coalitions. The values for each coalition by scenario are given in Table B.1 in Appendix B.

The results indicate that high damages due to climate change encourage cooperation, as the grand coalition is stable for the *mean* and *pess* scenarios and only three blocking coalitions exist in the *opt* scenario, confirming the results of Chapter 3. In contrast, there are many blocking coalitions if damages are low, particularly in the *opt* and *mean* scenarios. The best coalition in these two scenarios consists of only five regions, with three regions blocking cooperation.

That higher damages tend to favor cooperation is a direct consequence of region's incentives. Higher damages also mean higher benefits from mitigation for all regions. Therefore, even regions with economic disincentives for global mitigation efforts, like the blocking countries above, might prefer global cooperation to "All Singletons", if this greatly reduces damage costs.

Damage Scenario	**Technology Scenario**	**Best coalition**	**Global emission level for best coalition (GtCO_2)**	**# blocking coalitions**	**singleton regions in any blocking coalitions**
	opt	$N\setminus\{$EUR, ANZ, JPN$\}$	40.6	21	EUR, ANZ, JPN, CHN
Low	*mean*	$N\setminus\{$ANZ, JPN, CHN$\}$	42.6	20	EUR, ANZ, JPN, CHN
	pess	$N\setminus\{$ANZ$\}$	40.4	3	ANZ, JPN
	opt	$N\setminus\{$ANZ, JPN$\}$	34.0	6	EUR, ANZ, JPN, EXP
Default	*mean*	$N\setminus\{$ANZ, JPN$\}$	36.1	3	ANZ, JPN
	pess	$N\setminus\{$ANZ$\}$	35.7	1	ANZ
	opt	$N\setminus\{$ANZ, JPN$\}$	28.0	3	ANZ, JPN
High	*mean*	N	27.9	0	
	pess	N	28.8	0	

Table 4.3: Best coalition and blocking coalitions in all scenarios.

	BAU			**BC**			**GC**		
	pess	***mean***	***opt***	***pess***	***mean***	***opt***	***pess***	***mean***	***opt***
Consumption (BAU-*mean* = 100)	99.8	100.0	100.6	98.2	98.4	98.7	98.2	98.8	98.7
Emissions (BAU-*mean* = 100)	101.2	100.0	96.9	64.4	65.1	61.1	63.8	63.5	61.8
CO_2 price in coalition (weighted global price) US$/t$CO_2$				72.8	51.1	53.3	72.5	60.1	50.7
Electricity price (BAU-*mean* = 100)	101.5	100.0	96.2	109.2	104.6	95.6	109.1	104.2	95.6
Oil price (BAU-*mean* = 100)	101.3	100.0	97.1	89.9	90.3	88.1	89.8	89.7	88.3

Table 4.4: Key economic and ecological variables in 2050 for BAU, BC and GC under different technology scenarios and under default damages.

The *pess* scenario produces the lowest number of blocking coalitions among all the damages scenarios, while the *opt* scenario always produces the highest number. Overall, higher damages and more pessimistic technological assumptions both tend to favor stable global cooperation. The drivers behind these findings are investigated in the following sections.

4.2.2 Global effects and regional burden sharing

To analyse the direct effects of the technological assumptions and especially the indirect effects due to cooperation in more detail, we analyzed all default damages scenarios with the DART model. Comparing the best coalition (BC) to the case of global cooperation (GC) sheds light on the indirect effects due to cooperation. Table 4.4 summarizes the major global variables for these scenarios.

The effects of the different technological assumptions are small[2] for both global consumption and global emissions, and there is little difference between the GC and the BC cases. Thus, on a global level technological variations in the electricity sector have neither a significant direct nor a significant indirect effect due to changes in cooperation. Absolute consumption is slightly higher for the *opt* scenarios and lower for the *pess* scenarios. Direct mitigation costs, as reflected in carbon prices, are highest in the *pess* scenarios, but since this is not the case for the total effects reflected in the consumption levels, this is obviously offset by indirect effects, due to e.g. changes in comparative advantages, trade flows and energy market effects. Vice versa, emissions are slightly lower for *opt* and this is mostly also the case for *mean* scenarios compared to *pess* scenarios. The exception is that more cooperation in the *pess* scenario, compared to the *mean* scenario, leads to a lower global emission level in the *pess* scenario, though the difference between GC and BC remains below 3%. Note also that, due to carbon leakage, the

[2] For a detailed discussion of the role of the uncertainties in the power sector and a discussion why overall effects are only small see Weitzel (2015).

emissions of the non-cooperating region ANZ, which does not undertake any mitigation efforts in BC, are higher than in the BAU scenario. Both cooperation cases (BC and GC) entail significant emission reductions relative to BAU. Cooperation furthermore plays a role for the direct mitigation costs reflected in carbon prices. With less cooperation, the carbon price is higher for the coalition for the *opt* and *pess* scenarios, with a visible increase of almost 5% in the *opt* scenario, when both ANZ and JPN do not cooperate. Interestingly, under *mean* technology assumptions the price in BC is 15% lower than in GC. This is caused by the shape of the consumption function for $N\backslash\{\text{ANZ, JPN}\}$, which is steepest under *mean* assumptions, inducing the least ambitious relative emission target in the BC scenario (see Table 4.2) and therefore requires only a relatively low carbon price to reach the target. Table 4.4 also shows the electricity and oil prices for the the different scenarios. As expected, for BAU both prices are lower under optimistic technology assumptions. Also, the effects of emission reductions are significant in GC and technological assumptions matter. Electricity prices increase under mean and pessimistic technology assumptions, because more expensive renewable electricity is produced under climate constraints. For optimistic assumptions prices fall, because faster progress in learning about solar energy dominates other effects. Oil demand and prices under GC are highest for pessimistic technology assumptions. In the BC case, the different cooperation cases yield more diverse patterns. Figure 4.1 shows the resulting electricity production in 2050, in petawatt-hours (PWh). In all cases, more electricity is produced under more optimistic technological assumptions, and the share of renewables and CCS increases with emission reductions. For solar, there is a visible increase especially in the optimistic scenarios. One significant effect of cooperation is that fossil fuel use without CCS in the *pess* and *mean* BC scenarios is around 2%/ 7% higher than in the GC case. A major driver for this is the different level of carbon prices. These changes go hand in hand with differences in the use of CCS. CCS use is 1.4%/ 3.8% lower in BC than in GC for *pess*/*mean* technology assumptions, respectively, but 1.4%

higher for the *opt* scenario. Total fossil electricity production (fossil + CCS) is very similar in GC and BC and differs by no more than 2.1% under *mean* technology assumptions.

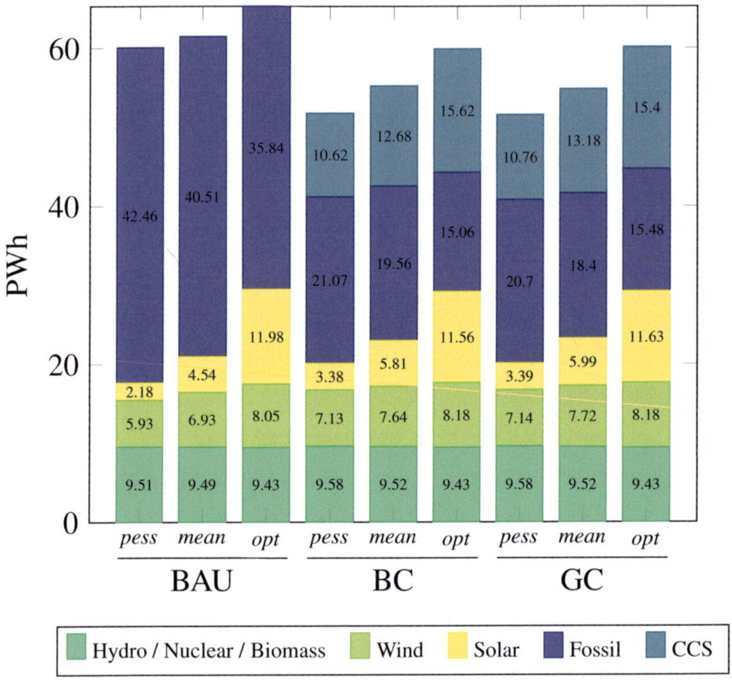

Figure 4.1: Global electricity production in 2050 by scenario (default damages scenarios).

Turning to the regional effects, Table 4.5 shows the change in consumption for the different regions in 2050 relative to the BAU scenario with the same technological assumptions. Indirect effects on the macro level can be seen by comparing the cooperation cases AS, BC and GC. As expected, differences between GC and BC are visible for ANZ and JPN, while these are small for the regions that do not change their cooperation behaviour. Absolute levels are heavily influenced by whether a region exports fossil fuels and loses export revenue under emission reductions (especially EXP and ANZ) or whether the region is an energy importer that profits from cheaper fossil fuels net of carbon prices when emissions are reduced (especially IND, JPN, EUR and CHN).

	AS			**BC**			**GC**		
	pess	*mean*	*opt*	*pess*	*mean*	*opt*	*pess*	*mean*	*opt*
NAM	0.0	0.0	0.0	-1.8	-1.9	-2.2	-1.8	-2.0	-2.1
EUR	0.4	0.4	0.3	-0.6	-1.4	-2.0	-0.6	-1.4	-1.9
ANZ	-3.3	-2.6	-1.9	-3.3	-2.7	-2.1	-5.0	-4.6	-4.1
JPN	0.7	0.6	0.3	-0.3	0.1	-1.4	-0.4	-1.1	-1.6
EXP	-1.7	-1.5	-1.0	-7.0	-6.4	-6.2	-7.1	-6.6	-6.1
CHN	0.0	0.0	0.0	0.1	0.2	-0.3	0.1	0.1	-0.1
IND	1.3	1.1	0.6	0.8	0.8	0.5	0.8	0.9	0.6
ROW	-0.4	-0.1	-0.2	-1.3	-1.3	-1.6	-1.3	-1.3	-1.5

Table 4.5: Change in consumption in 2050 by scenario, relative to the BAU scenario with the same technological assumptions, in % (default damages scenarios).

In the electricity sector, indirect effects on renewable production are visible, also mainly for ANZ and JPN. This is discussed in detail in the context of cooperation drivers in Section 4.2.3. The difference between BC and GC is smaller for the other regions that are only affected by non-cooperation of JPN and ANZ. In contrast, the global shift from fossil without CCS to fossil with CCS is especially apparent in the *mean* and *opt* scenarios. This can be seen in Table 4.6, which shows the change in fossil electricity production without and with CCS in BC compared to GC, in terawatt-hours (TWh).

Under pessimistic technology assumptions, significant differences between BC and GC in fossil electricity production with and without CCS are only found in ANZ and JPN. This changes under more optimistic assumptions. In the *mean* scenario, which features a big drop in the carbon price between BC and GC (see Table 4.4), NAM produces significantly more fossil electricity

	pess		*mean*		*opt*	
	w/o CCS	**with CCS**	**w/o CCS**	**with CCS**	**w/o CCS**	**with CCS**
NAM	-17	3	**73 (+38.9%)**	-23	0	2
EUR	-10	-3	12	-23	**-33 (-3.6%)**	30
ANZ	**418 (420%)**	**-93 (-100%)**	**485 (inf*)**	**-145 (-100%)**	**336 (inf*)**	**-159 (-98.3%)**
JPN	**17 (11.2%)**	**-20 (-9.2%)**	**332 (inf*)**	**-243 (-73.7%)**	**102 (inf*)**	**-99 (-26.3%)**
EXP	0	-6	0	-12	0	19
CHN	-23	2	168	**-57 (-12.2%)**	**-422 (-6.2%)**	**223 (27.5%)**
IND	-6	-14	78	-3	**-210 (-4.9%)**	**74 (15.1%)**
ROW	-4	-18	12	8	**-194 (-5.6%)**	**131 (3.9%)**
World	374	-147	**1.162 (+6.3%)**	**-499 (-3.8%)**	-421	220

Table 4.6: Change in electricity production from fossil energy sources with and without CCS in the BC case, compared to the GC case (in TWh, default damages scenarios).

*No fossil production without CCS in GC

Bold figures - % changes $\geq$ 3%, % change shown in brackets without CCS (and a little less with CCS) in BC. The same thing happens in CHN with the difference that the decrease in CCS electricity production is higher in relative terms. Under optimistic technology assumptions, the shifts are even larger. Here, the carbon price is higher in BC, and CHN, IND, ROW and to a lesser degree also EUR produce significantly less fossil electricity without CCS and more electricity with CCS.

In summary, the indirect effects of different technology assumptions are relatively small on a global level, but are visible in the energy systems on a regional level. Under pessimistic assumptions, the effects are visible primarily for ANZ and JPN, while under mean and optimistic assumptions, there are significant changes to the regional patterns of fossil electricity production with and without CCS.

4.2.3 Drivers of cooperation

To explain the drivers of cooperation and how the technological assumptions affect the incentives for cooperation, it is necessary to look at both climate damages and consumption losses from mitigation measures. To shed light on the latter, we again use the results from DART and compare the AS and the GC cases.

The greater the damages due to climate change for a region, the higher its incentives to mitigate emissions and engage in cooperation. For this reason, regions with generally higher damages (EXP, ROW) have a greater incentive to cooperate. Across scenarios this incentive is higher with higher global emissions (shown in Table 4.2) and higher resulting damages. While cooperation reduces emissions by 9.3 GtCO_2 and 9.2 GtCO_2 in the *pess* and *mean* scenarios, respectively, the reduction in the *opt* scenario is only 8 GtCO_2. Thus the incentives to cooperate are lower in the *opt* scenario, so that it is no surprise that this technology scenario produces the highest number of blocking coalitions. To recall, the regional order of damages can be seen in Figure 3.2 in Chapter 3.

Consumption losses, measured here for the year 2050, are driven by three factors (see Peterson and Weitzel, 2015): direct mitigation costs, indirect mitigation costs, which are mostly driven by the effects on fossil fuel exports and imports, and finally the cost of or income from permit trading, which is not relevant for our analysis. Theoretically, the incentives resulting from cheaper renewables and CCS are unclear and depend, for example, on market shares and production with and without emission reductions.
We investigated the incentives of regions in more detail. Regions are (a) affected to varying degrees by changes in technological assumptions and (b) experience different consumption losses when moving from "All Singletons" to global cooperation. Figure 4.2 shows both effects.

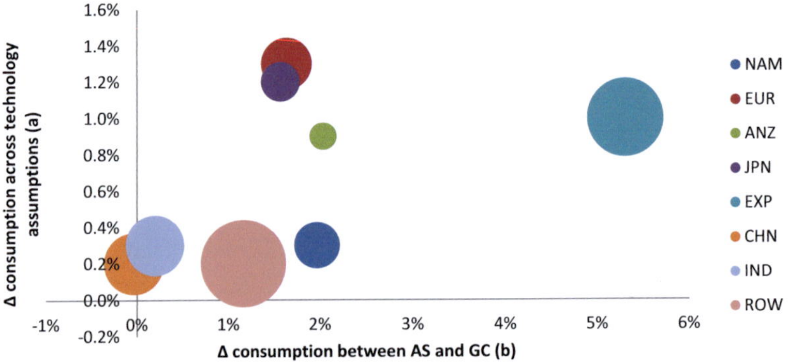

Bubble size corresponds to the default damages of a region for a temperature increase of 2°C.

Figure 4.2: Effects of technology scenarios, consumption losses, and damages for all regions (default damages scenarios).

The effect of technological assumptions (a) is measured as the difference in consumption loss across the different technology scenarios in the GC case, as shown in Table 4.5. Since the difference in consumption between AS and GC (b) drives the cooperation decision in the game-theoretical model, this is also derived from Table 4.5[3]. Finally, the incentive to cooperate is influenced by the amount of damages in each region, as outlined above. The size of each region's bubble in Figure 4.2 corresponds to the default damages of a region for a temperature increase of 2°C.

For NAM, CHN, IND, and ROW, the effects of the different technological assumptions are rather low so that the incentives to cooperate remain stable across technology scenarios. These regions always support global cooperation since there are only small or medium consumption losses between GC and AS. ANZ with low climate damages never has an incentive to engage in cooperation, even though the difference between GC and AS is not so different from, e.g., NAM. For JPN and EUR there is a medium difference between AS and GC, but technological differences matter most. As Table 4.3 shows, the negative effects of emission reductions in the *opt* scenario (EUR and JPN) and the *mean* scenario (JPN) lead to some blocking behaviour. For EXP, the mitigation costs under cooperation are high, but so are the gains due to reduced damages, which dominate in *pess* and *mean*. In *opt*, there is some incentive to defect even though this shows the lowest differences between GC and AS.

For regional burden sharing, these results imply that technological assumptions directly affect the burden of EUR and JPN and to a smaller degree also of EXP and ANZ. In three of these cases, EXP, JPN and EUR, the technological assumptions also affect the willingness to cooperate and through this mechanism the burdens of other regions. In the case of EUR (EXP) this is only the case for two (one) suboptimal blocking coalitions under *opt* assumptions, while JPN defects for optimistic and mean assumptions in the best partition. ANZ, on the other hand, always blocks. The regional incentives to cooperate are analysed now in more detail for the four blocking regions. We start by discussing the incentives for ANZ and JPN, whose defections produce the best coalitions, and then move on to EUR and EXP.

[3] The difference between AS and GC in Figure 4.2 represents the average difference over all technology scenarios.

For **ANZ**, damages from climate change are low and provide little incentive to mitigate unilaterally. As the mitigation costs are in line with other single regions for modest emission targets, ANZ's ratio of mitigation costs and damages is so high that ANZ does not mitigate emissions at all in AS. The move from AS to GC thus means that its economy moves from zero carbon prices to prices of $250 - 280$US\$/tCO_2 in 2050, implying a reduction of emissions and emission intensity by 58% to 65% in the different technology scenarios in 2050. For comparison, emission reductions in GC compared to AS for all other regions except EXP are only around 20-30% (NAM, EUR, JPN, IND) or even negligible (ROW, CHN).

Figure 4.3 shows electricity generation in 2050 for the different scenarios. Since ANZ does not implement any carbon prices in BAU, AS, and BC, electricity production patterns are very similar. Fossil fuel production even increases in AS and BC, compared to BAU, because the lack of a carbon price in ANZ gives the region a comparative advantage relative to the other regions. By not joining the coalition, ANZ's energy system in BC is almost the same as in AS for *pess* and *mean*. Under optimistic technology assumptions, ANZ produces more solar and wind in AS than in BC, where ANZ has a larger comparative advantage in fossil fuel production, due to the large difference in carbon prices to the other regions. In the GC scenario, the energy system looks very different with drastically reduced fossil electricity production that is also mostly equipped with CCS.

The high absolute consumption losses as the result of emission reductions are also driven by reduced export revenues for fossil fuels (which are 30-45% lower in GC and BC compared to BAU in 2050 with the same technology assumptions). Under optimistic technology assumptions, changes in export revenues from fossil fuels also incentivize cooperation: In GC-*opt* they are almost 20% lower than in AS-*opt* in 2050. Under pessimistic and mean technology assumptions, however, export revenues are about 3% higher in GC than in AS, but these small changes do not lead to cooperation and the effects of increased carbon costs dominate.

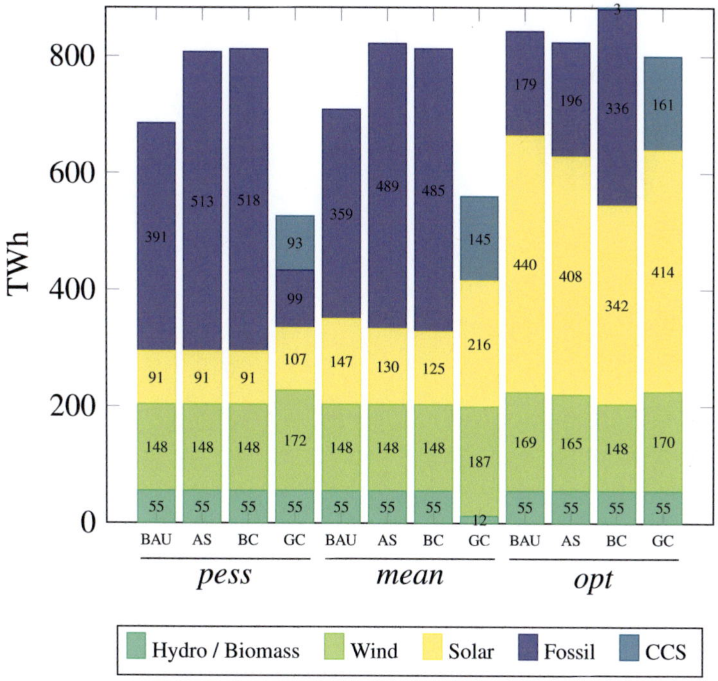

Figure 4.3: Electricity production in ANZ in 2050 by scenario.

JPN has only few domestic energy resources and relies on fossil fuel imports for over 90% of its energy needs (U.S. Energy Information Administration, 2015) so that it benefits from stricter emission reductions and reduced fossil fuel use. On the other hand it experiences the second lowest damages of all regions and thus benefits only marginally from additional emission reductions in the case of global cooperation, compared to "All Singletons". As Table 4.5 shows, the difference in economic costs between the two cases is relatively high under mean and optimistic technology assumptions, and lower under pessimistic assumptions, which explains why JPN does not defect in this case. Figure 4.4 shows JPN's electricity mix.

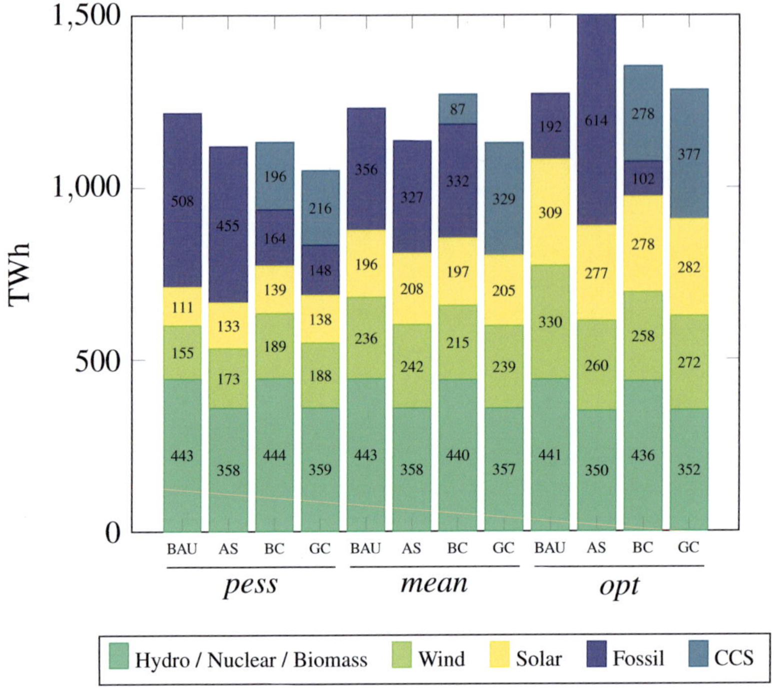

Figure 4.4: Electricity production in JPN in 2050 by scenario.

In the *mean* scenario, JPN reacts to global cooperation by switching its fossil fuel based electricity production to CCS, while leaving all other sources of electricity almost unchanged. This indicates that further expansion of non-fossil electricity production[4] is not economically viable for JPN, as the best locations for renewable electricity have already been exploited under "All Singletons". CCS remains the best mitigation option in the electricity sector, enhancing JPN's reliance on fossil fuel imports. JPN even increases its fossil fuel imports when aiming at ambitious emission targets under global coop-

[4] Note that for all countries and all scenarios electricity production from nuclear is fixed exogenously. This approach reflects that the use of nuclear power is a political decision rather than an economic one.

eration, because CCS requires higher resource input for the same amount of electricity due to efficiency losses. In sum, JPN does not benefit from reduced emissions or from lower fossil fuel imports in the case of global cooperation, but still has to pay for the costs of decarbonizing its electricity production. Therefore, it prefers "All Singletons" to global cooperation in the *mean* scenario.

A similar situation occurs in the *opt* scenario. As it is still not economically viable for JPN to substantially expand its renewable electricity production, JPN has to switch its fossil fuel based electricity production to incorporate CCS under global cooperation, while significantly reducing the total amount of electricity produced. Consequently, JPN again prefers "All Singletons" to global cooperation. The situation is more favorable in the *pess* scenario, where JPN's emission target (in absolute terms) under GC is less ambitious and hence JPN only has to apply CCS to part of its fossil fuel based electricity production, while slightly reducing the overall amount of electricity produced. These changes are quite modest compared to the transformation in the *mean* and *opt* scenarios. Consequently, JPN does not block global cooperation in the *pess* scenario.

As fossil fuel exporters, **EXP** is negatively affected by global emission reductions. EXP has a strong incentive to block global cooperation, because its revenues from exporting fossil fuels in 2050 are 5-6% higher under "All Singletons" than under global cooperation for all technological assumptions. Its emissions are 50% lower in GC than in AS and it faces large consumption losses when moving from AS to GC. The cooperation of EXP in *pess* and *mean*, and mostly also *opt*, is driven by the significant damages in EXP due to climate change. These damages also vary substantially between different technological scenarios. Table 4.7 shows the climate damages for EXP for all default damages scenarios, in the cases of "All Singletons" and global cooperation, as well as the corresponding relative damage reduction.

	pess	*mean*	*opt*
All Singletons	56.02	55.70	50.74
Global Cooperation	32.11	32.24	31.63
Damage reduction	-42.68%	-42.12%	-37.66%

Table 4.7: Damages in the EXP region by scenario in the cases of "All Singletons" and global cooperation (default damages, BAU-*mean* = 100).

While the damage reduction induced by global cooperation is similar in the *pess* and *mean* scenarios, it is significantly lower in the *opt* scenario. This is directly related to the change in global emissions for each scenario, as referenced above, which is lowest in the *opt* scenario. Consequently, the cooperation benefit for EXP is substantially lower in the *opt* scenario than in the other scenarios. This explains why EXP acts as a singleton in some blocking coalitions in the *opt* scenario, while it does not do so in the *mean* and *pess* scenarios.

EUR is characterized by a combination of medium damages and relatively high direct mitigation costs. It profits from lower costs for fossil fuel imports under global emission reductions, but these effects are not large in total (savings of a maximum of 5% in 2050 in GC relative to AS). Under pessimistic and mean technology assumptions, damages dominate again, but the gains from cooperation are smaller under optimistic assumptions, where emissions reductions due to global cooperation are lower (see the case of EXP). Also, the change in consumption is clearly the highest in the *opt* scenario (see Table 4.5), which explains why EUR sometimes defects.

In summary, technological assumptions make a difference for cooperation in JPN, EXP and EUR. The main drivers are

- smaller additional emission reduction under optimistic technological assumptions and the resulting smaller damage reduction through cooperation. This is relevant for EUR and EXP.

- larger increase in mitigation costs for global cooperation that results from changes in the energy system. This is relevant for JPN.

4.3 Conclusion

We found that the stability of global climate cooperation varies depending on the assumptions made about the development of key low-carbon power technologies, wind, solar photovoltaic and carbon capture and storage, and those made about climate related damages. Global cooperation was found to be stable in the scenarios with mean or pessimistic assumptions about the development of key low-carbon power technologies and when climate damages are high. In contrast, no stable outcome was achieved in scenarios assuming optimistic technological development (for all damage scenarios) or when climate damages were low or at the default level (for all technology assumptions). The best coalition did vary with assumptions about technological development for all damages scenarios.

The main blocking region in our analysis is Australia / New Zealand, which is not willing to participate in the grand coalition in any case in which global cooperation is not stable. In these cases (unstable grand coalition), Australia / New Zealand is not willing to mitigate any emissions at all, since the welfare losses due to carbon prices in this very coal-intensive region outweigh the (generally low) benefits of cooperation due to reduced climate damages.

For the second main blocking region, Japan, cooperation depends on the assumptions about the technological development of the key mitigation technologies. Under default damages, Japan only supports global cooperation for pessimistic technological assumptions, due to a relatively unambitious emission target, which mostly prevents the need for an expensive transformation of the electricity sector.

In general, under more optimistic assumptions about technological development, other regions (Europe and the region of fossil fuel exporting countries) were also found to be less cooperative and defect in some partitions. This is caused by the varying benefits of cooperation (in the form of damage reduction), which are lower under more optimistic assumptions about technological development. The result is similar to that in Helm and Schmidt (2015), who find that early investments in research and development decrease the attractiveness of cooperation.

These regional impacts mean that international burden sharing is affected by assumptions about technological development both directly through changing welfare effects and indirectly through varying cooperation behaviour. As we model technological uncertainty about electricity generation technologies, the electricity system is affected the most. For the default damages scenario, which was analysed in more detail, the effects are primarily visible in the domestic electricity system of blocking regions under pessimistic assumptions about technological development. For mean and optimistic assumptions about technological development, the global patterns of fossil fuel and CCS electricity production change significantly and most regions are affected. Renewable energy production depends more on the technological assumptions themselves and less on cooperation.

In sum, this chapter shows that different assumptions about climate damages and the costs of key mitigation technologies can substantially affect the results concerning technology deployment and regional burden sharing, and hence the stability of global climate cooperation. In situations of unstable global cooperation, non-global climate clubs have been proposed as a way of tackling for the climate cooperation problem (e.g. Grasso and Roberts, 2014; Nordhaus, 2015). Our findings generally support the proposition that a different solution might be needed. The idea of climate clubs is further investigated in Chapter 6.

5 Stability of global climate cooperation under uncertainty

While the previous chapter analysed the implications of different future pathways for technological development, it did not look at the direct impact of uncertainty on the stability of climate cooperation. However, it stands to reason that countries incorporate uncertainty into their decision making and that uncertainty might change optimal emission levels. Therefore, incentives to cooperate might also be affected, especially if countries have different preferences about behaviour under uncertainty.

Further, while Chapter 4 mainly considered the uncertain pathways of technological development, future damages from climate change are also highly uncertain. While several effects of climate change are well understood, their economic effects are still quite uncertain (IPCC, 2014a). Many current estimates also do not account for certain factors likely to influence the impact of climate change, such as changing weather patterns or tipping points (Burke et al., 2015; IPCC, 2014a).

In the past years, several game-theoretic models based on internal and external stability have been expanded to include uncertainty about one or multiple parameter values. Bramoullé and Treich (2009) find that uncertainty about the impact of a global pollutant can have a positive environmental effect, as risk averse polluters reduce their emissions. However, Benchekroun and van Long (2013) find that this result does not hold up in a dynamic game with a stock pollutant. Barrett (2013) analyses a threshold game and finds that uncertainty about the threshold causes cooperation to be unstable.

A few studies have included uncertainty about mitigation costs. Hong and Karp (2014) use a theoretical model with uncertainty in the mitigation cost parameter and find that higher risk aversion of countries increases membership in a stable climate agreement, but reduces mitigation levels. Kolstad and Ulph (2011) and Finus and Pintassilgo (2013) use a similar theoretical model with uncertainty in the benefit-cost ratio of mitigation. They find that such uncertainty can increase the size of a stable coalition, if countries are symmetric under uncertainty, but asymmetric after the true nature of the parameter is revealed. However, this negative effect of the removal of uncertainty can mostly be avoided by a suitable transfer scheme (Dellink and Finus, 2012). Dellink et al. (2008) employ a numerical model and find that uncertainty in the mitigation benefit parameters has a larger influence on the stability of coalitions than uncertainty in the mitigation cost parameters.

To the best of my knowledge, no attempt has been made to introduce uncertainty into a model of international climate cooperation using core stability. This is despite the good alignment of the concept with the international climate negotiations and the striking result of the deterministic model, as described in Chapter 2. However, the underlying concept of a cooperative game has been extended into a *cooperative game with stochastic payoffs* (Suijs et al., 1999; Timmer et al., 2005), including modified definitions of preferences, the objective function of coalitions, allocations, and of the core. Two distinct allocation concepts are put forward by Suijs et al. (1999) and Timmer et al. (2005).

This chapter provides the first inclusion of uncertainty in a model of international climate cooperation using core stability. In particular, this chapter determines whether the result of stable global cooperation in the deterministic model carries over into a model with uncertainty. The game is extended into a cooperative game with stochastic payoffs, based on adapted preferences and objective functions. I analyse two model setups, one including technological uncertainty and one including uncertainty in climate damages.

Further, I check the (non-)emptiness of the core for both allocation concepts put forward in the literature, for both types of uncertainty.
Section 5.1 gives a general overview of the model and the different game-theoretic concepts. Section 5.2 analyses the model with technological uncertainty, while Section 5.3 analyses uncertainty in climate damages. Section 5.4 situates the results in the general context of international climate negotiations and policy. Section 5.5 concludes.

5.1 Uncertainty in a model of climate cooperation

The model in this chapter is based on the original theoretical CT model. This means that the international economic effects that were the focus of Chapters 3 and 4 are no longer present in the model going forward. The absence of these effects allows for an independent analysis of the pure impact of uncertainty.
In the subsequent sections of this chapter, either the consumption or the damage function are modified to include uncertainty. They become a *stochastic variable*. Consequently, the utility of player i also becomes a stochastic variable U_i:

$$U_i(E_i, E_N) = C_i(E_i) - D_i(E_N). \tag{5.1}$$

In order to define the *cooperative game with stochastic payoffs*, some adjustments to the deterministic CT model are needed, following Suijs et al. (1999). As payoffs are now stochastic, a *preference ordering* $\succeq_i$ is needed, which indicates whether player i prefers one stochastic payoff to another. This chapter uses the specific preference ordering proposed by Suijs et al. (1999). Let $\alpha_i \in (0, 0.5]$ and $q_{\alpha_i}(X)$ be the α_i-quantile of payoff X. Then player i prefers payoff X to payoff Y if and only if the α_i-quantile of payoff X is larger than the α_i-quantile of payoff Y:

$$X \succeq_i Y :\Leftrightarrow q_{\alpha_i}(X) \geq q_{\alpha_i}(Y). \tag{5.2}$$

This means that $q_{\alpha_i}(X)$ is the *certainty equivalent* of payoff X, $ce_i(X)$. For payoffs with symmetric distribution[1], $\alpha_i = 0.5$ implies risk neutral behaviour and $\alpha_i < 0.5$ implies risk averse behaviour, i.e.

$$ce_i(X) < \mathbb{E}(X). \tag{5.3}$$

I will occasionally refer to the *level of risk aversion*, which is higher with lower α_i[2]. Note that $\alpha_i > 0.5$, i.e. risk loving behaviour, is excluded, for reasons that will become apparent later in the chapter.
To determine emissions and value for each possible coalition $S \subseteq N$, I follow the original CT model. Let $j \notin S$. Then player j maximizes (the certainty equivalent of) its individual utility:

$$\max_{E_j} ce_j(U_j(E_j, E_N)). \tag{5.4}$$

All players $i \in S$ maximize the sum of (the certainty equivalent of) the utility of all members:

$$\max_{(E_i)_{i \in S}} \sum_{i \in S} ce_i(U_i(E_i, E_N)). \tag{5.5}$$

These parallel optimizations provide deterministic emission levels for all players. The *value function* $V(S)$ provides the payoffs for each coalition

[1] This will be the case throughout the chapter.

[2] The level of risk aversion as used in this chapter should not be confused with the *degree of risk aversion*, which is defined as the ratio of second and first derivative of an agent's utility function (Pratt, 1964; Arrow, 1965).

$S \subseteq N$. It is given by the sum of the utility of all members of the coalition, and is therefore a stochastic variable:

$$V(S) = \sum_{i \in S} U_i(E_i, E_N). \tag{5.6}$$

5.1.1 Allocation concepts

In order to check whether a stable global agreement is possible, I continue to use core stability. For the deterministic case, the core contains all allocations of the value of the grand coalition N, such that no coalition can achieve a higher payoff by defecting from the grand coalition. This requires the definition of the concept of an *allocation*. For games with stochastic payoffs, two different concepts of an allocation exist: the concept of *pure payoff allocation* by Timmer et al. (2005) and the concept of *expectation and risk allocation* by Suijs et al. (1999).

The concept of pure payoff allocation defines an allocation of $V(S)$ as a vector of multiples of $V(S)$ (Timmer et al., 2005). Let $h \in \mathbb{R}^{|S|}$ with $\sum_{i \in S} h_i = 1$. Then player $i \in S$ receives $h_i V(S)$.

In the concept of expectation and risk allocation (Suijs et al., 1999), an allocation is defined by two vectors, one for the expected value of the stochastic payoff, and one for the risk. Let $(d, r) \in \mathbb{R}^{|S|} \times \mathbb{R}_+^{|S|}$ with

$$\sum_{i \in S} d_i = \mathbb{E}(V(S)), \tag{5.7a}$$

$$\sum_{i \in S} r_i = 1. \tag{5.7b}$$

Then player $i \in S$ receives

$$d_i + r_i(V(S) - \mathbb{E}(V(S))). \tag{5.8}$$

The pure payoff allocation concept is a direct translation from the deterministic allocation concept, as every player receives a share of the coalition value.

However, as the coalition value is now stochastic, this means that a player can only receive a payoff if she also takes on risk. For risk averse players, the certainty equivalent of the received payoff is reduced by this presence of risk. The expectation and risk allocation concept remedies this drawback by allowing for an independent allocation of the expected value and the risk of the stochastic payoff. As a consequence, it is possible for very risk averse players to offload (some of) their risk on to less risk averse players, improving (the certainty equivalent of) total utility. On the other hand, risk neutral players can "insure" other players against risk by taking it on themselves, and receive some compensation for this service.

For both allocation concepts, an allocation X of $V(N)$ is in the core of the game, if for no coalition $S \subset N$ there exists an allocation Y of $V(S)$, such that $Y_i \succ X_i$ for all players $i \in S$. In other words, all members of a coalition S need to agree on a deviation from the grand coalition N.

For the concept of pure payoff allocation, several convexity concepts exist, which all imply that the core of the game is not empty (Timmer et al., 2005). For the concept of expectation and risk allocation, the core of the game is not empty if and only if (Suijs et al., 1999)

$$\max_{i \in N} q_{\alpha_i}(V(N)) \geq \sum_{S \subset N} \delta_S \max_{i \in S} q_{\alpha_i}(V(S)), \tag{5.9}$$

where δ_S is a *balanced map*, i.e.

$$\sum_{S \subset N} \delta_S \mathbb{1}_{i \in S} = 1 \; \forall i \in N. \tag{5.10}$$

In the following sections, I will apply both allocation concepts to stochastic models of climate cooperation. Section 5.2 considers technological uncertainty, while Section 5.3 considers uncertainty in climate damages.

5.2 Technological uncertainty

This section considers uncertainty in mitigation costs, i.e. in the consumption function. For the mean μ, I use a quadratic function in emission reductions. Uncertainty increases with emission reductions, as more new technologies need to be applied. The distribution is set, such that the standard deviation, σ, increases quadratically with emission reductions, in line with the deterministic mitigation costs. A normal distribution is used. Specifically, the model is

$$C_i(E_i) \sim \mathcal{N}\left(\underbrace{C_i^0 - \gamma_i(E_i^0 - E_i)^2}_{\mu}, \underbrace{(\theta(E_i^0 - E_i)^2)^2}_{\sigma^2}\right), \tag{5.11}$$

with

- C_i^0: baseline consumption level
- E_i^0: baseline emission level
- γ_i: mitigation cost parameter
- θ: amount of uncertainty parameter
- μ: mean of normal distribution
- σ^2: variance of normal distribution

For $\alpha \leq 0.5$, this formulation ensures that, in terms of consumption, a higher emission level is preferred to a lower emission level, i.e. emission reductions are costly[3].

Damages from climate change are assumed to be known with certainty in this section. They increase quadratically with global emissions $E_N = \sum_{i=1}^{n} E_i$:

$$D_i(E_N) = \pi_i E_N^2, \tag{5.12}$$

[3] For $\alpha > 0.5$, this would not necessarily be the case, as the higher risk resulting from emission reductions is preferred to lower risk. Therefore, this case is excluded throughout the chapter.

where π_i is the damage cost parameter. The use of quadratic functions for both consumption and damages follows the literature (e.g. Diamantoudi and Sartzetakis, 2006; Eichner and Pethig, 2015) and ensures that no country or coalition has a dominant strategy[4], while the game remains analytically solvable.

Taking consumption and damage together, utility is given by

$$\begin{aligned} U_i(E_i, E_N) &= C_i(E_i) - D_i(E_N) \\ &\sim \mathcal{N}\left(C_i^0 - \gamma_i(E_i^0 - E_i)^2 - \pi_i E_N^2, (\theta(E_i^0 - E_i)^2)^2\right). \end{aligned} \tag{5.13}$$

As utility is normally distributed, the certainty equivalent of utility is

$$\begin{aligned} ce_i(U_i(E_i, E_N)) &= \mu + \sigma z(\alpha_i) \\ &= C_i^0 - \gamma_i(E_i^0 - E_i)^2 - \pi_i E_N^2 + \theta(E_i^0 - E_i)^2 z(\alpha_i), \end{aligned} \tag{5.14}$$

where $z(\alpha_i)$ is the *probit function*

$$z(\alpha_i) = \sqrt{2}\, erf^{-1}(2\alpha_i - 1), \tag{5.15}$$

$$erf(x) = \frac{2}{\sqrt{\pi}} \int_0^x e^{-t^2}\, dt. \tag{5.16}$$

$erf(x)$ is the so-called *error function.* $z(\alpha_i)$ is strictly increasing and $z(0.5) = 0$. Consequently, $z(\alpha_i) \leq 0$ for the range of α_i considered in this chapter.

Players determine their emission levels by optimizing the certainty equivalent of utility. Proposition 1 shows the resulting emission levels and the impact of uncertainty.

Proposition 1. *Let $S \subset N$. For the game with technological uncertainty,*

[4] In games with linear damage functions, a country's optimal level of emissions is independent of the level of emissions of the other players. Therefore, this optimal level of emissions is a dominant strategy.

(i) emission levels of individual players ($E_i(S)$) and global emissions ($E_N(S)$) are given by

$$E_N(S) = \frac{E_N^0}{\pi_S \sum_{i\in S} \frac{1}{\gamma_i - \theta z(\alpha_i)} + \sum_{j\notin S} \frac{\pi_j}{\gamma_j - \theta z(\alpha_j)} + 1}, \tag{5.17a}$$

$$E_i(S) = E_i^0 - \frac{\pi_S}{\gamma_i - \theta z(\alpha_i)} E_N(S) \;\; \forall i \in S, \tag{5.17b}$$

$$E_j(S) = E_j^0 - \frac{\pi_j}{\gamma_j - \theta z(\alpha_j)} E_N(S) \;\; \forall j \notin S, \tag{5.17c}$$

with $\pi_S = \sum_{i\in S} \pi_i$.

(ii) increases in the amount of uncertainty (θ) or in the level of risk aversion ($-z(\alpha)$) influence emission levels like an increase of the mitigation cost (γ).

(iii) increases in the amount of uncertainty (θ) or in the level of risk aversion ($-z(\alpha)$) lead to higher emission levels.

For reasons of readability, all theoretical proofs can be found in Appendix C.1.

Proposition 1 (ii) and (iii) follow intuitively from the fact that all players are risk averse or risk neutral. As emission reductions cause higher uncertainty, an additional "cost" of mitigation is created. This cost is treated similarly to the deterministic mitigation cost γ. As the damage function is unchanged compared to the deterministic case, the benefit from emission reductions is also unchanged. Consequently, the optimal emission levels under technological uncertainty are higher than without uncertainty.

5.2.1 Stability of global cooperation under pure payoff allocation

I now consider the stability of global cooperation in the game with technological uncertainty. Specifically, I check whether the core of the cooperative game with stochastic payoffs is non-empty for all cases, as in the deterministic case. First, I consider the game under pure payoff allocation. Proposition 2 shows that the result from the deterministic case cannot be transferred to the uncertain setup.

Proposition 2. *Under pure payoff allocation, the core of the cooperative game with stochastic payoffs and technological uncertainty can be empty.*

The proof is given by the following simple counter-example.

Example 1. *Let* $N = \{1, .., 4\}$ *and*

$$\alpha = \begin{bmatrix} 0.001 \\ 0.1 \\ 0.5 \\ 0.5 \end{bmatrix}, \quad \gamma = \pi = E^0 = \begin{bmatrix} 1 \\ 1 \\ 1 \\ 1 \end{bmatrix}, \quad C^0 = \begin{bmatrix} 10 \\ 10 \\ 10 \\ 10 \end{bmatrix}. \tag{5.18}$$

The resulting game is given in Table C.2 in Appendix C.2.

The four players in Example 1 only differ in their risk preferences. Player 1 is very risk averse, player 2 is modestly risk averse, while players 3 and 4 are risk neutral. As a result of their different levels of risk aversion, the certainty equivalent of a payoff differs between the players. Figure 5.1 shows the relation between the share of $V(N)$ a player receives and the respective certainty equivalent of the payoff, for all players.

A high share of $V(N)$ increases the payoff in expectation, but also increases the level of risk. We see that player 1 actually prefers a payoff of zero to a small share of $V(N)$, due to its high level of risk aversion. For a share larger than roughly 0.05, the increase in expectation has the larger effect and player 1 prefers the higher share. Still, the larger risk for higher shares of $V(N)$ causes the certainty equivalent of the payoff to increase at the smallest rate of all players. Player 2 experiences the same phenomenon, but the impact

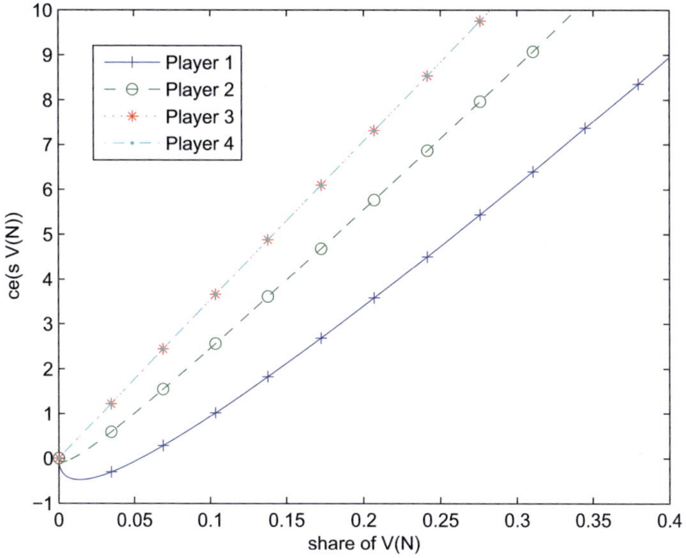

Figure 5.1: Certainty equivalent of payoff for varying share of $V(N)$, for all players in Example 1.

of risk is much smaller. For players 3 and 4, who are risk neutral, only the expected value of their share of $V(N)$ matters, and consequently the certainty equivalent of their payoff increases linearly with the share of $V(N)$.

To now show that the core of this game is empty, I compare the payoff of the grand coalition N to the payoffs of all singleton coalitions $\{i\}$. Specifically, I determine the minimum share of $V(N)$ each player needs to equal its payoff in the singleton case. For example, player 1 compares its payoff to the payoff of singleton coalition $\{1\}$. The corresponding certainty equivalent is 8.5319. In Figure 5.1, one can see that player 1 would need a share of 0.3857 of $V(N)$ or higher to prefer a proposed global allocation to the singleton payoff.

This calculation can be done for all players. The certainty equivalent of the singleton payoffs and the resulting minimum shares of $V(N)$ are shown in Table 5.1.

	Player 1	Player 2	Player 3	Player 4
Singleton payoff	8.5319	8.3033	7.6406	7.6406
Minimum share	0.3857	0.2865	0.2162	0.2162

Table 5.1: Singleton payoffs and minimum shares of $V(N)$ to satisfy corresponding singleton coalition for all players in Example 1.

The sum of the minimum shares of all players is 1.1046. As this is larger than one, no global allocation can satisfy all singleton coalitions simultaneously. Therefore, the core of the game is empty. The result is driven by the risk averse players 1 and 2. For them to join the grand coalition, both need a share of $V(N)$ substantially larger than 0.25 to compensate for the technological uncertainty associated with reaching low emission levels. While the risk neutral players 3 and 4 would be content with less than a uniform allocation, they cannot lower their share enough to allow sufficient redistribution to the risk averse players.

The result is also driven by the heterogeneity of risk aversion between the four players. If all players were as risk averse as player 1, the emission level in the grand coalition would remain higher, reducing technological uncertainty. Consequently, each player would be content with a share of $V(N)$ of 0.25 and the core of the game would not be empty. Similarly, if all players were risk neutral, the game would be similar to the deterministic case and therefore the core would not be empty. Overall, the combination of very risk averse players with risk neutral players causes the emptiness of the core in Example 1, as the wishes of both groups of players cannot be sufficiently reconciled in the grand coalition.

5.2.2 Stability of global cooperation under expectation and risk allocation

The previous section showed that under pure payoff allocation, the core of the game can be empty. This is caused by the inability for very risk averse players to receive an appropriate payoff without also taking on risk. The expectation and risk allocation concept in this section allows independent allocation of expectation and risk. This reinstates the result of core non-emptiness from the deterministic case. For the analytical proof, two simplifying assumptions are needed.

Assumption 1. *(i) All players are symmetric in all parameters except α_i, the level of risk aversion.*
(ii) At least one player is risk-neutral, i.e. $\alpha_i = 0.5$.

Proposition 3. *Under expectation and risk allocation and Assumption 1, the core of the cooperative game with stochastic payoffs and technological uncertainty is non-empty.*

Numerical simulations suggest that Proposition 3 also holds when Assumption 1 is not fulfilled. No counter-example was found.
Intuitively, Proposition 3 is a direct result from the possibility of independent risk allocation. This allows the least risk averse player to take on all risk in the grand coalition. If this player is risk neutral, the game is similar to the deterministic case and the deterministic core allocation is also in the core of the stochastic game. If the least risk averse player is not risk neutral, the acceptance of risk by this player in the grand coalition still creates a total utility surplus, compared to smaller coalitions. Most of this utility surplus can then be allocated to the least risk averse player as compensation for the acceptance of risk, so that this player also agrees to global cooperation. As the other players are made better off by being allowed to offload risk, this mechanism allows for a core stable allocation.

5.3 Uncertainty in climate damages

This section considers uncertainty in the damage function. In a reversal of the setup in the last section, the consumption function is known with certainty,

$$C_i(E_i) = C_i^0 - \gamma_i(E_i^0 - E_i)^2, \tag{5.19}$$

while the damage function is normally distributed

$$D_i(E_N) \sim \mathcal{N}\left(\pi_i E_N^2, (\kappa_i E_N^2)^2\right), \tag{5.20}$$

with parameter κ_i for the amount of uncertainty. Similar to the last section, $\alpha_i \leq 0.5$ ensures that, when considering damages, a lower global emission level is preferred to a higher global emission level, i.e. emission reductions reduce climate damages.
Utility is given by

$$\begin{aligned} U_i(E_i, E_N) &= P_i(E_i) - D_i(E_N) \\ &\sim \mathcal{N}\left(P_i^0 - \gamma_i(E_i^0 - E_i)^2 - \pi_i E_N^2, (\kappa_i E_N^2)^2\right) \end{aligned} \tag{5.21}$$

with certainty equivalent

$$ce_i(U_i(E_i, E_N)) = C_i^0 - \gamma_i(E_i^0 - E_i)^2 - \pi_i E_N^2 + \kappa_i E_N^2 z(\alpha_i). \tag{5.22}$$

Proposition 4 shows the emission levels resulting from the optimization of the certainty equivalents of utility and the effect of uncertainty.

Proposition 4. *Let $S \subset N$. For the game with uncertainty in climate damages,*

(i) emission levels of individual players and global emissions are given by

$$E_N(S) = \frac{E_N^0}{(\pi_S - (\kappa z(\alpha))_S)\sum_{i\in S}\frac{1}{\gamma_i} + \sum_{j\notin S}\frac{\pi_j - \kappa_j z(\alpha_j)}{\gamma_j} + 1}, \tag{5.23a}$$

$$E_i(S) = E_i^0 - \frac{\pi_S - (\kappa z(\alpha))_S}{\gamma_i} E_N(S), \ \forall i \in S \tag{5.23b}$$

$$E_j(S) = E_j^0 - \frac{\pi_j - \kappa_j z(\alpha_j)}{\gamma_j} E_N(S) \ \forall j \notin S, \tag{5.23c}$$

with $\pi_S = \sum_{i\in S}\pi_i$ and $(\kappa z(\alpha))_S = \sum_{i\in S}\kappa_i z(\alpha_i)$.

(ii) increases in the amount of uncertainty (κ) or in the level of risk aversion ($-z(\alpha)$) influence emission levels like an increase of the damage cost (π).

(iii) increases in the amount of uncertainty (κ) or in the level of risk aversion ($-z(\alpha)$) lead to lower emission levels.

Similar to Section 5.2, Proposition 4 (ii) and (iii) follow directly from the risk aversion of the players. As uncertainty is tied to the global emission level, emission reductions reduce uncertainty in this setup. Therefore, an extra benefit of mitigation is created by the inclusion of uncertainty, which is added to the deterministic benefit of mitigation, π. Consequently, emission levels are lower than without uncertainty.

5.3.1 Stability of global cooperation under pure payoff allocation

Again, I first consider the (non-)emptiness of the core of the cooperative game with stochastic payoffs under pure payoff allocation. In contrast to the game with technological uncertainty, global cooperation in the game with uncertainty in climate damages reduces total risk compared to the singletons case, as global emission levels are lowest under global cooperation. This can be seen in the standard deviation (σ), which increases quadratically with global emissions. Therefore, the impossibility of risk redistribution under the pure payoff allocation concept is not as detrimental to stable global cooperation as under technological uncertainty, because less risk needs to be redistributed. Consequently, the core of the game is non-empty for simple games similar to Example 1. However, games with empty core still exist, as Proposition 5 shows.

Proposition 5. *Under pure payoff allocation, the core of the cooperative game with stochastic payoffs and uncertainty in climate damages can be empty.*

The proof is given by the following counter-example.

Example 2. *Let* $N = \{1,2,3\}$ *and*

$$\alpha = \begin{bmatrix} 0.001 \\ 0.1 \\ 0.5 \end{bmatrix}, \quad \kappa = \begin{bmatrix} 0.01 \\ 0.1 \\ 0.5 \end{bmatrix}, \quad \gamma = \begin{bmatrix} 1 \\ 1 \\ 1 \end{bmatrix}, \quad \pi = \begin{bmatrix} 0.1 \\ 0.01 \\ 0.001 \end{bmatrix}$$

$$C^0 = 10^4 \begin{bmatrix} 1 \\ 5 \\ 5 \end{bmatrix}, \quad E^0 = 10^2 \begin{bmatrix} 1 \\ 1 \\ 1 \end{bmatrix}. \tag{5.24}$$

The resulting game is given in Table C.3 in Appendix C.2.

The three players in Example 2 differ in their risk preferences, with player 1 being very risk averse, player 2 being modestly risk averse and player 3 being risk neutral. They also differ in their personal amount of risk (κ) and in the deterministic damage cost (π). Player 1 is very risk averse, but experiences relatively little risk, while having the highest deterministic damage cost. Player 2's amount of risk and deterministic damage cost are both modestly high, similar to the level of risk aversion. Player 3 is risk neutral, while his amount of risk is the highest of all players and the deterministic damage cost is the lowest. Figure 5.2 again shows the relation between the share of $V(N)$ a player receives and the payoff.

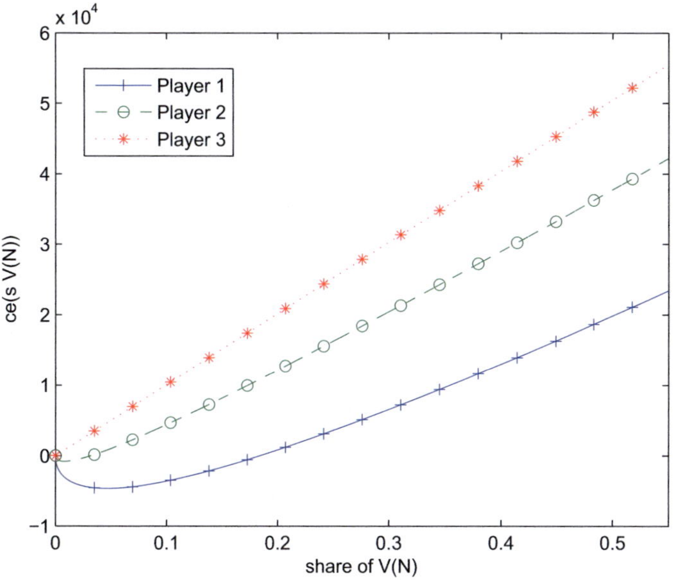

Figure 5.2: Certainty equivalent of payoff for varying share of $V(N)$, for all players in Example 2.

The picture is similar to the technological uncertainty case. Player 1 needs a share of $V(N)$ of roughly 0.2 or larger in order prefer the payoff to zero, due to the detrimental impact of risk. Player 2 experiences the same mechanism, but the effect is much smaller, while for player 3 the payoff increases linearly with the share of $V(N)$.

	Player 1	Player 2	Player 3
Singleton payoff	0.17E+04	4.12E+04	4.99E+04
Minimum share	0.2170	0.5390	0.4948

Table 5.2: Singleton payoffs and minimum shares of $V(N)$ to satisfy corresponding singleton coalition for all players in Example 2.

For the determination of core emptiness, the minimum shares of $V(N)$ to satisfy the singleton coalition of each player can be calculated, similar to Example 1. The results are shown in Table 5.2 and the sum of all minimum shares is 1.2508. Consequently, the core of the game is empty. In contrast to Example 1, the result is not driven by the most risk averse player, who actually requires less than a uniform allocation share, as the singleton payoff is relatively low. This is due to the low baseline consumption level C^0, which for player 1 is substantially lower than for players 2 and 3. A high share of $V(N)$ is rather required by player 2, because the modest level of risk aversion still means that the payoff growth in Figure 5.2 is substantially less than for the risk neutral player 3. Further, the singleton payoff of player 2 is relatively high, because the baseline consumption level is among the highest of all players. Consequently, a very high share of $V(N)$ is needed to compensate player 2 for the effect of risk.

Again, heterogeneity between the players is required for the result of core emptiness. If the players were symmetric in all parameters, the chosen emission level in the grand coalition, and its associated level of risk, would conform with the wishes of all players equally. Then, a uniform allocation of $V(N)$ to all players would be stable and the core of the game would not be empty. Asymmetry in the parameters can concentrate the detrimental effects of risk on one or a few players and thereby cause an empty core.

5.3.2 Stability of global cooperation under expectation and risk allocation

Finally, I check whether the expectation and risk allocation concept reinstates the result of core non-emptiness from the deterministic case, as it did under technological uncertainty. This is indeed the case, as Proposition 6 shows.

Proposition 6. *Under expectation and risk allocation, the core of the cooperative game with stochastic payoffs and uncertainty in climate damages is non-empty.*

The intuitive reasoning behind the result is similar to the technological uncertainty setup, as the independence of risk allocation allows the least risk averse player to take on all risk in the grand coalition. This creates a total utility surplus, which can be used to compensate the least risk averse player for the acceptance of risk, making all players better off under global cooperation.

5.4 Discussion

This section situates the theoretical results in the general context of international climate policy. Uncertainty continues to play a large role in the climate policy discourse, as the economic effects of climate change are still quite uncertain and many current estimates do not account for some factors likely to influence the impact of climate change, such as changing weather patterns or tipping points (Burke et al., 2015; IPCC, 2014a). Further, the future development of low-carbon technologies, and their costs, remain highly uncertain. For example, carbon capture and storage usually plays a prominent role in long-term scenarios compatible with ambitious emission reduction targets, but faces several technical, economic and political uncertainties (Watson et al., 2014; Koelbl et al., 2014). On the other hand, some low-carbon technologies have surprised with rapid cost reductions, such as the 80% drop in the costs of photovoltaic modules in mature markets between 2008 and 2012 (International Energy Agency, 2014a).

In this context, the results of this chapter lend themselves to two conclusions. First, the results suggest that global emission levels react differently to technological uncertainty and uncertainty in climate damages, in a situation with risk averse actors. While technological uncertainty introduces an additional mitigation cost, the presence of uncertainty in climate damages introduces an additional mitigation benefit. Consequently, global emission levels are higher under technological uncertainty, and lower under uncertainty in climate damages, compared to the situation without uncertainty. This suggests that research on low-carbon technologies, reducing mitigation costs and technological uncertainty, could be particularly effective in lowering global GHG emissions. On the other hand, some amount of uncertainty in climate damages helps to reduce emission levels, as risk averse actors react to uncertainty by increasing their mitigation efforts. While this result is also supported by the analysis of Bramoullé and Treich (2009), based on internal and external stability, Benchekroun and van Long (2013) find that it no longer holds up in a dynamic game with a stock pollutant. Further, in the actual climate policy discourse, uncertainty about the effects of climate change is often used to justify a delay of mitigation efforts, notably by US President George W. Bush in his announcement that he would not support the Kyoto Protocol (White House, 2001). Supporters of the precautionary principle, on the other hand, argue that high climate uncertainty should compel ambitious mitigation efforts (e.g. Grant and Quiggin, 2014; Lewandowsky et al., 2014).
Second, the results on core stability in this chapter suggest that the ability of risk redistribution between countries is a key determinant for stability of a global climate agreement. For both technological uncertainty and uncertainty in climate damages, global cooperation can be unstable under pure payoff allocation, where risk cannot be detached from the payoff. However, if the expectation and risk allocation concept is used, where risk can be freely distributed, a stable global agreement always exists.

This suggests that risk redistribution should be incorporated in the international climate regime. In particular, stable cooperation might be aided by the willingness of some countries to shoulder some of the risk of other countries, in addition to their own. Arguably, developed countries are better equipped to deal with with unexpected events than developing countries, due to higher wealth and well established governmental structures. Therefore, developed countries could shoulder additional risk, in exchange for more ambitious emission reductions from developing countries. This would both reduce the global impact of climate uncertainty and harmonize international emission reduction efforts.

The redistribution of risk might be achieved via the Warsaw International Mechanism on Loss and Damage (WIM) (e.g. UNFCCC, 2013), which was established at COP19 in 2013 and intends to address climate loss and damage in developing countries. The importance of loss and damage was further recognized in the Paris Agreement, which includes an independent article devoted to the subject (UNFCCC, 2015a, art. 8). While the WIM currently focuses on knowledge and dialogue, it was requested at COP21 "to establish a clearing house for risk transfer" (UNFCCC, 2015b, para. 48). The mandate of the WIM could further be enhanced at a scheduled review at COP22.

5.5 Conclusion

This chapter integrates technological uncertainty and uncertainty in climate damages into the model of international climate negotiations using core stability, by Chander and Tulkens (1997). This requires adjustments of several concepts of cooperative game theory, most prominently the concept of an allocation, for which two distinct concepts are put forward in the literature. I find that the deterministic result of core non-emptiness does not necessarily carry over to the uncertain setup, if the pure payoff allocation concept is used. However, the expectation and risk allocation concept reinstates the deterministic result, by allowing independent allocations of expected value of a payoff and of its risk. The possibility of risk redistribution, for example through the Warsaw International Mechanism on Loss and Damage, might therefore improve the opportunity for global agreement in the international climate negotiations.

The model in this chapter could be extended or modified in a few ways. First, the shape of the consumption and the damage functions could be generalized or changed. Second, other probability distributions and preference orderings could be used. Third, technological uncertainty and uncertainty under climate damages could both be considered in a joint model, or other types of uncertainty could be introduced.

6 Cooperation of climate clubs

The previous chapters introduced several real-world properties into the CT model to enhance its level of realism and to better align it with the absence of a global agreement on country-level emission targets found under the current international climate regime. This chapter analyses a potential alternative to the current structure of international climate negotiations, so-called *climate clubs*.

The idea of moving the climate negotiations from the UNFCCC to other, non-global fora has been suggested by several scholars (see e.g. Bodansky, 2002; Asheim et al., 2006; Naím, 2009; Victor, 2009; Eckersley, 2012; Weischer et al., 2012; Grasso and Roberts, 2014; Hovi et al., 2016). The literature suggests that advantages of climate clubs over global negotiations might be faster negotiations, higher ambition from the club members, better participation from private actors and more equitable agreements (Biermann et al., 2009). Simple game-theoretic models indeed imply that negotiations in small groups can aid the coordination between countries, and that global negotiations can be supported by prior agreements of a few countries (Smead et al., 2014). An analysis of UNFCCC high-level segment speeches suggests that climate clubs could reduce negotiation complexity by eliminating secondary demands from country positions (Bagozzi, 2014). Most climate clubs try to ensure that they act complementary to the UNFCCC (Widerberg and Pattberg, 2015).

However, from an empirical perspective, not enough is known about the effectiveness of different forms of climate governance to evaluate the proposed advantages of climate clubs (Jordan et al., 2015). Biermann et al. (2009)

point out several problems of climate clubs, such as "forum shopping" by powerful states and the potential for a "race to the bottom" between competing clubs. Biermann et al. (2009) conclude that fragmentation of the global climate governance might do more harm than good.
The number of climate clubs has increased substantially since 2005, as negotiations on a global agreement began under the UNFCCC (Weischer et al., 2012). Many of these clubs focus on specific issues, such as the promotion of renewable energy or energy efficiency, or the reduction of deforestation or short-lived greenhouse gases (Widerberg and Stenson, 2013). In a survey of climate negotiation participants (Hjerpe and Nasiritousi, 2015), the two most frequently mentioned clubs were *state clubs*: the Major Economies Forum On Energy And Climate (MEF), which brings together the 17 largest economies of the world, and the Group of Twenty (G20). The topic of climate change was featured in the final declaration of all G20 leaders' summits since the introduction of regular summits in 2008[1].
Some studies have used internal and external stability to analyse cooperation among smaller country groups. For exclusive membership games, Finus et al. (2005) find that exclusive membership stabilizes some coalitions, compared with open membership. However, these coalitions only marginally improve emission reductions over the the case of no cooperation. Asheim et al. (2006) examine two parallel regional agreements and find that the two agreements are able to improve participation over a single agreement. Nordhaus (2015) studies clubs with penalty tariffs on non-participants. He finds that the penalty greatly enhances participation in the club and that this structure makes emission reductions near the global optimal level possible. However, such a penalty might not be compatible with the rules of the World Trade Organization (WTO) (see Jaspers and Falkner, 2013, for an overview of the literature on the compatibility of climate policy with WTO rules).

[1] See Shaw (2011) for an overview of G20 decisions on climate change.

In all of these studies, the participation of countries in a coalition evolves during the course of the game, that is the membership of the climate club changes. However, some of the clubs that are discussed as potential fora for a climate agreement have a fixed set of members and exist independently of the climate issue. The best example is given by the G20, which is often cited as a potential climate club (Naím, 2009; Hjerpe and Nasiritousi, 2015). It was founded as a forum for international economic cooperation and its membership has not changed since its inception. Consequently, participation in such a club is not the result of a game of climate cooperation, as previous studies assert. Rather, the club and its members are given, and the question becomes whether stable climate cooperation in the club is possible. The analysis of this question requires a different framework, which accounts for a given club with fixed membership.

In this chapter, I analyse the stability of climate cooperation in pre-existing state clubs with fixed membership, such as the G20. Countries are divided into two distinct groups: those who are supposed to come to an agreement on legally binding commitments for all countries in this group (the *club members*) and the remaining countries, who benefit from commitments made by the club members, but do not commit to emission reductions themselves (the *outsiders*).

As decision making in state clubs like the G20 requires approval of all members, an agreement would have to include all club members. Therefore, I analyse the existence of a stable agreement using the core stability concept by Chander and Tulkens (1997), which incorporates such a unanimity rule. So far, this concept has only been used to study global cooperation. I modify the model of global cooperation for the study of cooperation among state clubs, using the concept of a *subgame*. While this concept has been used to study several types of cooperative games[2], it has so far not been employed

[2] The subgame concept was introduced by Shapley and Shubik (1969) to study market games. Inter alia, it has also been used to study partition, packing and covering games (Deng et al., 2000; Bietenhader and Okamoto, 2006)

in the context of the game of climate cooperation. I provide an analytical solution to the game with quadratic functions and determine the set of parameters for which a stable agreement among club members exists. I first assume that countries inside the club and countries outside the club are symmetric among their respective group. This assumption is later dropped and the impact of heterogeneous countries on the stability of a club agreement is shown. Finally, I apply the model to the case of the G20, using mitigation cost estimates from a techno-economic model and damage cost estimates from an integrated assessment model.
The model is presented in Section 6.1. Section 6.2 gives theoretical results for the symmetric and the asymmetric case. Section 6.3 shows the application of the model to the case of the G20. Section 6.4 concludes and gives an outlook for future work.

6.1 The model

The setup is again based on the original CT model, without any of the modifications described in the previous chapters. I model negotiations of climate clubs as a *subgame*[3] of the cooperative game in the CT model. The following definition is due to Peleg and Sudhölter (2007).

Definition 1. *Let* (N,v) *be a game. A* ***subgame*** *of* (N,v) *is a game* (T,v^T) *where* $\emptyset \neq T \subseteq N$ *and* $v^T(S) = v(S)$ *for all* $S \subseteq T$*. The subgame* (T,v^T) *is also denoted by* (T,v)*.*

Let $T \subset N$ be the set of club members and let $R = N \setminus T$ contain the outsiders. Then, the subgame (T,v) assesses the existence of a stable agreement among club members, while outsiders behave as they would in the global game. In accordance with the behaviour outlined above, outsiders maximize individual utility, while their payoff depends, inter alia, on the level of emissions

[3] Note that the subgame concept used in this chapter is different from the concept of a subgame of a non-cooperative game in extensive form. Therefore, it also bears no relation to the notion of a "subgame-perfect equilibrium".

of T. Therefore, R benefits from cooperation in T. However, decreasing emissions from T lead to increasing emissions from members of R, as they re-optimize their individual utility, making cooperation among T less beneficial and potentially unstable.
The existence of a stable agreement among the club members is tested by computing the utility of each *subcoalition* $S \subset T$, and comparing it to the utility of the *club coalition* T. This comparison determines the (non-)emptiness of the core of the subgame, which is the focus of the theoretical examination in the next section.

6.2 Theoretical results

For the theoretical analysis, I use quadratic consumption and damage functions, as introduced in Chapter 5. We will see that the (non-)emptiness of the core of the subgame crucially depends on the parameters for emission mitigation costs and for damages caused by emissions, γ and π. The setup is

$$C_i(E_i) = \begin{cases} C_i^0 - \gamma_i(E_i^0 - E_i)^2, & E_i < E_i^0 \\ C_i^0, & E_i \geq E_i^0 \end{cases} \quad \forall i \in N \tag{6.1a}$$

$$D_i(E_N) = \pi_i E_N^2 \quad \forall i \in N, \tag{6.1b}$$

with

- C_i^0: baseline consumption level
- E_i^0: baseline emission level
- γ_i: mitigation cost parameter
- π_i: damage cost parameter
- $E_N = \sum_{i=1}^n E_i$: global emissions

For convenience, define $s := |S|$ and $t := |T|$. The theoretical analysis begins by assuming symmetry of countries inside each of the two groups (T and R). This allows for the computation of conditions for the non-emptiness of the core of the subgame. In a second step, I allow individual parameters for countries inside a group and show how the core of the game changes with the introduction of heterogeneity.

6.2.1 Symmetric countries

In this section, I assume symmetry of countries inside each group, meaning that the parameters of all countries inside a group are equal:

$$\gamma_l = \gamma_i,\ \pi_l = \pi_i,\ C_l^0 = C_i^0 \quad \forall i,l \in T, \tag{6.2a}$$

$$\gamma_l = \gamma_j,\ \pi_l = \pi_j,\ C_l^0 = C_j^0 \quad \forall j,l \in R. \tag{6.2b}$$

For clarity, the index i represents a country in T, j represents a country in R, with l being an arbitrary third country. In order to determine conditions for the non-emptiness of the core, I first consider the symmetric allocation and later show that no other allocation needs to be considered.

Lemma 1. *Let*

$$y \in \mathbb{R}^t, \quad y_i \equiv \frac{v(T)}{t} \tag{6.3}$$

be the symmetric allocation of the subgame (T,v).

(i) In the setup above, the symmetric allocation lies in the core if and only if

$$a(\gamma_i,\gamma_j,\pi_i,\pi_j,s,t,n) \leq 0 \ \forall s = 1,..,t-1, \tag{6.4}$$

where

$$\begin{aligned} &a(\gamma_i,\gamma_j,\pi_i,\pi_j,s,t,n)\\ &=\Bigg[\frac{t+s}{t^2\frac{\pi_i}{\gamma_i}+1}(n-t)^2\left(\frac{\pi_j}{\gamma_j}\right)^2+2(n-t)\frac{\pi_j}{\gamma_j}\\ &+(2-s-t)(s^2\frac{\pi_i}{\gamma_i}+1)+(t-s)\frac{\pi_i}{\gamma_i}\Bigg]\frac{(t-s)\frac{\pi_i}{\gamma_i}}{s^2\frac{\pi_i}{\gamma_i}+1}. \end{aligned} \tag{6.5}$$

(ii) $a(\gamma_i,\gamma_j,\pi_i,\pi_j,s,t,n)$ *is monotonically increasing in* $\frac{\pi_j}{\gamma_j}$.

For reasons of readability, all proofs can be found in Appendix D.1.
As a only depends on the fractions $\frac{\pi_i}{\gamma_i}$ and $\frac{\pi_j}{\gamma_j}$, set $\gamma_i=\gamma_j=1$ without loss of generality and write $a(\pi_i,\pi_j,s,t,n):=a(1,1,\pi_i,\pi_j,s,t,n)$.
For a set game (i.e. n and t fixed), one can calculate the combinations of π_i and π_j for which the symmetric allocation lies in the core. Let

$$\mathscr{P}_s=\{(\pi_i,\pi_j)\in\mathbb{R}^2_+\mid a(\pi_i,\pi_j,s,t,n)\leq 0\}. \tag{6.6}$$

Then

$$\mathscr{P}=\bigcap_{s=1}^{t-1}\mathscr{P}_s \tag{6.7}$$

is this set. We will later see that it is the set of parameter combinations that lead to a non-empty core.
Let s,t and n be fixed. As $a(\pi_i,\pi_j,s,t,n)$ is continuous for $\pi_i,\pi_j>0$, the boundary between $\mathscr{P}_s$ and $\mathbb{R}^2_+\setminus\mathscr{P}_s$ can be identified. It corresponds to

$$a(\pi_i,\pi_j,s,t,n)=0$$

and, as Lemma 2 (i) shows, it can be interpreted as a function $\bar{\pi}_j(\pi_i,s,t,n)$.
Some useful features of this function are shown in Lemma 2 (ii).

Lemma 2. *(i) The function $\bar{\pi}_j(\pi_i, s, t, n)$ is well defined by*

$$a(\pi_i, \bar{\pi}_j(\pi_i, s, t, n), s, t, n) = 0,\ \pi_i > 0, \bar{\pi}_j(\pi_i, s, t, n) > 0.$$

(ii) $\bar{\pi}_j(\pi_i, s, t, n)$ is monotonically increasing in π_i and s.

As $a(\pi_i, \pi_j, s, t, n)$ is monotonically increasing in π_j, all parameter combinations (π_i, π_j) with $\pi_j > \bar{\pi}_j(\pi_i, s, t, n)$ do not satisfy condition (6.4). For the symmetric allocation to be in the core, this condition has to be satisfied for all s. Together with the fact that $\bar{\pi}_j(\pi_i, s, t, n)$ is monotonically increasing in s, we get the result that $s = 1$ is the only relevant case. In addition, no other allocations have to be considered, as Proposition 7 shows.

Proposition 7.

$$\mathscr{P} = \mathscr{P}_1 \tag{6.8}$$

is the set of parameters that lead to a non-empty core of the game.

I now consider the effect of a change in the parameters π_i and π_j on the stability of cooperation of the club. This is best done by first visualizing the set $\mathscr{P}$. Figure 6.1 shows $\mathscr{P}$ (blue area) for a game with 3 club members and 2 outsiders.

From the fact that $a(\pi_i, \pi_j, s, t, n)$ is monotonically increasing in π_j, we get the, somewhat counterintuitive, result that a *higher* damage cost parameter of the outsiders R (and thus *lower* emission levels in the uncooperative equilibrium) leads to *less* potential cooperation[4] among the club members T. In contrast, as $\bar{\pi}_j(\pi_i, s, t, n)$ is increasing in π_i, higher damages within the club lead to *more* potential cooperation. The reason lies in the *leakage* effect. Higher damages in R lead to a steeper slope of the best-reply function for countries in R[5]. This means that countries in R react more strongly to cooperation in T (and the accompanying emission reductions) by increasing

[4] By "less (more) potential cooperation", I simply mean the fact that, with increasing parameter, the game reaches a point at which the core becomes (non-)empty.

[5] See proof to Lemma 1.

emissions themselves. The result is less potential cooperation in T. Increases in π_i do not influence the best-reply function of countries in R and therefore do not cause a stronger leakage effect. Consequently, a different effect determines the result of an increase in π_i: the gains of cooperation for members of T grow and hence lead to games with a non-empty core. These effects are similar to the behaviour of stable coalition size in models based on the internal and external stability concept.

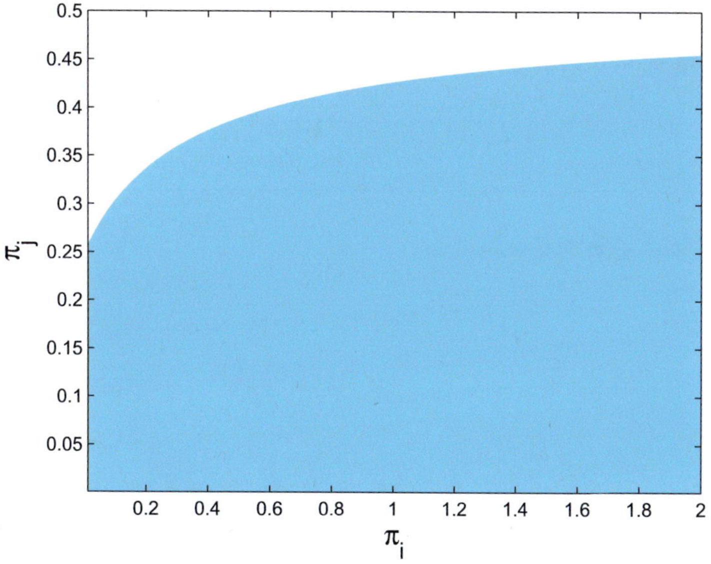

Figure 6.1: The blue area represents $\mathscr{P}$ for $t = 3, n = 5$.

Taken together, the results imply that it is especially important to involve those countries with high climate damages and/or low mitigation costs in the club attempting to negotiate a climate agreement, as it enhances the parameter space leading to the existence of a stable agreement. While it is in the self-interest of countries with high climate damages to participate in those negotiations, countries with low mitigation costs might need to be motivated externally, for example by the prospect of transfer payments for emission reductions.

Upper limit of π_j

The shape of $\mathscr{P}$ in Figure 6.1 suggests that the boundary value might converge to a fixed value for large π_i. Indeed, there exists such an absolute upper limit $\bar{\pi}_j^{ul}$, independent of π_i. To show the existence of $\bar{\pi}_j^{ul}$, consider the shape of the boundary of $\mathscr{P}$ and write $\bar{\pi}_j(\pi_i,t,n)$ for $\bar{\pi}_j(\pi_i,1,t,n)$. The following Proposition states the main results about this function and its limits.

Proposition 8. *Let $\bar{\pi}_j(\pi_i,t,n)$ be defined by*

$$a(\pi_i,\bar{\pi}_j(\pi_i,t,n),1,t,n)=0,\;\; \pi_i>0 \textit{ and } \bar{\pi}_j>0. \tag{6.9}$$

Then

(i) $\bar{\pi}_j(\pi_i,t,n)$ *is well defined and*

$$\bar{\pi}_j(\pi_i,t,n)=\frac{t\left(\sqrt{t^2\pi_i^2+(t^2+1)\pi_i+1}-t\pi_i\right)-1}{(t+1)(n-t)}. \tag{6.10}$$

(ii)

$$\lim_{\pi_i\to 0}\bar{\pi}_j(\pi_i,t,n)=\frac{t-1}{(t+1)(n-t)}=:\bar{\pi}_j^{ll} \tag{6.11}$$

(iii)

$$\lim_{\pi_i\to\infty}\bar{\pi}_j(\pi_i,t,n)=\frac{t-1}{2(n-t)}=:\bar{\pi}_j^{ul} \tag{6.12}$$

(iv) $\bar{\pi}_j^{ll}$ *and* $\bar{\pi}_j^{ul}$ *are monotonically increasing in t (for $2\le t<n$) and approach infinity as $t\to n$.*

Proposition 8 (ii) and (iii) confirm the existence of upper and lower limits of the boundary function. This means that if $\pi_j>\bar{\pi}_j^{ul}$, the core of the game is always empty, irrespective of π_i. In other words, if damages from climate change are very high outside of the club, the club will not cooperate.

In this case the main beneficiaries from emission reductions are not part of the club and cooperation in the club would only be met by corresponding emission increases outside of it, as outlined in the previous section. On the other hand, the existence of the lower limit means that if $\pi_j < \bar{\pi}_j^{ll}$, that is damages outside of the club are very low, cooperation is always possible. In this case, outsiders will not change their behaviour very much if the club cooperates, as they are not heavily affected by climate change. Therefore, the club comprises all relevant countries and the game of club cooperation becomes "global", in the sense that it includes all countries affected by climate change. As a result, the game is similar to the original CT model and its result of a non-empty core.
Proposition 8 (iv) also shows that the results are consistent with the result of the game of global cooperation. As the number of outsiders shrinks and the number of club members approaches all players, the set of parameter combinations that lead to a non-empty core expands towards the whole parameter space. This means that, in the limit of club size, a stable agreement exists for all parameter combinations.

6.2.2 Asymmetric countries

In this section, I drop the assumption of symmetry of countries and allow for individual parameters for each country. This means that the model is characterized by the number of countries n, the number of club members t and the parameter vector

$$\pi \in \mathbb{R}^n_+. \tag{6.13}$$

I continue to assume $\gamma \equiv 1$. Proposition 9 shows results for global emissions E_N in the cases of no cooperation or full cooperation among club members, when heterogeneity is present.

Proposition 9. *Let*

$$\pi_T := \sum_{i \in T} \pi_i, \quad \pi_R := \sum_{j \in R} \pi_j.$$

and $i \in T$. Assume coalition $S \subset T$ forms. Then

$$E_N = \frac{E_N^0}{\pi_T + \pi_R + 1} \text{ if } S = \{i\} \tag{6.14}$$

and

$$E_N = \frac{E_N^0}{t\pi_T + \pi_R + 1} \text{ if } S = T. \tag{6.15}$$

These instances represent the case of no cooperation (formation of singleton coalitions) and the case of full cooperation among club members, respectively.

Proposition 9 shows that global emissions do not depend on the individual values of the damage parameter. Rather, they only depend on the parameter sum of both groups. This means that individual parameters π_i can be varied, while holding π_T and π_R constant, without changing global emissions in the cooperative case. I use this property to study the impact of heterogeneity on the value of coalitions and therefore the existence of a stable allocation.
Due to the increased complexity of the case of asymmetric countries, conditions for a non-empty core cannot easily be calculated. Instead, I draw on Proposition 7 and focus on the set of singleton coalitions. Specifically, I check whether

$$\sum_{i \in T} v(\{i\}) > v(T), \tag{6.16}$$

which is a sufficient condition for an *emtpy* core. The set of parameters for which condition (6.16) is not satisfied is called $\tilde{\mathscr{P}}$. To be clear, this means that, while $\pi \notin \tilde{\mathscr{P}}$ is a sufficient condition for an empty core, $\pi \in \tilde{\mathscr{P}}$ is only a necessary condition for a non-empty core. However, Proposition 7 showed that

$$\tilde{\mathscr{P}} = \mathscr{P} \tag{6.17}$$

in the symmetric case. Similar to Lemma 1, the elements of $\tilde{\mathscr{P}}$ are determined by a quadratic function in π_R:

Lemma 3. *Let $\pi \in \mathbb{R}^n_+$. Then $\pi \in \tilde{\mathscr{P}}$ if and only if*

$$a(\pi) = \sum_{i \in T} a_i(\pi_i, \pi_T, \pi_R) \leq 0, \tag{6.18}$$

where

$$\begin{aligned} a_i(\pi_i, \pi_T, \pi_R) = & \left[\frac{1}{\pi_i^2 + \pi_i} - \frac{1}{\pi_T^2 + \pi_i} \right] \pi_R^2 \\ & + \left[\frac{\pi_T + 1}{\pi_i^2 + \pi_i} - \frac{t\pi_T + 1}{\pi_T^2 + \pi_i} \right] 2\pi_R \\ & + \frac{(\pi_T + 1)^2}{\pi_i^2 + \pi_i} - \frac{(t\pi_T + 1)^2}{\pi_T^2 + \pi_i}. \end{aligned} \tag{6.19}$$

By design, condition (6.18) is equivalent to condition (6.4) in the symmetric case. Lemma 3 shows that heterogeneity of countries in R does not influence membership in $\tilde{\mathscr{P}}$, as the condition only depends on π_R, the sum of parameters in R. The utility of club members is only influenced by the sum of emissions of outsiders, not their distribution. As the sum of emissions of outsiders does not depend on the distribution of parameters among outsider countries, the cooperation decision is not influenced by this distribution. However, it is clear that heterogeneity of countries in the club influences the core. Proposition 10 investigates this influence.

Proposition 10. *Let $\pi \in \mathbb{R}^n_+$, $l, h \in T$ with*

$$\pi_l \leq \frac{\pi_T}{t}, \quad \pi_h \geq \frac{\pi_T}{t}, \tag{6.20}$$

and let $d > 0$ with

$$d \leq \pi_l, \quad d \leq \pi_T - \pi_h. \tag{6.21}$$

Define $\tilde{\pi} \in \mathbb{R}^n_+$ by

$$\begin{aligned} \tilde{\pi}_l &= \pi_l - d, \\ \tilde{\pi}_h &= \pi_h + d, \\ \tilde{\pi}_i &= \pi_i \quad \forall i \neq l, i \neq h. \end{aligned} \tag{6.22}$$

Then $a(\tilde{\pi}) > a(\pi)$.

$\tilde{\pi}$ is designed such that $\tilde{\pi}_T = \pi_T$ and $\tilde{\pi}_R = \pi_R$, meaning that the transformation "adds" heterogeneity without altering the sum of parameters in each group. The repeated application of Proposition 10 can construct any vector with these total group values. Therefore, the specific definition of $\tilde{\pi}$ represents no loss of generality about the considered parameter vector.

Proposition 10 shows that the “addition” of heterogeneity in the club leads to an increase in $a(\pi)$. The drivers behind this increase can be best visualized with a numeric example. Building on Figure 6.1, Figure 6.2 shows the impact of heterogeneity in the case of $t = 3, n = 5$. π_T and π_R are kept constant, while one country's share of π_T is increased. The remaining part of π_T is divided equally between the other two club members. Focusing on the total net value $a(\pi)$, we see that in the symmetric case (share of $\frac{1}{3}$) we have $a(\pi) < 0$, meaning that a stable agreement exists. However, $a(\pi)$ increases with heterogeneity between the countries in T and $a(\pi)$ is positive for shares larger than 0.55, resulting in an empty core of the corresponding game.

This increase of $a(\pi)$ is driven by countries two and three, those with a decreasing share of π_T. Note that $a_2(\pi) = a_3(\pi)$ and $a(\pi) = \sum_{i=1}^{3} a_i(\pi)$. As the ratio of damage cost and mitigation cost of countries two and three reduces, the gains of cooperation become smaller and $a_2(\pi)$ and $a_3(\pi)$ rise. The opposite is true for country one: its ratio of damage cost and mitigation cost increases, leading to higher gains of cooperation and lower $a_1(\pi)$. However, this decrease is not big enough to offset the increases in $a_2(\pi)$ and $a_3(\pi)$. Consequentially, $a(\pi)$ increases with heterogeneity.

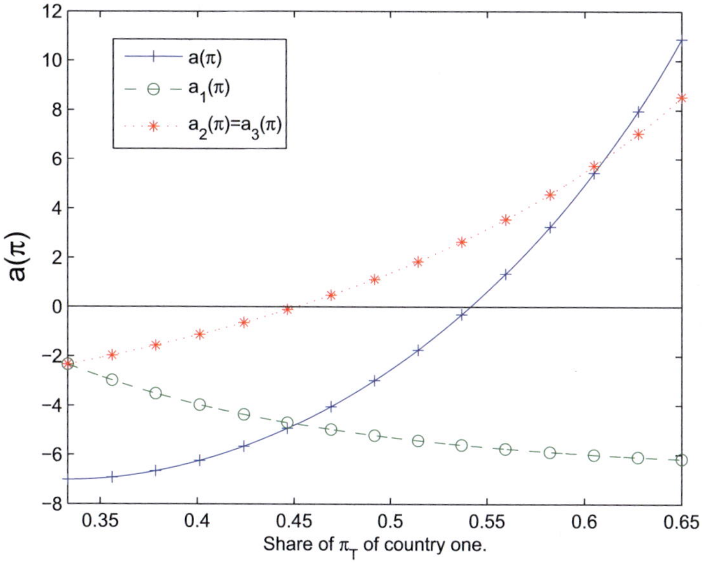

Figure 6.2: $a(\pi)$ for varying heterogeneity between club members. $\pi_T = 1$, $\pi_R = 0.2$, $t = 3$, $n = 5$.

As the result of Proposition 10 holds for all π_T and π_R, the non-empty core condition (6.18) is violated for some parameter combinations previously in $\tilde{\mathscr{P}}$ after the execution of transformation (6.22). Therefore, the set $\tilde{\mathscr{P}}$ shrinks with increased heterogeneity, as visualized in Figure 6.3. It shows $\tilde{\mathscr{P}}$ for different distributions of π_T upon the countries in T. These shares of countries are varied between subfigures only, meaning

$$\hat{\pi}_i = \frac{\pi_i}{\pi_T},\ i \in T \tag{6.23}$$

is constant for each subfigure.

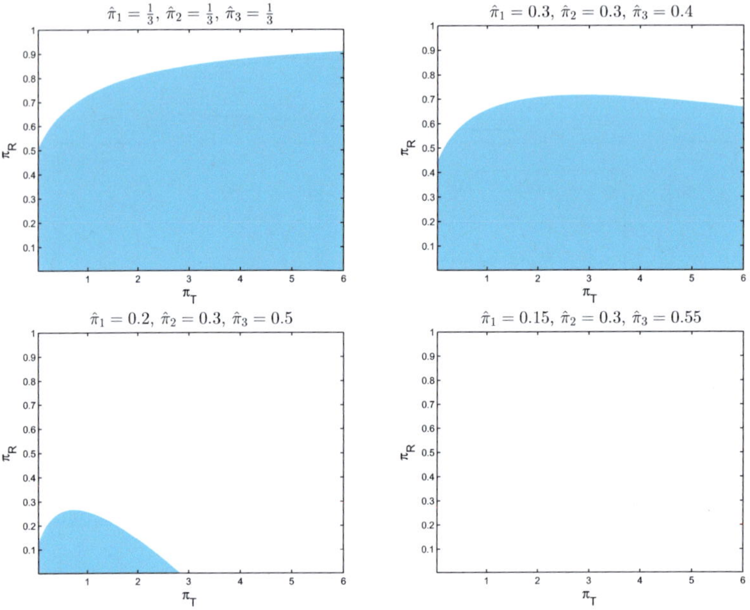

Figure 6.3: $\tilde{\mathscr{P}}$ for different levels of heterogeneity in T.

The shrinking of $\tilde{\mathscr{P}}$ with increased heterogeneity causes a different shape of the boundary of $\tilde{\mathscr{P}}$. While a high π_R still leads to less cooperation in T (as in the symmetric case), the same is true for a high π_T, unlike the symmetric case. An intuitive explanation for this phenomenon is that, for asymmetric countries, the "absolute" differences in the parameters become more pronounced with higher π_T, which reinforces the effect that more heterogeneity causes less cooperation. As the last subfigure shows, high diversity between countries in T can even lead to a game for which the core is empty for all combinations of π_T and π_R.

The results about cooperation of asymmetric countries align with the findings of Driessen et al. (2011), who show that, in a cooperative oligopoly game, higher heterogeneity of marginal costs decreases the size of the core. This is also supported by the model of internal and external stability by Na and Shin (1998), who find that coalitions are more likely to form among similar countries. However, Finus and Pintassilgo (2013) show that, in a more general game with transfers, asymmetry can lead to larger stable agreements. The latter view is also backed by Smead et al. (2014), who study a bargaining game of equilibrium selection and find a positive impact of heterogeneity between players on the chances of reaching an agreement.

6.3 Application of the model to the Group of Twenty

The Group of Twenty (G20) is the most frequently mentioned forum for climate action outside of the UNFCCC in a survey of participants at UNFCCC COPs (Hjerpe and Nasiritousi, 2015). It is also the biggest of the proposed state clubs (Widerberg and Stenson, 2013) and climate change has been a topic of discussion at all of its summits since 2008. Therefore, I use it for an application of the theoretical model. The model could also be applied to all other state clubs.

I start the analysis by estimating mitigation cost and damage cost parameters, using the POLES and RICE models. Subsequently, this data is applied to the theoretical model, beginning with the assumption of symmetric countries inside a group. Finally, this assumption is dropped and the impact of heterogeneity is evaluated.

6.3.1 Parameter estimation

Mitigation cost estimation

I use scenario runs from the POLES model[6] to generate mitigation cost curves for different countries. The employed scenario was produced in 2013.

[6] Prospective Outlook on Long-term Energy Systems model (POLES) is a global simulation model for the energy sector, developed by Enerdata in collaboration with JRC-IPTS and University of Grenoble's CNRS. For a detailed description of the model, see Kitous et al. (2010) or `http://www.enerdata.net/enerdatauk/solutions/energy-models/poles-model.php`.

In the baseline, this scenario assumes that dynamic economic growth is restored from 2015 onwards and no global climate agreement is reached, resulting in soaring GHG emissions around the world. From this baseline, mitigation cost curves are produced by the successive introduction of a carbon price.

The POLES scenario runs up to the year 2050. As the largest impacts of climate change are expected to happen in the very long-term, I use a simple procedure to extend the emission paths up to 2300, similar to Chapter 3. Up to 2100, baseline emissions are extrapolated based on the linear trend of per capita emissions for each country. Population values are taken from the scenario of medium fertility from the UN World Population Prospects (United Nations, 2012). For later years, I follow the extension procedure for RCP8.5 (Meinshausen et al., 2011; IPCC, 2014b). This means constant emissions up to 2150, followed by linear reduction of global emissions to the level that is consistent with stable atmospheric concentrations in 2250. Emissions stay at this level for the rest of the time period.

For each carbon price, I extend the corresponding emission path based on the linear extension of the relative reduction amount below baseline emissions. The reduction stops when net-zero emissions are reached. Mitigation costs are calculated as the area under the marginal mitigation cost curve for each year and country.

Afterwards, emission reductions for each carbon price are accumulated over the whole time period, 2013 to 2300. Mitigation costs are also aggregated, using a discount rate as described below. The result is a mitigation cost curve for each country, with each carbon price providing one data point. I then estimate the mitigation cost parameter γ as the best fit for a quadratic function to these data points.

For the symmetric case, all G20 countries are assigned the average emission reductions and average mitigation costs of G20 countries. Similarly, all non-G20 countries are assigned the average values of non-G20 countries.

The discount rate used for the aggregation of mitigation costs is determined by the Ramsey formula (Arrow et al., 2012). Similar to Chapter 3, the rate of pure time preference and the elasticity of the marginal utility of consumption are based on the median values from a recent survey of economists (Drupp et al., 2015). The per capita growth rate of consumption up to a specific year is approximated using GDP projections from the POLES model. The GDP projections are extended up to 2300 based on the linear trend of per capita values, similar to the extension procedure for emissions described above. For years after 2100, population projections from the UN World Population to 2300 report are used (United Nations, 2004).

Damage cost estimation

I use the RICE model (Nordhaus, 2010) to estimate the damage cost parameter π for each country. RICE provides cumulative emissions and the corresponding temperature increase. It also gives damage functions, depending on temperature increase, for 12 world regions. For each country and cumulative emission level, I use these functions to calculate damages, as percent of output. I then compute absolute damages using GDP projections from the POLES model. These projections are aggregated over time, again using a discount rate determined by the Ramsey formula. Finally, absolute damages are given by multiplying the aggregated GDP value with the relative damage amount calculated from RICE.

After this procedure, I estimate the damage cost parameter π as the best fit for a quadratic function to the data points combining cumulative emissions and absolute damages. For the symmetric case, damages are uniformly distributed among all countries in a group, analogue to the mitigation cost estimation.

6.3.2 Existence of a stable agreement

For the application to the model, I consider 130 countries for which there is sufficient data available to perform the parameter estimation. However, the EU is treated as one country and individual EU member states are therefore removed from the list of countries[7]. As a result, the group T includes 16 countries (15 non-EU members of the G20, plus the EU). The remaining 87 countries comprise the set R. For the full list of countries, see Table 6.2 for G20 countries and Table D.1 in Appendix D.2 for non-G20 countries.

Symmetric case

Table 6.1 shows the results of the parameter estimation in the symmetric case. The large differences in the magnitude of the parameters are a result of the different number of countries in each group and the fact that most big emitters are part of the G20.

	γ	π	Ratio $\frac{\pi}{\gamma}$
G20 countries	7,835	148	1.89 E-2
non-G20 countries	149,549	6	4.29 E-5

Table 6.1: Mitigation cost parameter γ and damage cost parameter π in the symmetric case. Values of γ and π in $\frac{EUR}{10^{15}*(tCO_2)^2}$.

In order to determine if the core of the *G20 game* is empty or not, the estimated parameters need to be compared to the set of parameters, which lead to a game with non-empty core, $\mathscr{P}$. Figure 6.4 shows this set for the G20 configuration, $n = 103, t = 16$. The location of the estimated parameter ratios from Table 6.1 is shown as a red dot.

[7] In particular, the United Kingdom is still considered as a member state of the EU and is therefore not included as an individual G20 member.

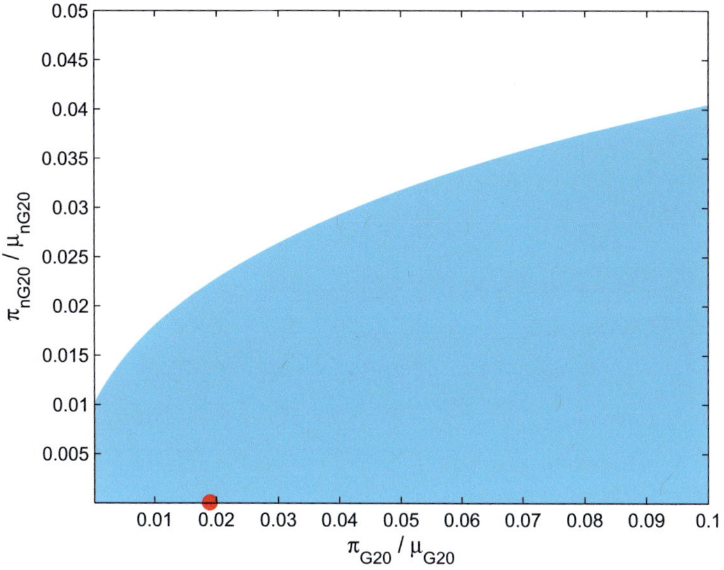

Figure 6.4: $\mathscr{P}$ for $n = 103, t = 16$ and estimated parameter ratios from Table 6.1.

I find that the estimated parameter ratios lie squarely in $\mathscr{P}$. Specifically, the ratio of parameters for non-G20 countries is so small that the core of the game is non-empty, irrespective of the ratio of parameters for G20 countries (see Proposition 8). In essence, the collective of G20 countries is large enough, in terms of expected absolute damages from climate change and ability to reduce emissions, that the behaviour of non-G20 countries does not change their incentive to cooperate. Therefore, in the highly stylized scenario of the symmetric case, a stable agreement among G20 countries exists.

Asymmetric case

Table 6.2 shows the results of the parameter estimation for individual G20 countries. The results for non-G20 countries can be found in Table D.1 in Appendix D.2.

Country	γ	π	Ratio $\frac{\pi}{\gamma}$
Argentina	50,130	28	5.67E-04
Australia	22,842	25	1.09E-03
Brazil	26,265	48	1.81E-03
Canada	24,296	30	1.24E-03
China	1,083	901	8.32E-01
European Union	10,362	236	2.28E-02
India	1,979	415	2.10E-01
Indonesia	30,187	36	1.18E-03
Japan	33,513	127	3.78E-03
Republic of Korea	70,577	52	7.32E-04
Mexico	75,342	37	4.88E-04
Russian Federation	6,259	34	5.36E-03
Saudi Arabia	69,241	15	2.23E-04
South Africa	48,941	18	3.59E-04
Turkey	26,873	52	1.94E-03
United States	9,034	319	3.54E-02

Table 6.2: Mitigation cost parameter γ and damage cost parameter π for G20 countries. Values of γ and π in $\frac{EUR}{10^{15} * (tCO_2)^2}$.

The parameter estimation shows a high degree of heterogeneity between G20 countries. China, the EU, India and the US especially stand out among the group. These countries have the four highest damage cost parameters, resulting from high GDP and, consequently, high absolute damages. They also have four of the five lowest mitigation cost parameters, resulting from high emission levels and the accompanying large mitigation opportunities. As a result, the ratio of damage cost and mitigation cost in these four countries is one or two orders of magnitude larger than the ratio in other countries.

Consequently, the conclusion about stability of climate cooperation in the case of asymmetric countries differs considerably from the case of symmetric countries. As Proposition 10 showed, "adding" heterogeneity between countries can lead to an empty core of the game. The G20 game is such a case. If the estimated parameters from Table 6.2 are used as the basis of the game, the core of the game is empty. This result is based solely on the heterogeneity of countries. If the ratio of mitigation cost and damage cost parameters is increased or decreased by an equal percentage for all G20 countries, leaving the heterogeneity between countries constant, the core stays empty. The same is true for a variation of non-G20 parameters. Therefore, I find that heterogeneity among G20 countries makes a potential climate agreement among the club unstable.

6.4 Conclusion

In order to account for the special structure of climate negotiations in preexisting state clubs with fixed membership, I analysed subgames of the cooperative game by Chander and Tulkens (1997). I find that, contrary to the model of global negotiations, a stable agreement does not exist for all parameter combinations. Instead, existence is determined by the ratio of damage and mitigation cost parameters. The set of parameters, for which a stable agreement exists, decreases in size as the extent of the club shrinks, due to lower gains of cooperation in the club. Additionally, changes in the cost parameters of both groups (club members and outsiders) lead to vastly different effects. Parameters of non-cooperative outsiders change the result in a counterintuitive way, as higher damage costs lead to less potential cooperation. Parameters of club members influence cooperation in a much more intuitive sense, as higher damages and lower mitigation costs enhance the prospect of a stable agreement. However, the parameters of the outsiders play a larger role and can prevent the existence of a stable agreement, when exceeding a certain upper limit.

The introduction of asymmetry in the cost parameters of both groups has a neutral or negative effect on stability of cooperation in the club. While asymmetry in the parameters of outsider countries does not influence cooperation inside the club, asymmetry in the parameters of the club members hurts the chances of cooperation. This can even lead to a situation in which the heterogeneity of countries prevents the existence of a stable agreement, irrespective of all other parameters.

Application of the model to the G20 leads to such a situation: when symmetric countries are assumed, the model predicts cooperation in the group. However, when this assumption is dropped, the core of the subgame is empty and no stable agreement exists.

Overall, the model is a lot less optimistic about the existence of a stable agreement in a climate club than in a global negotiation environment. This was expected as the model mainly considers the impact of potential free-riding of outsiders on an agreement among club members, making cooperation harder. The negative effects as outlined in this chapter therefore have to be evaluated against proposed advantages of climate clubs like faster negotiations and better participation from private actors (Biermann et al., 2009), as well as barriers in global negotiations like the blocking power of small countries with special circumstances. In addition, the model could be evaluated for different function shapes and other groups of countries. The model could also be extended in a number of ways. It does not include international macroeconomic effects of emission reduction measures in a country or multiple countries, as were considered in Chapter 3. Also, the model does not include uncertainty about the values of future mitigation costs or future damages, as was considered in Chapter 5. These issues are left for further research.

7 Conclusions and outlook

Global GHG emissions need to be substantially reduced to avoid dangerous climate change. As emission reductions in one country also benefit all other countries, international cooperation is needed for effective emission mitigation. This thesis analysed the incentives of countries to cooperate on emission reductions and the prospect of a global climate agreement.

In particular, the thesis analysed the stability of global climate cooperation using the concept of core stability. This concept nicely reproduces the requirement of consensus for decisions under the UNFCCC. However, the standard model is quite abstract and misses several important real-world properties. This thesis introduced five such properties into the model of international climate cooperation based on core stability.

First, consumption of a country was allowed to depend on the emission levels of all countries, not just emissions of the country itself. A numerical model was constructed, allowing for the calculation of the emission level and utility of each country for each possible coalition of countries. The model was applied using consumption functions from a global CGE model and thus includes international economic effects of emission reduction measures, for example technological learning and fossil fuel market effects. Such effects were missed in previous theoretical and numerical models.

It was found that these effects can indeed make global cooperation unstable, in contrast to the original model without international economic effects. The result is driven by fossil fuel exporting regions: in the case of global cooperation on climate change, low demand for fossil fuels would decrease its price and, consequently, the revenue of fossil fuel exporters. While these regions could be compensated for their agreement to global cooperation, other regions could also form a *coalition of the willing* without the fossil fuel exporters. Such a coalition would achieve emission reductions almost as high as a global coalition, while not having to compensate fossil fuel exporters. Therefore, no global agreement can satisfy all regions simultaneously, making it unstable.

The result arises for two damage scenarios covering the range of damage estimates by the IPCC. In contrast, in a scenario with damages twice as high as the upper end of the IPCC range, global cooperation is stable. As high damages imply high gains from cooperation, the incentive to cooperate is larger than the negative impacts of fossil fuel market effects in this scenario.

Second, the numerical model was used to identify the impact of different pathways for the future development of key low-carbon technologies. In addition to a scenario with mean values for several parameters, two scenarios generated by the CGE model, representing the most optimistic and most pessimistic parameters values found in the literature, were considered. These were again combined with three scenarios about climate damages, resulting in a total of nine scenarios analysed.

It was found that different assumptions about future technology development can influence the stability of global climate cooperation. Under high damages and mean or pessimistic technological assumptions, global cooperation is stable. Under high damages and optimistic assumptions, as well as under low or medium damages irrespective of technological assumptions, global cooperation is not stable. More optimistic technology assumptions reduce the gains of cooperation, due to relatively large unilateral emission reductions, and thus decrease the stability of global cooperation.

Further, the key drivers of cooperation stability vary by region, depending on each region's economic profile. While fossil-fuel exporting regions lose revenue under global cooperation, changes in the energy system can also cause substantial costs in other regions. The extent of climate damages can also

cause support or disapproval for global cooperation, if regional damages, and the associated gains of cooperation, are high or low, respectively.
Third, the original theoretical model was extended to include uncertainty and its influence on the decision making of countries. A cooperative game was constructed using concepts from the game-theoretical literature, including the application of competing allocation concepts. Distinct models were constructed for technological uncertainty and for uncertainty about climate damages. For each combination of uncertainty type and allocation concept, (non-)emptiness of the core of the game was shown either by an example of a game with empty core or by a proof of balancedness of the game.
The analysis showed that the incorporation of uncertainty can lead to unstable global cooperation, if risk is distributed between countries together with the expected value of a payoff. The result is driven by risk averse countries, who incur an additional "cost" when having to take on uncertainty. When the risk preferences of countries differ substantially, this cost can prohibit global cooperation. However, if the model allows for independent distribution of risk, the deterministic result of stable global cooperation is reinstated. In this case, the least risk averse country can act as an insurer by taking on the risk of other countries for a fee. This creates a global benefit and allows for a stable global agreement.
The analysis also showed that the results about stability of global cooperation are similar for technological uncertainty and uncertainty in climate damages. The different types of uncertainty do however influence emission levels in opposite directions. While technological uncertainty introduces an additional mitigation cost, the presence of uncertainty in climate damages introduces an additional mitigation benefit. Consequently, global emission levels are higher under technological uncertainty, and lower under uncertainty in climate damages, compared to the situation without any uncertainty.
Fourth, a potential alternative to the global UNFCCC process was analysed, non-global climate clubs. For the analysis, the original global model was adapted to the situation of climate negotiations in an arbitrary group of coun-

tries, using the concept of a subgame of a cooperative game. The theoretical model was first examined under the simplifying assumption of symmetric countries. It was shown that cooperation can be unstable, in contrast to the global model, depending on mitigation cost and damage cost parameters. Furthermore, the assumption of symmetry was dropped and the introduction of asymmetry in the cost parameters of different countries was shown to have a neutral or negative effect on stability of cooperation in the club. While asymmetry in the parameters of countries outside of the club does not influence cooperation inside the club, asymmetry in the parameters of the club members hurts the chances of cooperation. This can cause cooperation in the climate club to be unstable, even if it had been stable under the assumption of symmetric countries.

The application of the climate club model to the G20 showed that such a situation is not far-fetched. While cooperation is assessed to be stable under the assumption of symmetric countries, the numerical parameter estimation for asymmetric countries leads to cooperation being unstable.

The following sections provide overarching conclusions and implications drawn from the results of this thesis, as well as a critical reflection of the applied methods and an outlook for further research.

7.1 Conclusions

The thesis shows that the introduction of several real-world properties into the core stability model of climate cooperation substantially changes the results. Global climate cooperation is found to be unstable in certain scenarios after the introduction of international economic effects and of uncertainty. Climate clubs also do not necessarily offer a way to stable cooperation. These results show that the core stability model is a useful tool to study important determinants of the stability of climate cooperation. It can therefore complement the rich literature on internal and external stability.

From a more applied point of view, efforts can be made to design the international climate negotiations such that the barriers to climate cooperation featured in this thesis can be overcome.
For example, the evaluation of the impact of international economic effects shows that special consideration has to be given to large fossil fuel exporting countries. As fossil fuel revenues often provide a large portion of the state budget, these countries might expect to be compensated for their loss of fossil fuel export revenue under a global climate agreement. While other countries might be reluctant towards the idea of direct monetary compensation, more indirect measures, such as support for the economic transformation of fossil fuel exporting countries towards a more sustainable business model, might be able to attract support.
Further, the analysis of the influence of uncertainty shows that varying risk preferences between countries can be an obstacle to stable global cooperation. However, it can be overcome by risk redistribution between countries, which could be facilitated through the Warsaw International Mechanism on Loss and Damage under the UNFCCC. The uncertainty analysis also highlights the positive effects of research on low-carbon technologies, which reduces both the cost of mitigation efforts and the uncertainty of mitigation.
Finally, the examination of climate clubs shows that such clubs might not be an appropriate instrument to overcome barriers to global cooperation. In particular, groups like the G20 do not seem to offer any advantage, as most of the competing interests on a global level are still present in the G20. Therefore, the current support of such groups for the global negotiations under the UNFCCC seems to justified.
Overall, the thesis shows that several obstacles complicate the path to global cooperation on GHG emission reductions. However, the thesis only considered the pure economic inventive of countries. In reality, the perception of fairness plays a huge role in the climate negotiations. Some factors considered in this respect are the historical responsibility of developed countries, the ability to pay for GHG reductions of richer countries, and the capacity

to reduce emissions of countries with cheap mitigation options. As the difference between stable and unstable global cooperation is often only a small fraction of global economic output (see e.g. Chapter 3), the acceptance of certain fairness principles can help overcome this difference. The structure of national contributions in the Paris Agreement could manage to bring different perceptions together, as each country can submit what it perceives as fair. Therefore, this structure might be able to include fairness principles in a way that helps to make global climate cooperation stable.

7.2 Critical reflection and outlook

The analyses in this thesis introduced several aspects into the model of core stability and greatly enhanced its level of realism. However, this should just be seen as an intermediate step, as some limitations remain.
Although numerical models were used to consider a long time period, the decision about emission levels and whether to cooperate in the game-theoretical models is only made once. However, the international climate negotiations under the UNFCCC are a dynamic process with decisions made at every COP. The Paris Agreement stipulates the submission of contributions every five years, meaning that emission targets are set on a regular basis. Therefore, an extension to a dynamic game-theoretical framework with negotiations at each time period, as used by Germain et al. (2003), could further enhance the realism of the model.
Another remaining limitation is inherent in cooperative game theory and thereby also in core stability. It is assumed that, once an agreement is reached, countries will comply with it. Such an agreement might therefore not be "self-enforcing" in the sense of internal and external stability. Also, the possibility of renegotiation is ignored. While the unanimity requirement of negotiations under the UNFCCC somewhat lessens the importance of these issues, they are by no means irrelevant, as the withdrawal of Canada from the Kyoto Protocol shows.

The models used in this thesis also contain a few simplifications in order to remain solvable in a reasonable amount of time. First, the number of world regions in the numerical model used in Chapters 3 and 4 is not high enough for a detailed analysis of countries' blocking incentives. In particular, the aggregation of many fossil fuel exporting countries to one region ignores the substantial difference in projected climate damages between different countries. Therefore, a higher regional resolution of the model would be highly desirable.

Second, the time horizon of the CGE model is too short for a sensible consideration of climate damages in that period. Therefore, the time period had to be extended using a rather simple procedure. Preferably, the CGE model would have covered a time period long enough for an integration of climate damages, such that no extension procedures would have been needed.

Further, the model does not include a full feedback of the optimization of emission levels to the consumption side, in the way that integrated assessment models do. If such a feedback were implemented, the impacts of climate change on the economy, and on certain sectors of the economy, could be assessed in interaction with the effects of mitigation measures. For example, agriculture is one sector likely to be heavily influenced by climate change (IPCC, 2014a). Consequently, countries in which agriculture accounts for a large share of the economy would be directly affected from climate change. However, as many agricultural products are internationally traded, other countries would be affected indirectly. Therefore, the combination of a CGE model with feedback of climate effects based on emission levels would enhance the level of realism depicted by the model.

The theoretical models used in Chapters 5 and 6 could also be extended or modified in a few ways. First, the shape of the consumption and damage functions could be changed. Some theoretical studies of climate cooperation assume that damages change linearly with emissions (e.g. Breton et al., 2006; Kolstad and Ulph, 2011; Dellink and Finus, 2012; Nordhaus, 2015). The specific functions could also be replaced by general functions satisfy-

ing certain properties. It might still be possible to show some of the simpler results with these general functions, although the proofs of the main results might not be replicable with general functions.
In the theoretical model of uncertainty in Chapter 5, other probability distributions and preference orderings could be used. For example, one might consider a bounded probability distribution to ensure that emission reductions reduce consumption and that emissions cause climate damages for all possible values of the random variable. In that case, the restriction of the preference ordering to risk averse or risk neutral players could be avoided.
Further, technological uncertainty and uncertainty of climate damages could be considered in a joint model. This would directly show the opposite impacts of both types of uncertainty on emission levels. However, the stability of global climate cooperation would likely not be changed, as the established results for both types of uncertainty are similar.
In addition to the separate analyses of international economic effects, uncertainty and climate clubs, the properties could also be studied together in a joint model. While different technological pathways were considered together with international economic effects in Chapter 4, this did not include the impact of uncertainty on decision making of countries as in Chapter 5. A combination of both aspects could identify ways for countries to reduce or distribute uncertainty in a way that is most beneficial to their economic structure. Also, the introduction of both aspects in a model of cooperation in climate clubs could consider specially designed clubs. For example, international economic effects could inspire a climate club of the "coalition of the willing" without fossil fuel exporting countries. Further, a club of the most risk averse or of the least risk averse countries might be willing to cooperate under uncertainty.
Finally, several other real-world properties have not yet been considered in a model of core stability. For example, the ability to adapt to the impacts of climate change alters the incentives of countries, because an alternative to emission mitigation that only benefits the executing country is available

(Benchekroun et al., 2011; Lazkano et al., 2016). Future climate change might not occur in a predictable pattern, but rather trigger certain tipping points, leading to irreversible impacts. The existence of such tipping points can change the incentive structure of the climate cooperation game (Barrett, 2013). The ability of countries to control emissions not just via a cap, but also via a tax can also change the cooperation incentives (Eichner and Pethig, 2015). In addition, certain mitigation measures exhibit benefits additional to their emission reductions, and the impact of these additional benefits on the stability of climate cooperation is ambiguous (Finus and Rübbelke, 2013). Further, the influence of different forms of financial transfers could be explored. While the model in this thesis assumes a simple monetary transfer, actual climate finance also occurs in various other forms. Examples are projects under the UNFCCC's Clean Development Mechanism or the Global Environment Facility, bilateral offset mechanisms as pioneered by Japan, or funds such as the Adaptation Fund and the Green Climate Fund. It would therefore be worthy to explicitly model the finance flows and explore whether some forms of climate finance are more conducive to stable climate cooperation than others.

A Appendix to Chapter 3

Region	Consumption (NPV)
NAM	1,471.4
EUR	1,110.4
ANZ	69.2
JPN	176.4
EXP	850.8
CHN	845.3
IND	630.1
ROW	2,557.7
Global	7,711.1

Table A.1: NPV of cumulative baseline consumption for each region in trillion 2007 US$.

Region	Allocated amount
NAM	39.90
EUR	33.56
ANZ	0.64
JPN	3.35
EXP	58.99
CHN	27.42
IND	10.97
ROW	278.27

Table A.2: Core-stable payoff vector in the high damages scenario, in utility loss (NPV, trillion 2007 US$).

Note: the payoff vector was found by manual allocation of the surplus of the grand coalition, beginning with the "All Singletons" case and adjustment based on coalitions with an incentive to deviate. It is just one example of infinitely many core-stable payoff vectors of this game.

B Appendix to Chapter 4

	Low Damages			Default Damages			High Damages		
	pess	mean	opt	pess	mean	opt	pess	mean	opt
N	184.5	189.0	194.8	291.8	298.4	303.3	449.3	453.1	457.4
N\{ANZ}	182.2	187.4	193.5	290.6	297.5	301.7	450.4	454.2	455.8
N\{ANZ,JPN}	183.0	184.2	192.4	292.2	297.3	296.8	454.8	458.7	451.5
N\{EUR,ANZ,JPN}	184.9	186.0	186.6	303.3	308.1	301.5	475.3	487.1	476.9
N\{ANZ,JPN,CHN}	186.3	184.1	194.6	298.9	300.9	307.5	483.8	485.2	477.6
All Singletons	206.1	202.0	231.7	348.3	343.2	318.9	548.3	548.4	503.1

Table B.1: Global value loss caused by selected coalitions, by scenario (in value loss compared to BAU consumption, in trillion 2007 US$). The best coalition in each scenario is highlighted in red.

C Appendix to Chapter 5

C.1 Proofs

C.1.1 Proof of Proposition 1

Proof. Let $S \subset N, i \in S, j \notin S$. Then j optimizes the certainty equivalent of individual utility. $E_j(S)$ and $E_N(S)$ denote emissions of player j and global emissions, respectively, given that coalition S has formed.

$$
\begin{aligned}
ce_j(U_j(E_j(S), E_N(S))) &= C_j^0 - \gamma_j(E_j^0 - E_j(S))^2 - \pi_j E_N(S)^2 + \theta(E_j^0 - E_j(S))^2 z(\alpha_j) \\
0 \overset{!}{=} \frac{\partial ce_j(U_j(E_j(S), E_N(S)))}{\partial E_j(S)} &= 2\gamma_j(E_j^0 - E_j(S)) - 2\pi_j E_N(S) + 2\theta z(\alpha_j)(E_j^0 - E_j(S)) \\
\Rightarrow (\gamma_j - \theta z(\alpha_j))(E_j^0 - E_j(S)) &= \pi_j E_N(S) \\
\Rightarrow E_j(S) &= E_j^0 - \frac{\pi_j}{\gamma_j - \theta z(\alpha_j)} E_N(S)
\end{aligned}
$$

Player i optimizes the sum of all certainty equivalents of utility of the members of S:

$$\sum_{l\in S} ce_l(U_l(E_l(S),E_N(S))) = \sum_{l\in S} C_l^0 - \gamma_l(E_l^0 - E_l(S))^2 - \pi_l E_N(S)^2 + \theta(E_l^0 - E_l(S))^2 z(\alpha_l) \tag{C.1}$$

$$0 \stackrel{!}{=} \frac{\partial \sum_{l\in S} ce_l(C_l(E_l(S)) - D_l(E_N(S)))}{\partial E_i(S)} = 2\gamma_i(E_i^0 - E_i(S)) - 2\underbrace{\sum_{l\in S}\pi_l}_{=:\pi_S} E_N(S) - 2\theta z(\alpha_i)(E_i^0 - E_i(S))$$

$$\Rightarrow \pi_S E_N(S) = (\gamma_i - \theta z(\alpha_i))(E_i^0 - E_i(S))$$

$$\Rightarrow E_i(S) = E_i^0 - \frac{\pi_S}{\gamma_i - \theta z(\alpha_i)} E_N(S)$$

The sum of individual emissions of all players gives global emissions $E_N(S)$:

$$\begin{aligned}
E_N(S) &= \sum_{l\in N} E_l(S) = \sum_{i\in S} E_i(S) + \sum_{j\notin S} E_j(S) \\
&= \sum_{i\in S} E_i^0 - \frac{\pi_S}{\gamma_i - \theta z(\alpha_i)} E_N(S) + \sum_{j\notin S} E_j^0 - \frac{\pi_j}{\gamma_j - \theta z(\alpha_j)} E_N(S) \\
&= E_N^0 - \underbrace{\left(\pi_S \sum_{i\in S} \frac{1}{\gamma_i - \theta z(\alpha_i)} + \sum_{j\notin S} \frac{\pi_j}{\gamma_j - \theta z(\alpha_j)}\right)}_{=:\chi(S)} E_N(S) \\
\Rightarrow E_N(S) &= \frac{E_N^0}{\chi(S)+1}
\end{aligned}$$

$\chi(S)$ is the reduction factor of global emissions, showing Proposition 1 (i). The second and third parts of the Proposition follows directly from (i).

□

C.1.2 Proof of Proposition 3

Proof. As mentioned in Section 5.1.1, the core of the game is not empty if and only if condition (5.9) is fulfilled.

In our setup, the maximum quantile of a payoff is

$$\max_{i\in S} q_{\alpha_i}(V(S)) = \max_{i\in S} \mu(S) + \sigma(S)z(\alpha_i) = \mu(S) + \sigma(S)\max_{i\in S} z(\alpha_i) \tag{C.2}$$

$$= \mu(S) + \sigma(S)z\left(\max_{i\in S} \alpha_i\right), \tag{C.3}$$

as z is monotonically increasing in α. Assuming at least one risk-neutral player, this leads to

$$z\left(\max_{i\in N} \alpha_i\right) = z(0.5) = 0 \tag{C.4}$$

and

$$z\left(\max_{i\in S} \alpha_i\right) \leq 0 \quad \forall S \subset N. \tag{C.5}$$

As $\sigma(S) \geq 0$, condition 5.9 is implied by

$$\mu(N) \geq \sum_{S\subset N} \delta_S\, \mu(S)$$

$$\Leftrightarrow \quad C_N^0 - \pi_N\left(\pi_N \sum_{i\in N} \frac{\gamma_i}{(\gamma_i - \theta z(\alpha_i))^2} + 1\right) E_N(N)^2$$

$$\geq \sum_{S\subset N} \delta_S C_S^0 - \pi_S\left(\pi_S \sum_{i\in S} \frac{\gamma_i}{(\gamma_i - \theta z(\alpha_i))^2} + 1\right) E_N(S)^2 \tag{C.6}$$

Global emissions under different coalitions are related by

$$E_N(S) = \frac{E_N^0}{\chi(S)+1} = \frac{E_N^0}{(\chi(N)+1)\frac{\chi(S)+1}{\chi(N)+1}} = E_N(N)\frac{\chi(N)+1}{\chi(S)+1} \tag{C.7}$$

Using (C.7), condition (C.6) becomes

$$\begin{aligned} -\pi_N\left(\pi_N\sum_{i\in N}\frac{\gamma_i}{(\gamma_i-\theta z(\alpha_i))^2}+1\right)E_N(N)^2 &\geq -\sum_{S\subset N}\delta_S\pi_S\left(\pi_S\sum_{i\in S}\frac{\gamma_i}{(\gamma_i-\theta z(\alpha_i))^2}+1\right)\left(E_N(N)\frac{\chi(N)+1}{\chi(S)+1}\right)^2 \\ \Leftrightarrow \quad \pi_N\left(\pi_N\sum_{i\in N}\frac{\gamma_i}{(\gamma_i-\theta z(\alpha_i))^2}+1\right) &\leq \sum_{S\subset N}\delta_S\pi_S\left(\pi_S\sum_{i\in S}\frac{\gamma_i}{(\gamma_i-\theta z(\alpha_i))^2}+1\right)\left(\frac{\chi(N)+1}{\chi(S)+1}\right)^2 \\ \Leftrightarrow \quad \pi_N\left(\pi_N\sum_{i\in N}\frac{\gamma_i}{(\gamma_i-\theta z(\alpha_i))^2}+1\right) &\leq \sum_{S\subset N}\delta_S\pi_S\left(\pi_S\sum_{i\in S}\frac{\gamma_i}{(\gamma_i-\theta z(\alpha_i))^2}+1\right)\left(\frac{\pi_N\sum_{i\in N}\frac{1}{\gamma_i-\theta z(\alpha_i)}+1}{\pi_S\sum_{i\in S}\frac{1}{\gamma_i-\theta z(\alpha_i)}+\sum_{j\notin S}\frac{\pi_j}{\gamma_j-\theta z(\alpha_j)}+1}\right)^2 \end{aligned}$$

Using symmetry and defining $s := |S|$ and $n := |N|$ for convenience, we have

$$\begin{aligned}
&\Leftrightarrow \; n\pi\left(n\pi\sum_{i\in N}\frac{\gamma}{(\gamma-\theta z(\alpha_i))^2}+1\right)\\
&\leq \sum_{S\subset N}\delta_S s\pi\left(s\pi\sum_{i\in S}\frac{\gamma}{(\gamma-\theta z(\alpha_i))^2}+1\right)\left(\frac{n\pi\sum_{i\in N}\frac{1}{\gamma-\theta z(\alpha_i)}+1}{s\pi\sum_{i\in S}\frac{1}{\gamma-\theta z(\alpha_i)}+\sum_{j\notin S}\frac{\pi}{\gamma-\theta z(\alpha_j)}+1}\right)^2\\
&=\pi\left(n\pi\sum_{i\in N}\frac{\gamma}{(\gamma-\theta z(\alpha_i))^2}+1\right)\sum_{S\subset N}\delta_S s\frac{\left(s\pi\sum_{i\in S}\frac{\gamma}{(\gamma-\theta z(\alpha_i))^2}+1\right)}{\left(n\pi\sum_{i\in N}\frac{\gamma}{(\gamma-\theta z(\alpha_i))^2}+1\right)}\left(\frac{n\pi\sum_{i\in N}\frac{1}{\gamma-\theta z(\alpha_i)}+1}{s\pi\sum_{i\in S}\frac{1}{\gamma-\theta z(\alpha_i)}+\sum_{j\notin S}\frac{\pi}{\gamma-\theta z(\alpha_j)}+1}\right)^2
\end{aligned}$$

Define

$$A := \left(s\pi\sum_{i\in S}\frac{\gamma}{(\gamma-\theta z(\alpha_i))^2}+1\right)\left(n\pi\sum_{i\in N}\frac{1}{\gamma-\theta z(\alpha_i)}+1\right)^2, \tag{C.8a}$$

$$B := \left(n\pi\sum_{i\in N}\frac{\gamma}{(\gamma-\theta z(\alpha_i))^2}+1\right)\left(s\pi\sum_{i\in S}\frac{1}{\gamma-\theta z(\alpha_i)}+\sum_{j\notin S}\frac{\pi}{\gamma-\theta z(\alpha_j)}+1\right)^2. \tag{C.8b}$$

In the next step, I show that

$$\sum_{S\subset N}\delta_S s\frac{A}{B}\geq n, \tag{C.9}$$

completing the proof.

For $S = N$, we immediately have $A = B$. Let $S \subsetneq N$. Then

$$\begin{aligned}
A = & \left(s\pi \sum_{i\in S} \frac{\gamma}{(\gamma - \theta z(\alpha_i))^2} + 1 \right) \left(n\pi \sum_{i\in N} \frac{1}{\gamma - \theta z(\alpha_i)} + 1 \right)^2 \\
= & \pi^3 \left[sn^2 \left(\sum_{i\in N} \frac{1}{\gamma - \theta z(\alpha_i)} \right)^2 \left(\sum_{i\in S} \frac{\gamma}{(\gamma - \theta z(\alpha_i))^2} \right) \right] \\
& + \pi^2 \left[2sn \left(\sum_{i\in N} \frac{1}{\gamma - \theta z(\alpha_i)} \right) \left(\sum_{i\in S} \frac{\gamma}{(\gamma - \theta z(\alpha_i))^2} \right) + n^2 \left(\sum_{i\in N} \frac{1}{\gamma - \theta z(\alpha_i)} \right)^2 \right] \\
& + \pi \left[s \left(\sum_{i\in S} \frac{\gamma}{(\gamma - \theta z(\alpha_i))^2} \right) + 2n \left(\sum_{i\in N} \frac{1}{\gamma - \theta z(\alpha_i)} \right) \right] \\
& + 1 \\
=: & a_3\pi^3 + a_2\pi^2 + a_1\pi + 1,
\end{aligned}$$

and

$$
\begin{aligned}
B = \quad & \left(n\pi \sum_{i\in N} \frac{\gamma}{(\gamma-\theta z(\alpha_i))^2} + 1\right)\left(s\pi \sum_{i\in S} \frac{1}{\gamma-\theta z(\alpha_i)} + \pi \sum_{j\notin S} \frac{1}{\gamma-\theta z(\alpha_j)} + 1\right)^2 \\
= \pi^3 n & \left(\sum_{i\in N} \frac{\gamma}{(\gamma-\theta z(\alpha_i))^2}\right) \\
& \left[s^2\left(\sum_{i\in S} \frac{1}{\gamma-\theta z(\alpha_i)}\right)^2 + \left(\sum_{j\notin S} \frac{1}{\gamma-\theta z(\alpha_j)}\right)^2 + 2s\left(\sum_{i\in S} \frac{1}{\gamma-\theta z(\alpha_i)}\right)\left(\sum_{j\notin S} \frac{1}{\gamma-\theta z(\alpha_j)}\right)\right] \\
+\pi^2 & \left[2ns\left(\sum_{i\in S} \frac{1}{\gamma-\theta z(\alpha_i)}\right)\left(\sum_{i\in N} \frac{\gamma}{(\gamma-\theta z(\alpha_i))^2}\right) + 2n\left(\sum_{j\notin S} \frac{1}{\gamma-\theta z(\alpha_j)}\right)\left(\sum_{i\in N} \frac{\gamma}{(\gamma-\theta z(\alpha_i))^2}\right)\right. \\
& \left. + s^2\left(\sum_{i\in S} \frac{1}{\gamma-\theta z(\alpha_i)}\right)^2 + \left(\sum_{j\notin S} \frac{1}{\gamma-\theta z(\alpha_j)}\right)^2 + 2s\left(\sum_{i\in S} \frac{1}{\gamma-\theta z(\alpha_i)}\right)\left(\sum_{j\notin S} \frac{1}{\gamma-\theta z(\alpha_j)}\right)\right] \\
+\pi & \left[n\left(\sum_{i\in N} \frac{\gamma}{(\gamma-\theta z(\alpha_i))^2}\right) + 2s\left(\sum_{i\in S} \frac{1}{\gamma-\theta z(\alpha_i)}\right) + 2\left(\sum_{j\notin S} \frac{1}{\gamma-\theta z(\alpha_j)}\right)\right] \\
+1 & \\
=: \; & b_3\pi^3 + b_2\pi^2 + b_1\pi + 1
\end{aligned}
$$

As an intermediate step, I show $a_1 \geq b_1$ and $a_2 \geq b_2$. Using

$$\frac{1}{\gamma - \theta z(\alpha_i)} = \frac{\gamma - \theta z(\alpha_i)}{(\gamma - \theta z(\alpha_i))^2} \overset{\theta z(\alpha_i) \leq 0}{\geq} \frac{\gamma}{(\gamma - \theta z(\alpha_i))^2}, \tag{C.10}$$

we have

$$
\begin{aligned}
a_1 =& s\left(\sum_{i\in S}\frac{\gamma}{(\gamma-\theta z(\alpha_i))^2}\right)+2n\left(\sum_{i\in N}\frac{1}{\gamma-\theta z(\alpha_i)}\right)\\
=& s\left(\sum_{i\in S}\frac{\gamma}{(\gamma-\theta z(\alpha_i))^2}\right)+2n\left(\left(\sum_{i\in S}\frac{1}{\gamma-\theta z(\alpha_i)}\right)+\left(\sum_{j\notin S}\frac{1}{\gamma-\theta z(\alpha_j)}\right)\right)\\
=& s\left(\sum_{i\in S}\frac{\gamma}{(\gamma-\theta z(\alpha_i))^2}\right)+2(n-s)\left(\sum_{i\in S}\frac{1}{\gamma-\theta z(\alpha_i)}\right)+2s\left(\sum_{i\in S}\frac{1}{\gamma-\theta z(\alpha_i)}\right)\\
&+2(n-1)\left(\sum_{j\notin S}\frac{1}{\gamma-\theta z(\alpha_j)}\right)+2\left(\sum_{j\notin S}\frac{1}{\gamma-\theta z(\alpha_j)}\right)\\
\overset{(C.10)}{\geq}& s\left(\sum_{i\in S}\frac{\gamma}{(\gamma-\theta z(\alpha_i))^2}\right)+2(n-s)\left(\sum_{i\in S}\frac{\gamma}{(\gamma-\theta z(\alpha_i))^2}\right)+2s\left(\sum_{i\in S}\frac{1}{\gamma-\theta z(\alpha_i)}\right)\\
&+2(n-1)\left(\sum_{j\notin S}\frac{\gamma}{(\gamma-\theta z(\alpha_i))^2}\right)+2\left(\sum_{j\notin S}\frac{1}{\gamma-\theta z(\alpha_j)}\right)\\
\overset{n\geq 2}{\geq}& n\left(\sum_{i\in S}\frac{\gamma}{(\gamma-\theta z(\alpha_i))^2}\right)+2s\left(\sum_{i\in S}\frac{1}{\gamma-\theta z(\alpha_i)}\right)+n\left(\sum_{j\notin S}\frac{\gamma}{(\gamma-\theta z(\alpha_i))^2}\right)+2\left(\sum_{j\notin S}\frac{1}{\gamma-\theta z(\alpha_j)}\right)\\
=& n\left(\sum_{i\in N}\frac{\gamma}{(\gamma-\theta z(\alpha_i))^2}\right)+2s\left(\sum_{i\in S}\frac{1}{\gamma-\theta z(\alpha_i)}\right)+2\left(\sum_{j\notin S}\frac{1}{\gamma-\theta z(\alpha_j)}\right)\\
=& b_1
\end{aligned}
$$

and

$$\begin{aligned}
a_2 =& 2sn\left(\sum_{i\in N}\frac{1}{\gamma-\theta z(\alpha_i)}\right)\left(\sum_{i\in S}\frac{\gamma}{(\gamma-\theta z(\alpha_i))^2}\right)+n^2\left(\sum_{i\in N}\frac{1}{\gamma-\theta z(\alpha_i)}\right)^2\\
=& 2sn\left[\left(\sum_{i\in S}\frac{1}{\gamma-\theta z(\alpha_i)}\right)\left(\sum_{i\in S}\frac{\gamma}{(\gamma-\theta z(\alpha_i))^2}\right)+\left(\sum_{j\notin S}\frac{1}{\gamma-\theta z(\alpha_j)}\right)\left(\sum_{i\in S}\frac{\gamma}{(\gamma-\theta z(\alpha_i))^2}\right)\right]\\
&+n^2\left[\left(\sum_{i\in S}\frac{1}{\gamma-\theta z(\alpha_i)}\right)^2+2\left(\sum_{i\in S}\frac{1}{\gamma-\theta z(\alpha_i)}\right)\left(\sum_{j\notin S}\frac{1}{\gamma-\theta z(\alpha_j)}\right)+\left(\sum_{j\notin S}\frac{1}{\gamma-\theta z(\alpha_j)}\right)^2\right]\\
\geq& 2sn\left(\sum_{i\in S}\frac{1}{\gamma-\theta z(\alpha_i)}\right)\left(\sum_{i\in S}\frac{\gamma}{(\gamma-\theta z(\alpha_i))^2}\right)+2n\left(\sum_{j\notin S}\frac{1}{\gamma-\theta z(\alpha_j)}\right)\left(\sum_{i\in S}\frac{\gamma}{(\gamma-\theta z(\alpha_i))^2}\right)\\
&+s^2\left(\sum_{i\in S}\frac{1}{\gamma-\theta z(\alpha_i)}\right)^2+2(n^2-s-sn)\left(\sum_{i\in S}\frac{1}{\gamma-\theta z(\alpha_i)}\right)\left(\sum_{j\notin S}\frac{1}{\gamma-\theta z(\alpha_j)}\right)\\
&+2s\left(\sum_{i\in S}\frac{1}{\gamma-\theta z(\alpha_i)}\right)\left(\sum_{j\notin S}\frac{1}{\gamma-\theta z(\alpha_j)}\right)+2sn\left(\sum_{i\in S}\frac{1}{\gamma-\theta z(\alpha_i)}\right)\left(\sum_{j\notin S}\frac{1}{\gamma-\theta z(\alpha_j)}\right)\\
&+(n^2-2n-1)\left(\sum_{j\notin S}\frac{1}{\gamma-\theta z(\alpha_j)}\right)^2+2n\left(\sum_{j\notin S}\frac{1}{\gamma-\theta z(\alpha_j)}\right)^2+\left(\sum_{j\notin S}\frac{1}{\gamma-\theta z(\alpha_j)}\right)^2
\end{aligned}$$

$$\begin{aligned}
&\geq 2sn\left(\sum_{i\in S}\frac{1}{\gamma-\theta z(\alpha_i)}\right)\left(\sum_{i\in S}\frac{\gamma}{(\gamma-\theta z(\alpha_i))^2}\right)+2sn\left(\sum_{i\in S}\frac{1}{\gamma-\theta z(\alpha_i)}\right)\left(\sum_{j\notin S}\frac{\gamma}{(\gamma-\theta z(\alpha_j))^2}\right)\\
&\quad+2n\left(\sum_{j\notin S}\frac{1}{\gamma-\theta z(\alpha_j)}\right)\left(\sum_{i\in S}\frac{\gamma}{(\gamma-\theta z(\alpha_i))^2}\right)+2n\left(\sum_{j\notin S}\frac{1}{\gamma-\theta z(\alpha_j)}\right)\left(\sum_{j\notin S}\frac{\gamma}{(\gamma-\theta z(\alpha_j))^2}\right)\\
&\quad+s^2\left(\sum_{i\in S}\frac{1}{\gamma-\theta z(\alpha_i)}\right)^2+2s\left(\sum_{i\in S}\frac{1}{\gamma-\theta z(\alpha_i)}\right)\left(\sum_{j\notin S}\frac{1}{\gamma-\theta z(\alpha_j)}\right)+\left(\sum_{j\notin S}\frac{1}{\gamma-\theta z(\alpha_j)}\right)^2\\
&=2sn\left(\sum_{i\in S}\frac{1}{\gamma-\theta z(\alpha_i)}\right)\left(\sum_{i\in N}\frac{\gamma}{(\gamma-\theta z(\alpha_i))^2}\right)+2n\left(\sum_{j\notin S}\frac{1}{\gamma-\theta z(\alpha_j)}\right)\left(\sum_{i\in N}\frac{\gamma}{(\gamma-\theta z(\alpha_i))^2}\right)\\
&\quad+s^2\left(\sum_{i\in S}\frac{1}{\gamma-\theta z(\alpha_i)}\right)^2+2s\left(\sum_{i\in S}\frac{1}{\gamma-\theta z(\alpha_i)}\right)\left(\sum_{j\notin S}\frac{1}{\gamma-\theta z(\alpha_j)}\right)+\left(\sum_{j\notin S}\frac{1}{\gamma-\theta z(\alpha_j)}\right)^2\\
&=b_2,
\end{aligned}$$

where

$$n^2-s-sn\geq 0 \quad \text{and}$$
$$n^2-2n-1\geq 0$$

hold for $n\geq 3$ and $s\leq(n-1)$.

To show condition (C.9), I distinguish two cases. If $A \geq B$, then

$$\sum_{S \subset N} \delta_S s \frac{A}{B} \geq \sum_{S \subset N} \delta_S s = \sum_{S \subset N} \delta_S \sum_{i \in N} \mathbb{1}_{i \in S} = \sum_{i \in N} \underbrace{\sum_{S \subset N} \delta_S \mathbb{1}_{i \in S}}_{=1} = n.$$

If $A < B$, then

$$\sum_{S \subset N} \delta_S s \frac{A}{B} = \sum_{S \subset N} \delta_S s \frac{a_3 \pi^3 + a_2 \pi^2 + a_1 \pi + 1}{b_3 \pi^3 + b_2 \pi^2 + b_1 \pi + 1} \geq \sum_{S \subset N} \delta_S s \frac{a_3 \pi^3}{b_3 \pi^3}$$

as

$$a_2 \pi^2 + a_1 \pi + 1 \geq b_2 \pi^2 + b_1 \pi + 1.$$

Further, we have

$$
\begin{aligned}
&\sum_{S\subset N} \delta_S s \frac{a_3 \pi^3}{b_3 \pi^3} \\
=&\sum_{S\subset N} \delta_S s \frac{s n^2 \left(\sum_{i\in N} \frac{1}{\gamma-\theta z(\alpha_i)}\right)^2 \left(\sum_{i\in S} \frac{\gamma}{(\gamma-\theta z(\alpha_i))^2}\right)}{n\left(\sum_{i\in N} \frac{\gamma}{(\gamma-\theta z(\alpha_i))^2}\right)\left[s\left(\sum_{i\in S} \frac{1}{\gamma-\theta z(\alpha_i)}\right)+\left(\sum_{j\notin S} \frac{1}{\gamma-\theta z(\alpha_j)}\right)\right]^2} \\
=&\frac{n^2}{n\left(\sum_{i\in N} \frac{\gamma}{(\gamma-\theta z(\alpha_i))^2}\right)} \sum_{S\subset N} \delta_S s^2 \frac{\left(\sum_{i\in N} \frac{1}{\gamma-\theta z(\alpha_i)}\right)^2 \left(\sum_{i\in S} \frac{\gamma}{(\gamma-\theta z(\alpha_i))^2}\right)}{\left[s\left(\sum_{i\in S} \frac{1}{\gamma-\theta z(\alpha_i)}\right)+\left(\sum_{j\notin S} \frac{1}{\gamma-\theta z(\alpha_j)}\right)\right]^2} \\
=&\frac{n}{\left(\sum_{i\in N} \frac{\gamma}{(\gamma-\theta z(\alpha_i))^2}\right)} \sum_{S\subset N} \delta_S \left(\sum_{i\in S} \frac{\gamma}{(\gamma-\theta z(\alpha_i))^2}\right) \frac{\left(s\sum_{i\in N} \frac{1}{\gamma-\theta z(\alpha_i)}\right)^2}{\left[s\left(\sum_{i\in S} \frac{1}{\gamma-\theta z(\alpha_i)}\right)+\left(\sum_{j\notin S} \frac{1}{\gamma-\theta z(\alpha_j)}\right)\right]^2} \\
\geq&\frac{n}{\left(\sum_{i\in N} \frac{\gamma}{(\gamma-\theta z(\alpha_i))^2}\right)} \sum_{S\subset N} \delta_S \left(\sum_{i\in S} \frac{\gamma}{(\gamma-\theta z(\alpha_i))^2}\right) \\
=&\frac{n}{\left(\sum_{i\in N} \frac{\gamma}{(\gamma-\theta z(\alpha_i))^2}\right)} \left(\sum_{i\in N} \frac{\gamma}{(\gamma-\theta z(\alpha_i))^2}\right) \\
=&n,
\end{aligned}
$$

showing condition (C.9) and completing the proof. □

C.1.3 Proof of Proposition 4

Proof. Let $S \subset N, i \in S, j \notin S$. Then j optimizes the certainty equivalent of individual utility.

$$\begin{aligned} ce_j(U_j(E_j(S),E_N(S))) &= C_j^0 - \gamma_j(E_j^0 - E_j(S))^2 - \pi_j E_N(S)^2 + \kappa_j E_N^2 z(\alpha_j) \\ 0 \stackrel{!}{=} \frac{\partial ce_j(U_j(E_j(S),E_N(S)))}{\partial E_j(S)} &= 2\gamma_j(E_j^0 - E_j(S)) - 2\pi_j E_N(S) + 2\kappa_j z(\alpha_j) E_N(S) \\ \Rightarrow \quad \gamma_j(E_j^0 - E_j(S)) &= (\pi_j - \kappa_j z(\alpha_j)) E_N(S) \\ \Rightarrow \quad E_j(S) &= E_j^0 - \frac{\pi_j - \kappa_j z(\alpha_j)}{\gamma_j} E_N(S) \end{aligned}$$

Player i optimizes the sum of all certainty equivalents of utility of the members of S:

$$\sum_{l \in S} ce_l(U_l(E_l(S),E_N(S))) = \sum_{l \in S} C_l^0 - \gamma_l(E_l^0 - E_l(S))^2 - \pi_l E_N(S)^2 + \kappa_l E_N^2 z(\alpha_l)$$

$$\begin{aligned} 0 &\stackrel{!}{=} \frac{\partial \sum_{l \in S} ce_l(U_l(E_l(S),E_N(S)))}{\partial E_i(S)} \\ &= 2\gamma_i(E_i^0 - E_i(S)) - 2\underbrace{\sum_{l \in S} \pi_l}_{=:\pi_S} E_N(S) + 2\underbrace{\sum_{l \in S} \kappa_l z(\alpha_l)}_{=:(\kappa z(\alpha))_S} E_N(S) \end{aligned}$$

$$\Rightarrow \quad \gamma_i(E_i^0 - E_i(S)) = (\pi_S - (\kappa z(\alpha))_S) E_N(S)$$

$$\Rightarrow \quad E_i(S) = E_i^0 - \frac{\pi_S - (\kappa z(\alpha))_S}{\gamma_i} E_N(S)$$

The sum of individual emissions of all players gives global emissions $E_N(S)$:

$$\begin{aligned} E_N(S) &= \sum_{l \in N} E_l(S) = \sum_{i \in S} E_i(S) + \sum_{j \notin S} E_j(S) \\ &= \sum_{i \in S} E_i^0 - \frac{\pi_S - (\kappa z(\alpha))_S}{\gamma_i} E_N(S) + \sum_{j \notin S} E_j^0 - \frac{\pi_j - \kappa_j z(\alpha_j)}{\gamma_j} E_N(S) \\ &= E_N^0 - \underbrace{\left((\pi_S - (\kappa z(\alpha))_S) \sum_{i \in S} \frac{1}{\gamma_i} + \sum_{j \notin S} \frac{\pi_j - \kappa_j z(\alpha_j)}{\gamma_j} \right)}_{=: \psi(S)} E_N(S) \end{aligned}$$

$$\Rightarrow \quad E_N(S) = \frac{E_N^0}{\psi(S) + 1}$$

$\psi(S)$ is the reduction factor of global emissions, showing Proposition 4 (i). The second and third parts of the Proposition follows directly from (i).

□

C.1.4 Proof of Proposition 6

Proof. As mentioned in Section 5.1.1, the core of the game is not empty if and only if condition (5.9) is fulfilled.

We have

$$\max_{i\in S} ce_i(V(S)) = \max_{i\in S} \mu(S) + z(\alpha_i)\sigma(S) = \mu(S) + z(\max_{i\in S} \alpha_i)\sigma(S). \tag{C.11}$$

For simplicity, define

$$z_{max}(S) := z(\max_{i\in S} \alpha_i), (z\kappa)_S := \sum_{i\in S} z_i \kappa_i, \left(\frac{1}{\gamma}\right)_S := \sum_{i\in S} \frac{1}{\gamma_i}. \tag{C.12}$$

Then condition (5.9) is equivalent to

$$
\begin{aligned}
& C_N^0 - \left(\pi_N + (\pi_N - (z\kappa)_N)^2 \left(\frac{1}{\gamma}\right)_N \right) E_N(N)^2 + z_{max}(N) \sqrt{\sum_{i\in N} \kappa_i^2 E_N(N)^2} \\
& \geq \sum_{S\subset N} \delta_S \left[C_S^0 - \left(\pi_S + (\pi_S - (z\kappa)_S)^2 \left(\frac{1}{\gamma}\right)_S \right) E_N(S)^2 + z_{max}(S) \sqrt{\sum_{i\in S} \kappa_i^2 E_N(S)^2} \right] \\
\Leftrightarrow \quad & \left[\pi_N - z_{max}(N) \sqrt{\sum_{i\in N} \kappa_i^2} + (\pi_N - (z\kappa)_N)^2 \left(\frac{1}{\gamma}\right)_N \right] E_N(N)^2 \\
& \leq \sum_{S\subset N} \delta_S \left[\pi_S - z_{max}(S) \sqrt{\sum_{i\in S} \kappa_i^2} + (\pi_S - (z\kappa)_S)^2 \left(\frac{1}{\gamma}\right)_S \right] E_N(S)^2 \\
\Leftrightarrow \quad & \pi_N - z_{max}(N) \sqrt{\sum_{i\in N} \kappa_i^2} + (\pi_N - (z\kappa)_N)^2 \left(\frac{1}{\gamma}\right)_N \\
& \leq \sum_{S\subset N} \delta_S \left[\pi_S - z_{max}(S) \sqrt{\sum_{i\in S} \kappa_i^2} + (\pi_S - (z\kappa)_S)^2 \left(\frac{1}{\gamma}\right)_S \right] \left(\frac{\psi(N)+1}{\psi(S)+1} \right)^2 \\
\Leftrightarrow \quad & \pi_N - z_{max}(N) \sqrt{\sum_{i\in N} \kappa_i^2} + (\pi_N - (z\kappa)_N)^2 \left(\frac{1}{\gamma}\right)_N \\
& \leq \sum_{S\subset N} \delta_S \left[\pi_S - z_{max}(S) \sqrt{\sum_{i\in S} \kappa_i^2} + (\pi_S - (z\kappa)_S)^2 \left(\frac{1}{\gamma}\right)_S \right] \left(\frac{(\pi_N - (z\kappa)_N) \left(\frac{1}{\gamma}\right)_N + 1}{(\pi_S - (z\kappa)_S) \left(\frac{1}{\gamma}\right)_S + \sum_{j\notin S} \frac{\pi_j - z_j\kappa_j}{\gamma_j} + 1} \right)^2
\end{aligned}
\tag{C.13}
$$

I first show condition (C.13) for the special case of the *All Singletons* map, i.e.

$$\delta_S^{\text{Singl}} = \begin{cases} 1, & S = \{i\}, i \in N \\ 0, & \text{otherwise.} \end{cases} \tag{C.14}$$

Then the right hand side of (C.13) is equal to

$$\sum_{i \in N} \frac{\left(\pi_i - z_i \kappa_i + \frac{(\pi_i - z_i \kappa_i)^2}{\gamma_i}\right) \left((\pi_N - (z\kappa)_N) \left(\frac{1}{\gamma}\right)_N + 1\right)^2}{\left(\sum_{l \in N} \frac{\pi_l - z_l \kappa_l}{\gamma_l} + 1\right)^2}$$

$$= \left((\pi_N - (z\kappa)_N) \left(\frac{1}{\gamma}\right)_N + 1\right) \sum_{i \in N} \frac{(\pi_i - z_i \kappa_i) \left(1 + \frac{\pi_i - z_i \kappa_i}{\gamma_i}\right) \left((\pi_N - (z\kappa)_N) \left(\frac{1}{\gamma}\right)_N + 1\right)}{\left(\sum_{l \in N} \frac{\pi_l - z_l \kappa_l}{\gamma_l} + 1\right)^2}$$

I now show

$$\sum_{i \in N} \frac{(\pi_i - z_i \kappa_i) \left(1 + \frac{\pi_i - z_i \kappa_i}{\gamma_i}\right) \left((\pi_N - (z\kappa)_N) \left(\frac{1}{\gamma}\right)_N + 1\right)}{\left(\sum_{l \in N} \frac{\pi_l - z_l \kappa_l}{\gamma_l} + 1\right)^2} \geq \pi_N - (z\kappa)_N, \tag{C.15}$$

which implies (C.13), as

$$\begin{aligned}
&\left((\pi_N - (z\kappa)_N)\left(\frac{1}{\gamma}\right)_N + 1\right)(\pi_N - (z\kappa)_N) \\
=&(\pi_N - (z\kappa)_N)^2\left(\frac{1}{\gamma}\right)_N + \pi_N - (z\kappa)_N \\
\geq&(\pi_N - (z\kappa)_N)^2\left(\frac{1}{\gamma}\right)_N + \pi_N - z_{max}(N)\sqrt{\sum_{i\in N}\kappa_i^2}
\end{aligned}$$

For simplicity, define

$$\tau_i := \pi_i - z_i\kappa_i. \tag{C.16}$$

Then (C.15) is equivalent to

$$\begin{aligned}
&\sum_{i\in N}\frac{\tau_i\left(1+\frac{\tau_i}{\gamma_i}\right)\left(\tau_N\left(\frac{1}{\gamma}\right)_N + 1\right)}{\left(\sum_{l\in N}\frac{\tau_l}{\gamma_l}+1\right)^2} \geq \tau_N \\
\Leftrightarrow &\sum_{i\in N}\tau_i\left(1+\frac{\tau_i}{\gamma_i}\right)\left(\tau_N\left(\frac{1}{\gamma}\right)_N + 1\right) \geq \tau_N\left(\sum_{l\in N}\frac{\tau_l}{\gamma_l}+1\right)^2
\end{aligned}$$

We have

$$
\begin{aligned}
&\sum_{i\in N}\tau_i\left(1+\frac{\tau_i}{\gamma_i}\right)\left(\tau_N\left(\frac{1}{\gamma}\right)_N+1\right)=\sum_{i\in N}\tau_i\left(1+\frac{\tau_i}{\gamma_i}\right)\left(\sum_{j\in N}\tau_j\sum_{k\in N}\frac{1}{\gamma_k}+1\right)\\
&=\sum_{i,j,k\in N}\frac{\tau_i^2\tau_j}{\gamma_i\gamma_k}+\sum_{i,j,k\in N}\frac{\tau_i\tau_j}{\gamma_k}+\sum_{i\in N}\frac{\tau_i^2}{\gamma_i}+\sum_{i\in N}\tau_i\\
&=\sum_{i,j\in N}\frac{\tau_i^2\tau_j}{\gamma_i^2}+\sum_{\substack{i,j,k\in N\\k\neq i}}\frac{\tau_i^2\tau_j}{\gamma_i\gamma_k}+\sum_{i,j\in N}\frac{\tau_i\tau_j}{\gamma_i}+\sum_{i,j\in N}\frac{\tau_i\tau_j}{\gamma_j}+\sum_{\substack{i,j,k\in N\\k\neq i\\k\neq j}}\frac{\tau_i\tau_j}{\gamma_k}+\sum_{i\in N}\frac{\tau_i^2}{\gamma_i}+\sum_{i\in N}\tau_i\\
&\geq\sum_{i,j\in N}\frac{\tau_i^2\tau_j}{\gamma_i^2}+\sum_{\substack{i,j,k\in N\\k\neq i}}\frac{\tau_i\tau_k\tau_j}{\gamma_i\gamma_k}+2\sum_{i,j\in N}\frac{\tau_i\tau_j}{\gamma_i}+\sum_{i\in N}\tau_i\\
&=\sum_{i\in N}\tau_i\left(\sum_{j\in N}\frac{\tau_j^2}{\gamma_j^2}+\sum_{\substack{j\in N\\k\neq j}}\frac{\tau_j\tau_k}{\gamma_j\gamma_k}+2\sum_{j\in N}\frac{\tau_j}{\gamma_j}+1\right)\\
&=\sum_{i\in N}\tau_i\left(\left(\sum_{j\in N}\frac{\tau_j}{\gamma_j}\right)^2+2\sum_{j\in N}\frac{\tau_j}{\gamma_j}+1\right)=\tau_N\left(\sum_{l\in N}\frac{\tau_l}{\gamma_l}+1\right)^2,
\end{aligned}
$$

showing (C.15).

For the general case, define

$$g(S) := \frac{\pi_S - z_{max}(S)\sqrt{\sum_{l\in S}\kappa_l^2} + (\pi_S - (z\kappa)_S)^2\left(\frac{1}{\gamma}\right)_S}{\left[(\pi_S - (z\kappa)_S)\left(\frac{1}{\gamma}\right)_S + \sum_{l\notin S}\frac{\pi_l - z_l\kappa_l}{\gamma_l} + 1\right]^2}. \tag{C.17}$$

From the singleton case, we have

$$\left((\pi_N - (z\kappa)_N)\left(\frac{1}{\gamma}\right)_N + 1\right)^2 \sum_{S\subset N}\delta_S^{\text{Singl}} g(S) \geq (\pi_N - (z\kappa)_N)^2\left(\frac{1}{\gamma}\right)_N + \pi_N - z_{max}(N)\sqrt{\sum_{i\in N}\kappa_i^2}. \tag{C.18}$$

Let

$$\hat{\delta}_S = \begin{cases} \varepsilon, & S = \{i,j\} \\ 1-\varepsilon, & S = \{i\}, S = \{j\} \\ \delta_S^{\text{Singl}}, & \text{otherwise} \end{cases} \tag{C.19}$$

for some $\varepsilon > 0$. $\hat{\delta}$ thus is a balanced map that shifts some weight from the singleton coalitions of the players i and j to the joint coalition of these two players. I now show that $\hat{\delta}$ also satisfies condition (C.13). Two cases need to be distinguished:

$$\text{Case 1:} \quad g(\{i,j\}) \geq g(\{i\}) + g(\{j\}) \tag{C.20}$$

Then

$$\begin{aligned}
&\left((\pi_N - (z\kappa)_N)\left(\frac{1}{\gamma}\right)_N + 1\right)^2 \sum_{S\subset N} \hat{\delta}_S g(S) \\
\overset{(C.20)}{\geq} &\left((\pi_N - (z\kappa)_N)\left(\frac{1}{\gamma}\right)_N + 1\right)^2 \sum_{S\subset N} \delta_S^{\text{Singl}} g(S) \\
\overset{(C.18)}{\geq} &(\pi_N - (z\kappa)_N)^2 \left(\frac{1}{\gamma}\right)_N + \pi_N - z_{max}(N)\sqrt{\sum_{i\in N} \kappa_i^2},
\end{aligned}$$

showing (C.13).

$$\text{Case 2:} \quad g(\{i,j\}) < g(\{i\}) + g(\{j\}) \tag{C.21}$$

Define a new game, denoted by $\sim$, in which players i and j are replaced by a single player, called W, i.e.

$$\tilde{N} = N \backslash \{i,j\} \cup \{W\}. \tag{C.22a}$$

Let

$$\tilde{z}_W := z_{max}(\{i,j\}), \tag{C.22b}$$

$$\tilde{\kappa}_W := \sqrt{\kappa_i^2 + \kappa_j^2}, \tag{C.22c}$$

$$\tilde{E}_W^0 := E_i^0 + E_j^0, \tag{C.22d}$$

$$\tilde{C}_W^0 := C_i^0 + C_j^0, \tag{C.22e}$$

while the parameters for other players stay as in the original game. Choose $\tilde{\pi}_W$ and $\tilde{\gamma}_W$ as solutions to the system of inequalities

$$\left((\pi_N - (z\kappa)_N)\left(\frac{1}{\gamma}\right)_N + 1\right)^2 \left[g(\{i,j\}) + \sum_{\substack{l\in N\\ l\neq i,j}} g(\{l\})\right] \geq \left((\tilde{\pi}_{\tilde{N}} - (\tilde{z}\tilde{\kappa})_{\tilde{N}})\left(\frac{1}{\tilde{\gamma}}\right)_{\tilde{N}} + 1\right)^2 \left[\tilde{g}(W) + \sum_{\substack{l\in N\\ l\neq i,j}} \tilde{g}(\{l\})\right], \tag{C.23a}$$

$$(\tilde{\pi}_{\tilde{N}} - (\tilde{z}\tilde{\kappa})_{\tilde{N}}))^2 \left(\frac{1}{\tilde{\gamma}}\right)_{\tilde{N}} + \tilde{\pi}_{\tilde{N}} \geq (\pi_N - (z\kappa)_N)^2 \left(\frac{1}{\gamma}\right)_N + \pi_N. \tag{C.23b}$$

For example, in Example 2, one could choose $\tilde{\pi}_W$ and $\tilde{\gamma}_W$ as in Table C.1. A general solution for $\tilde{\pi}_W$ and $\tilde{\gamma}_W$ is not spelled out in this proof, due to length and complexity.

Thus

$$
\begin{aligned}
&\left((\pi_N - (z\kappa)_N)\left(\frac{1}{\gamma}\right)_N + 1\right)^2 \sum_{S\subset N} \hat{\delta}_S g(S) \\
&= \left((\pi_N - (z\kappa)_N)\left(\frac{1}{\gamma}\right)_N + 1\right)^2 \left[(1-\varepsilon)g(\{i,j\}) + \varepsilon(g(\{i\}) + g(\{j\})) + \sum_{\substack{l\in N\\ l\neq i,j}} g(\{l\})\right] \\
&\overset{(C.21)}{\geq} \left((\pi_N - (z\kappa)_N)\left(\frac{1}{\gamma}\right)_N + 1\right)^2 \left[g(\{i,j\}) + \sum_{\substack{l\in N\\ l\neq i,j}} g(\{l\})\right] \overset{(C.23a)}{\geq} \left((\tilde{\pi}_{\tilde{N}} - (\tilde{z}\tilde{\kappa})_{\tilde{N}})\left(\frac{1}{\tilde{\gamma}}\right)_{\tilde{N}} + 1\right)^2 \left[\tilde{g}(W) + \sum_{\substack{l\in N\\ l\neq i,j}} \tilde{g}(\{l\})\right] \\
&= \left((\tilde{\pi}_{\tilde{N}} - (\tilde{z}\tilde{\kappa})_{\tilde{N}})\left(\frac{1}{\tilde{\gamma}}\right)_{\tilde{N}} + 1\right)^2 \sum_{S\subset\tilde{N}} \tilde{\delta}_S^{\mathrm{Singl}} \tilde{g}(S) \overset{(C.18)}{\geq} (\tilde{\pi}_{\tilde{N}} - (\tilde{z}\tilde{\kappa})_{\tilde{N}}))^2 \left(\frac{1}{\tilde{\gamma}}\right)_{\tilde{N}} + \tilde{\pi}_{\tilde{N}} - z_{max}(N)\sqrt{\sum_{i\in N}\kappa_i^2} \\
&\overset{(C.23b)}{\geq} (\pi_N - (z\kappa)_N)^2 \left(\frac{1}{\gamma}\right)_N + \pi_N - z_{max}(N)\sqrt{\sum_{i\in N}\kappa_i^2},
\end{aligned}
$$

showing (C.13). The iterative application of transformation (C.19) can produce any balanced map δ, completing the proof. □

i	j	$\tilde{\pi}_W$	$\tilde{\gamma}_W$
1	2	2.00E-3	5.56E-2
1	3	2.00E-1	1.00E-1
2	3	1.50E-1	1.00E3

Table C.1: Values of $\tilde{\pi}_W$ and $\tilde{\gamma}_W$ that satisfy equations (C.23) in Example 2.

C.2 Additional tables

Coalition S	V(S)	
	μ	σ^2
{1}	8.7498	0.0050
{2}	8.5937	0.0514
{3}	7.6406	1.3917
{4}	7.6406	1.3917
{1,2}	17.4751	0.4565
{1,3}	15.8882	6.9740
{1,4}	15.8882	6.9740
{2,3}	15.8706	6.1752
{2,4}	15.8706	6.1752
{3,4}	15.0455	7.8550
{1,2,3}	25.4051	8.7419
{1,2,4}	25.4051	8.7419
{1,3,4}	24.8395	9.3169
{2,3,4}	25.0362	7.8691
{1,2,3,4}	35.3460	7.0608

Table C.2: Cooperative game with stochastic payoffs resulting from Example 1. Payoffs are normally distributed with $\mathcal{N}(\mu, \sigma^2)$.

Coalition S	V(S)	
	μ	σ^2
{1}	3.5E+03	3E+05
{2}	4.84E+04	3.11E+07
{3}	4.99E+04	7.783E+08
{1,2}	5.03E+04	1.46E+07
{1,3}	5.38E+04	5.244E+08
{2,3}	9.77E+04	5.340E+08
{1,2,3}	1.009E+05	1.962E+08

Table C.3: Cooperative game with stochastic payoffs resulting from Example 2. Payoffs are normally distributed with $\mathcal{N}(\mu, \sigma^2)$.

D Appendix to Chapter 6

D.1 Proofs

D.1.1 Proof of Lemma 1

Proof. (i) Calculate the value function of the game. Emissions are given by the first order conditions. Let $S \subseteq T$ and $i \in S$.

$$\max_{E_i} \sum_{l \in S} [C_l(E_l) - D_l(E_N)] \Rightarrow \frac{\partial C_i(E_i)}{\partial E_i} - \sum_{l \in S} \frac{\partial D_l(E_N)}{\partial E_i} = 0$$

$$\Rightarrow 2\gamma_i(E_i^0 - E_i) = 2 \underbrace{\sum_{l \in S} \pi_l}_{=:\pi_S} E_N \Rightarrow 2\gamma_i(E_i^0 - E_i) = 2s\pi_i E_N$$

$$\Rightarrow E_i = \frac{\gamma_i E_i^0 - s\pi_i E_N}{\gamma_i} = E_i^0 - \frac{s\pi_i}{\gamma_i} E_N$$

For $i \in T$, $i \notin S$ one gets

$$\max_{E_i} C_i(E_i) - D_i(E_N) \Rightarrow \frac{\partial C_i(E_i)}{\partial E_i} + \frac{\partial D_i(E_N)}{\partial E_i} = 0$$

$$\Rightarrow 2\gamma_i(E_i^0 - E_i) = 2\pi_i E_N \Rightarrow E_i = \frac{\gamma_i E_i^0 - \pi_i E_N}{\gamma_i} = E_i^0 - \frac{\pi_i}{\gamma_i} E_N.$$

And for $j \in R$, the resulting emissions are

$$\max_{E_j} C_j(E_j) - D_j(E_N) \Rightarrow \frac{\partial C_j(E_j)}{\partial E_j} + \frac{\partial D_j(E_N)}{\partial E_j} = 0$$

$$\Rightarrow 2\gamma_j(E_j^0 - E_j) = 2\pi_j E_N \Rightarrow E_j = \frac{\gamma_j E_j^0 - \pi_j E_N}{\gamma_j} = E_j^0 - \frac{\pi_j}{\gamma_j} E_N.$$

For convenience, define $\lambda_l = \frac{1}{\gamma_l}$ and $\lambda_S = \sum_{l \in S} \lambda_l$. Then sum over all players' emissions.

$$\Rightarrow \underbrace{\sum_{k=1}^{n} E_k}_{=E_N} = tE_i^0 + (n-t)E_j^0 - (s^2\lambda_i\pi_i + (t-s)\lambda_i\pi_i + (n-t)\lambda_j\pi_j)E_N$$

$$\Rightarrow E_N = \frac{tE_i^0 + (n-t)E_j^0}{s^2\lambda_i\pi_i + (t-s)\lambda_i\pi_i + (n-t)\lambda_j\pi_j + 1}.$$

With this, the value function can be calculated:

$$
\begin{aligned}
v(S) =& s\left[C_i^0 - \frac{1}{\lambda_i}\left(E_i^0 - (E_i^0 - s\lambda_i\pi_i E_N)\right)^2 - \pi_i E_N^2\right] \\
=& s\left[C_i^0 - \frac{1}{\lambda_i}\left(\frac{s\lambda_i\pi_i(tE_i^0 + (n-t)E_j^0)}{s^2\lambda_i\pi_i + (t-s)\lambda_i\pi_i + (n-t)\lambda_j\pi_j + 1}\right)^2 - \pi_i\left(\frac{tE_i^0 + (n-t)E_j^0}{s^2\lambda_i\pi_i + (t-s)\lambda_i\pi_i + (n-t)\lambda_j\pi_j + 1}\right)^2\right] \\
=& s\left[C_i^0 - \pi_i\frac{(s^2\lambda_i\pi_i + 1)(tE_i^0 + (n-t)E_j^0)^2}{(s^2\lambda_i\pi_i + (t-s)\lambda_i\pi_i + (n-t)\lambda_j\pi_j + 1)^2}\right]
\end{aligned}
$$

and

$$
\begin{aligned}
v(T) =& t\left[C_i^0 - \frac{1}{\lambda_i}\left(\frac{t\lambda_i\pi_i(tE_i^0 + (n-t)E_j^0)}{t^2\lambda_i\pi_i + (n-t)\lambda_j\pi_j + 1}\right)^2 - \pi_i\left(\frac{tE_i^0 + (n-t)E_j^0}{t^2\lambda_i\pi_i + (n-t)\lambda_j\pi_j + 1}\right)^2\right] \\
=& t\left[C_i^0 - \pi_i\frac{(t^2\lambda_i\pi_i + 1)(tE_i^0 + (n-t)E_j^0)^2}{(t^2\lambda_i\pi_i + (n-t)\lambda_j\pi_j + 1)^2}\right].
\end{aligned}
$$

The excess of the symmetric allocation is defined as

$$e(S,y,v) = v(S) - y(S) = v(S) - \frac{s}{t}v(T).$$

Clearly, y lies in the core of (T,v) if and only if

$$e(S,y,v) \leq 0 \; \forall S \subsetneq T.$$

In our case, this is equivalent to

$$
\begin{aligned}
& v(S) \leq \frac{s}{t} v(T) \\
\Leftrightarrow & -\frac{s^2\lambda_i\pi_i+1}{(s^2\lambda_i\pi_i+(t-s)\lambda_i\pi_i+(n-t)\lambda_j\pi_j+1)^2} \leq -\frac{t^2\lambda_i\pi_i+1}{(t^2\lambda_i\pi_i+(n-t)\lambda_j\pi_j+1)^2} \\
\Leftrightarrow & \frac{s^2\lambda_i\pi_i+1}{(s^2\lambda_i\pi_i+(t-s)\lambda_i\pi_i+(n-t)\lambda_j\pi_j+1)^2} \geq \frac{t^2\lambda_i\pi_i+1}{(t^2\lambda_i\pi_i+(n-t)\lambda_j\pi_j+1)^2} \\
\Leftrightarrow & \frac{(s^2\lambda_i\pi_i+(t-s)\lambda_i\pi_i+(n-t)\lambda_j\pi_j+1)^2}{s^2\lambda_i\pi_i+1} \leq \frac{(t^2\lambda_i\pi_i+(n-t)\lambda_j\pi_j+1)^2}{t^2\lambda_i\pi_i+1} \\
\Leftrightarrow & \frac{((n-t)\lambda_j\pi_j)^2+2(n-t)\lambda_j\pi_j(s^2\lambda_i\pi_i+(t-s)\lambda_i\pi_i+1)+(s^2\lambda_i\pi_i+(t-s)\lambda_i\pi_i+1)^2}{s^2\lambda_i\pi_i+1} \\
& \leq \frac{((n-t)\lambda_j\pi_j)^2+2(n-t)\lambda_j\pi_j(t^2\lambda_i\pi_i+1)+(t^2\lambda_i\pi_i+1)^2}{t^2\lambda_i\pi_i+1}
\end{aligned}
$$

$$
\begin{aligned}
\Leftrightarrow & \underbrace{\left(\frac{1}{s^2\lambda_i\pi_i+1}-\frac{1}{t^2\lambda_i\pi_i+1}\right)}_{>0}(n-t)^2(\lambda_j\pi_j)^2+\left(\underbrace{\frac{s^2\lambda_i\pi_i+(t-s)\lambda_i\pi_i+1}{s^2\lambda_i\pi_i+1}}_{>1}-\underbrace{\frac{t^2\lambda_i\pi_i+1}{t^2\lambda_i\pi_i+1}}_{=1}\right)2(n-t)\lambda_j\pi_j \\
& +\frac{(s^2\lambda_i\pi_i+(t-s)\lambda_i\pi_i+1)^2}{s^2\lambda_i\pi_i+1}-(t^2\lambda_i\pi_i+1) \leq 0
\end{aligned}
$$

Define the left hand side of the last inequality as $a(\lambda_i,\lambda_j,\pi_i,\pi_j,s,t,n)$. Due to the rearranging of the formula, it is the excess multiplied with a positive number.

The coefficients of the polynomial can be further simplified. One has

$$\frac{1}{s^2\lambda_i\pi_i+1}-\frac{1}{t^2\lambda_i\pi_i+1}=\frac{t^2\lambda_i\pi_i+1-(s^2\lambda_i\pi_i+1)}{(s^2\lambda_i\pi_i+1)(t^2\lambda_i\pi_i+1)}=\frac{(t^2-s^2)\lambda_i\pi_i}{(s^2\lambda_i\pi_i+1)(t^2\lambda_i\pi_i+1)}=\frac{(t+s)(t-s)\lambda_i\pi_i}{(s^2\lambda_i\pi_i+1)(t^2\lambda_i\pi_i+1)}$$
$$=\frac{(t-s)\lambda_i\pi_i}{s^2\lambda_i\pi_i+1}\,\frac{t+s}{t^2\lambda_i\pi_i+1},$$

$$\frac{s^2\lambda_i\pi_i+(t-s)\lambda_i\pi_i+1}{s^2\lambda_i\pi_i+1}-1=\frac{s^2\lambda_i\pi_i+(t-s)\lambda_i\pi_i+1-s^2\lambda_i\pi_i-1}{s^2\lambda_i\pi_i+1}=\frac{(t-s)\lambda_i\pi_i}{s^2\lambda_i\pi_i+1}$$

and

$$\frac{(s^2\lambda_i\pi_i+(t-s)\lambda_i\pi_i+1)^2}{s^2\lambda_i\pi_i+1}-(t^2\lambda_i\pi_i+1)=\frac{(t-s)\lambda_i\pi_i}{s^2\lambda_i\pi_i+1}\left[(2-s-t)(s^2\lambda_i\pi_i+1)+(t-s)\lambda_i\pi_i\right].$$

This leads to

$$a(\lambda_i,\lambda_j,\pi_i,\pi_j,s,t,n)=\left[\frac{t+s}{t^2\lambda_i\pi_i+1}(n-t)^2\left(\lambda_j\pi_j\right)^2+2(n-t)\lambda_j\pi_j+(2-s-t)(s^2\lambda_i\pi_i+1)+(t-s)\lambda_i\pi_i\right]\frac{(t-s)\lambda_i\pi_i}{s^2\lambda_i\pi_i+1}.$$

(ii) $a(\lambda_i,\lambda_j,\pi_i,\pi_j,s,t,n)$ is a quadratic polynomial of $(\lambda_j\pi_j)$. The coefficients, disregarding the constant term, are positive. Therefore, $a(\lambda_i,\lambda_j,\pi_i,\pi_j,s,t,n)$ is monotonically increasing in $(\lambda_j\pi_j)$. □

D.1.2 Proof of Lemma 2

Proof. (i) Using the implicit function theorem, $\bar{\pi}_j(\pi_i, s, t, n)$ is well defined if

$$\frac{\partial a(\pi_i, \pi_j, s, t, n)}{\partial \pi_j} \neq 0 \ \forall \pi_i > 0, \pi_j > 0.$$

Continuing from Lemma 1, one gets

$$\frac{\partial a}{\partial \pi_j} = \underbrace{\frac{(t-s)\pi_i}{s^2\pi_i + 1}}_{>0} \left[\underbrace{2\frac{t+s}{t^2\pi_i + 1}(n-t)^2\pi_j}_{>0} + \underbrace{2(n-t)}_{>0} \right] > 0.$$

(ii) In order to get an analytical solution for $\bar{\pi}_j(\pi_i, s, t, n)$, solve

$$a(\pi_i, \bar{\pi}_j, s, t, n) = 0$$

for $\bar{\pi}_j > 0$.

$$
\begin{aligned}
& a(\pi_i, \bar{\pi}_j, s, t, n) = 0 \\
\Leftrightarrow\ & \frac{t+s}{t^2\pi_i+1}(n-t)^2\bar{\pi}_j^2 + 2(n-t)\bar{\pi}_j + (2-s-t)(s^2\pi_i+1) + (t-s)\pi_i = 0 \\
\Leftrightarrow\ & \bar{\pi}_j^2 + 2\frac{t^2\pi_i+1}{(t+s)(n-t)}\bar{\pi}_j + \frac{((2-s-t)(s^2\pi_i+1)+(t-s)\pi_i)(t^2\pi_i+1)}{(t+s)(n-t)^2} = 0 \\
\Leftrightarrow\ & \bar{\pi}_j^2 + 2\frac{t^2\pi_i+1}{(t+s)(n-t)}\bar{\pi}_j + \frac{((t+s)(2-s-t)(s^2\pi_i+1)+(t^2-s^2)\pi_i)(t^2\pi_i+1)}{(t+s)^2(n-t)^2} = 0
\end{aligned}
$$

$$
\begin{aligned}
\Leftrightarrow\ \bar{\pi}_j &= -\frac{t^2\pi_i+1}{(t+s)(n-t)} \pm \sqrt{\frac{(t^2\pi_i+1)^2}{(t+s)^2(n-t)^2} - \frac{((t+s)(2-s-t)(s^2\pi_i+1)+(t^2-s^2)\pi_i)(t^2\pi_i+1)}{(t+s)^2(n-t)^2}} \\
&= \frac{-(t^2\pi_i+1) \pm \sqrt{(t^2\pi_i+1)(t^2\pi_i+1-((t+s)(2-s-t)(s^2\pi_i+1)+(t^2-s^2)\pi_i))}}{(t+s)(n-t)}
\end{aligned}
$$

As $\bar{\pi}_j > 0$, the term with positive root defines the boundary. With

$$
\begin{aligned}
& t^2\pi_i + 1 - ((t+s)(2-s-t)(s^2\pi_i+1) + (t^2-s^2)\pi_i) \\
=& 1 - (t+s)(2-s-t)(s^2\pi_i+1) + s^2\pi_i \\
=& 1 - (t+s-1)(2-s-t)(s^2\pi_i+1) - (2-s-t)(s^2\pi_i+1) + s^2\pi_i \\
=& (t+s-1)^2(s^2\pi_i+1),
\end{aligned}
$$

one gets

$$\bar{\pi}_j(\pi_i,s,t,n) = \frac{-(t^2\pi_i+1)+\sqrt{(t^2\pi_i+1)(t+s-1)^2(s^2\pi_i+1)}}{(t+s)(n-t)}$$
$$= \frac{-(t^2\pi_i+1)+(t+s-1)\sqrt{(t^2\pi_i+1)(s^2\pi_i+1)}}{(t+s)(n-t)}.$$

One can now show that $\bar{\pi}_j(\pi_i,s,t,n)$ is monotonically increasing in π_i:

$$\frac{\partial\bar{\pi}_j(\pi_i,s,t,n)}{\partial\pi_i} = \frac{1}{(t+s)(n-t)}\left[-t^2+(t+s-1)\frac{2s^2t^2\pi_i+s^2+t^2}{2\sqrt{(t^2\pi_i+1)(s^2\pi_i+1)}}\right]$$
$$= \frac{1}{(t+s)(n-t)}\left[-t^2+\frac{1}{2}(t+s-1)\left(\frac{(2s^2t^2\pi_i+s^2+t^2)(2s^2t^2\pi_i+s^2+t^2)}{(t^2\pi_i+1)(s^2\pi_i+1)}\right)^{\frac{1}{2}}\right]$$
$$= \frac{1}{(t+s)(n-t)}\left[-t^2+\frac{1}{2}(t+s-1)\left(\frac{4s^4t^4\pi_i^2+4s^2t^2\pi_i(s^2+t^2)+(s^2+t^2)^2}{s^2t^2\pi_i^2+(s^2+t^2)\pi_i+1}\right)^{\frac{1}{2}}\right]$$
$$\geq \frac{1}{(t+s)(n-t)}\left[-t^2+\frac{1}{2}(t+s-1)\left(\frac{(4t^2)(s^4t^2\pi_i^2+s^2\pi_i(s^2+t^2)+1)}{s^2t^2\pi_i^2+(s^2+t^2)\pi_i+1}\right)^{\frac{1}{2}}\right]$$
$$\geq \frac{1}{(t+s)(n-t)}\left[-t^2+\frac{1}{2}(t+s-1)\left(4t^2\right)^{\frac{1}{2}}\right] = \frac{1}{(t+s)(n-t)}\left[-t^2+(t+s-1)t\right] \geq 0,$$

where the first inequality holds as $(s^2+t^2)^2 \geq 4t^2$ for $t \geq 2, s \geq 1$. Finally, $\bar{\pi}_j(\pi_i,s,t,n)$ is monotonically increasing in s:

$$
\begin{aligned}
&\frac{\partial \bar{\pi}_j(\pi_i,s,t,n)}{\partial s} \\
=&\Bigg[\Bigg(\sqrt{(t^2\pi_i+1)(s^2\pi_i+1)}+(t+s-1)\frac{1}{2\sqrt{(t^2\pi_i+1)(s^2\pi_i+1)}}2s\pi_i(t^2\pi_i+1)\Bigg)\,(t+s)(n-t) \\
&-\Big((t+s-1)\sqrt{(t^2\pi_i+1)(s^2\pi_i+1)}-(t^2\pi_i+1)\Big)\,(n-t)\Bigg]\Bigg/((t+s)^2(n-t)^2) \\
=&\Bigg[(t+s)\sqrt{(t^2\pi_i+1)(s^2\pi_i+1)}+\frac{(t+s)(t+s-1)s\pi_i(t^2\pi_i+1)}{\sqrt{(t^2\pi_i+1)(s^2\pi_i+1)}} \\
&-(t+s-1)\sqrt{(t^2\pi_i+1)(s^2\pi_i+1)}+(t^2\pi_i+1)\Bigg]\Bigg/((t+s)^2(n-t)) \\
=&\Bigg[\sqrt{(t^2\pi_i+1)(s^2\pi_i+1)}+\frac{(t+s)(t+s-1)s\pi_i(t^2\pi_i+1)}{\sqrt{(t^2\pi_i+1)(s^2\pi_i+1)}}+(t^2\pi_i+1)\Bigg]\Bigg/((t+s)^2(n-t)) \\
\geq&0.
\end{aligned}
$$

□

D.1.3 Proof of Proposition 7

Proof.

$$\mathscr{P} = \mathscr{P}_1$$

follows directly from Lemma 1 and the fact that a is increasing in π_j. It remains to be shown that no other allocation has to be considered.

For this, assume that the symmetric allocation does not belong to the core of the game, so $(\pi_i, \pi_j) \notin \mathscr{P} = \mathscr{P}_1$. Let $i \in T$. Then

$$\begin{aligned} 0 < a(\pi_i, \pi_j, 1, t, n) &= v(\{i\}) - \frac{v(T)}{t} \\ \Leftrightarrow v(\{i\}) &> \frac{v(T)}{t} \\ \Rightarrow \sum_{i \in T} v(\{i\}) &> v(T). \end{aligned}$$

Therefore, no allocation can satisfy all singletons simultaneously. The core is empty. □

D.1.4 Proof of Proposition 8

Proof. (i) From the proof of Lemma 2, one has

$$\bar{\pi}_j(\pi_i, s, t, n) = \frac{-(t^2\pi_i + 1) + (t + s - 1)\sqrt{(t^2\pi_i + 1)(s^2\pi_i + 1)}}{(t+s)(n-t)}.$$

In the case of $s = 1$, this simplifies to

$$\bar{\pi}_j(\pi_i, 1, t, n) = \frac{-(t^2\pi_i + 1) + t\sqrt{(t^2\pi_i + 1)(\pi_i + 1)}}{(t+1)(n-t)}$$

$$= \frac{t\left(\sqrt{(t^2\pi_i + 1)(\pi_i + 1)} - t\pi_i\right) - 1}{(t+1)(n-t)} = \frac{t\left(\sqrt{t^2\pi_i^2 + (t^2+1)\pi_i + 1} - t\pi_i\right) - 1}{(t+1)(n-t)}.$$

(ii) Follows directly from (i).

(iii) In order to calculate the upper limit, first simplify the inner term

$$\sqrt{t^2\pi_i^2 + (t^2+1)\pi_i + 1} - t\pi_i = \left(\sqrt{t^2\pi_i^2 + (t^2+1)\pi_i + 1} - t\pi_i\right) \frac{\sqrt{t^2\pi_i^2 + (t^2+1)\pi_i + 1} + t\pi_i}{\sqrt{t^2\pi_i^2 + (t^2+1)\pi_i + 1} + t\pi_i}$$

$$= \left(t^2\pi_i^2 + (t^2+1)\pi_i + 1 - t^2\pi_i^2\right) \frac{1}{\sqrt{t^2\pi_i^2 + (t^2+1)\pi_i + 1} + t\pi_i} = \frac{(t^2+1)\pi_i + 1}{\sqrt{t^2\pi_i^2 + (t^2+1)\pi_i + 1} + t\pi_i}$$

$$= \frac{(t^2+1) + \frac{1}{\pi_i}}{\sqrt{t^2\pi_i^2 + (t^2+1)\frac{1}{\pi_i} + \frac{1}{\pi_i^2}} + t} \overset{\pi_i \to \infty}{\to} \frac{t^2+1}{\sqrt{t^2} + t} = \frac{t^2+1}{2t}.$$

This leads to

$$\begin{aligned}\lim_{\pi_i \to \infty} \bar{\pi}_j(\pi_i, t, n) &= \frac{t\frac{t^2+1}{2t} - 1}{(t+1)(n-t)} = \frac{\frac{t^2+1}{2} - 1}{(t+1)(n-t)} = \frac{t^2+1-2}{2(t+1)(n-t)} = \frac{(t^2-1)(t-1)}{2(t^2-1)(n-t)} \\ &= \frac{t-1}{2(n-t)} =: \bar{\pi}_j^{ul}.\end{aligned}$$

(iv) $\bar{\pi}_j^{ul}$ is obviously monotonically increasing in t. This is also true for $\bar{\pi}_j^{ll}$, as

$$\begin{aligned}\frac{\partial \bar{\pi}_j^{ll}}{\partial t} &= \frac{(-t^2+(n-1)t+n)-(t-1)(-2t+(n-1))}{(-t^2+(n-1)t+n)^2} = \frac{-t^2+(n-1)t+n+2t^2-(n-1)t-2t+(n-1)}{(-t^2+(n-1)t+n)^2} \\ &= \frac{t^2-2t+2n-1}{(-t^2+(n-1)t+n)^2} > 0 \quad \forall t \geq 2, n \geq 2.\end{aligned}$$

□

D.1.5 Proof of Proposition 9

Proof. Let $S \subset T, \lambda \equiv 1$. Similar to the proof of Lemma 1, one gets

$$\begin{aligned}E_i &= E_i^0 - \pi_S E_N \quad \forall i \in S \\ E_i &= E_i^0 - \pi_i E_N \quad \forall i \in T, i \notin S \\ E_j &= E_j^0 - \pi_j E_N \quad \forall j \in R\end{aligned}$$

and

$$E_N = \frac{E_N^0}{s\pi_S + \pi_{T\setminus S} + \pi_R + 1}.$$

In the cases of $S = \{i\}$ and $S = T$, the proposition follows directly. □

D.1.6 Proof of Lemma 3

Proof. Following Proposition 9, calculate the individual utility of $i \in S$:

$$\begin{aligned} v_i(S) =& C_i(E_i) - D_i(E_N) = C_i^0 - \left(E_i^0 - \left(E_i^0 - \pi_S \frac{E_N^0}{s\pi_S + \pi_{T\setminus S} + \pi_R + 1}\right)\right)^2 - \pi_i \left(\frac{E_N^0}{s\pi_S + \pi_{T\setminus S} + \pi_R + 1}\right)^2 \\ =& C_i^0 - (\pi_S^2 + \pi_i)\left(\frac{E_N^0}{s\pi_S + \pi_{T\setminus S} + \pi_R + 1}\right)^2 \end{aligned}$$

Therefore one gets

$$v_i(\{i\}) = C_i^0 - (\pi_i^2 + \pi_i)\left(\frac{E_N^0}{\pi_i + \pi_{T\setminus i} + \pi_R + 1}\right)^2 = C_i^0 - (\pi_i^2 + \pi_i)\left(\frac{E_N^0}{\pi_T + \pi_R + 1}\right)^2,$$

$$v_i(T) = C_i^0 - (\pi_T^2 + \pi_i)\left(\frac{E_N^0}{t\pi_T + \pi_R + 1}\right)^2$$

and

$$
\begin{aligned}
& v_i(\{i\}) > v_i(T) \\
\Leftrightarrow & \frac{\pi_T^2+\pi_i}{(t\pi_T+\pi_R+1)^2} > \frac{\pi_i^2+\pi_i}{(\pi_T+\pi_R+1)^2} \\
\Leftrightarrow & \frac{(\pi_T+\pi_R+1)^2}{\pi_i^2+\pi_i} > \frac{(t\pi_T+\pi_R+1)^2}{\pi_T^2+\pi_i} \\
\Leftrightarrow & \frac{\pi_T^2+\pi_R^2+1+2\pi_T\pi_R+2\pi_T+2\pi_R}{\pi_i^2+\pi_i} > \frac{t^2\pi_T^2+\pi_R^2+1+2t\pi_T\pi_R+2t\pi_T+2\pi_R}{\pi_T^2+\pi_i} \\
\Leftrightarrow & \left[\frac{1}{\pi_i^2+\pi_i}-\frac{1}{\pi_T^2+\pi_i}\right]\pi_R^2+\left[\frac{\pi_T+1}{\pi_i^2+\pi_i}-\frac{t\pi_T+1}{\pi_T^2+\pi_i}\right]2\pi_R+\frac{\pi_T^2+1+2\pi_T}{\pi_i^2+\pi_i}-\frac{t^2\pi_T^2+1+2t\pi_T}{\pi_T^2+\pi_i}>0 \\
\Leftrightarrow & \left[\frac{1}{\pi_i^2+\pi_i}-\frac{1}{\pi_T^2+\pi_i}\right]\pi_R^2+\left[\frac{\pi_T+1}{\pi_i^2+\pi_i}-\frac{t\pi_T+1}{\pi_T^2+\pi_i}\right]2\pi_R+\frac{(\pi_T+1)^2}{\pi_i^2+\pi_i}-\frac{(t\pi_T+1)^2}{\pi_T^2+\pi_i}>0
\end{aligned}
$$

Defining the left-hand-side of the equation as $a_i(\pi_i, \pi_T, \pi_R)$ leads to the desired result. □

D.1.7 Proof of Proposition 10

Proof. Define

$$F(x) = \frac{X}{x^2+x} - \frac{Y}{Z+x},$$

where X, Y and Z only depend on π_T, but not on π_i. Let

$$F^{total}(\pi) = \sum_{i \in T} F(\pi_i).$$

I show that $F^{total}(\tilde{\pi}) > F^{total}(\pi)$ for all three terms of $a(\pi)$, as derived in Lemma 3:

$$X = 1,\ Y = 1,\ Z = \pi_T^2;$$
$$X = \pi_T + 1,\ Y = t\pi_T + 1,\ Z = \pi_T^2;$$
$$X = (\pi_T + 1)^2,\ Y = (t\pi_T + 1)^2,\ Z = \pi_T^2.$$

One has

$$\frac{\partial F}{\partial x} = -\frac{X(2x+1)}{x^2(x+1)^2} + \frac{Y}{(Z+x)^2}.$$

I now show that

$$\frac{\partial F}{\partial x}(\pi_l) < \frac{\partial F}{\partial x}(\pi_h) \ \ \forall \pi_l < \frac{\pi_T}{t}, \pi_h > \frac{\pi_T}{t}.$$

Then, with $d > 0$ approaching zero, one has

$$F(\tilde{\pi}_l) - F(\pi_k) = -d\left(\frac{\partial F}{\partial x}(\pi_l)\right)$$
$$F(\tilde{\pi}_h) - F(\pi_h) = d\left(\frac{\partial F}{\partial x}(\pi_h)\right)$$
$$\Rightarrow F^{total}(\tilde{\pi}) - F^{total}(\pi) = d\left(-\frac{\partial F}{\partial x}(\pi_l) + \frac{\partial F}{\partial x}(\pi_h)\right) \geq 0.$$

Let $\pi_m = \frac{\pi_T}{t}$. I first show that

$$\frac{\partial F}{\partial x}(\pi_l) < \frac{\partial F}{\partial \pi}(\pi_m).$$

$$\frac{\partial^2 F}{\partial^2 x}(\pi_l) = \frac{2X(Z+\pi_l)^3((2\pi_l+1)(2\pi_l^2+3\pi_l+1)-\pi_l(\pi_l+1)^2)-2Y\pi_l^3(\pi_l+1)^4}{\pi_l^3(\pi_l+1)^4(Z+\pi_l)^3}.$$

The numerator can be rearranged. Using $\pi_T \geq t\pi_l$.

$$\begin{aligned}
&2X(Z+\pi_l)^3((2\pi_l+1)(2\pi_l^2+3\pi_l+1)-\pi_l(\pi_l+1)^2)-2Y\pi_l^3(\pi_l+1)^4\\
=&2X(\pi_T^6+3\pi_l\pi_T^4+3\pi_l^2\pi_T^2+\pi_l^3)(3\pi_l^3+6\pi_l^2+4\pi_l+1)-2Y(\pi_l^7+4\pi_l^6+6\pi_l^5+4\pi_l^4+\pi_l^3)\\
\geq&2X(t^6\pi_l^6+3t^4\pi_l^5+3t^2\pi_l^4+\pi_l^3)(3\pi_l^3+6\pi_l^2+4\pi_l+1)-2Y(\pi_l^7+4\pi_l^6+6\pi_l^5+4\pi_l^4+\pi_l^3)\\
=&2[\pi_l^9(t^2X(3t^4))+\pi_l^8(t^2X(pt^2+6t^4))+\pi_l^7(t^2X(4t^4+18t^2+12)-Y)+\pi_l^6(t^2X(t^4+12t^2+18+\frac{3}{t^2})-4Y)\\
&+\pi_l^5(t^2X(3t^2+12+\frac{6}{t^2})-6Y)+\pi_l^4(X(3t^2+4)-4Y)+\pi_l^3(X-Y)]
\end{aligned}$$

In the case $X = (\pi_T + 1)^2, Y = (t\pi_T + 1)^2$, this equals

$$
\begin{aligned}
&2[\pi_l^9(t^2X(3t^4)) + \pi_l^8(t^2X(pt^2+6t^4)) + \pi_l^7(t^2X(4t^4+18t^2+12) - Y) + \pi_l^6(t^2X(t^4+12t^2+18+\frac{3}{t^2}) - 4Y) \\
&\quad + \pi_l^5(t^2X(3t^2+12+\frac{6}{t^2}) - 6Y) + \pi_l^4((\pi_T^2+2\pi_T+1)(3t^2+4) - 4(t^2\pi_T^2+2t\pi_T+1)) \\
&\quad + \pi_l^3(\pi_T^2+2\pi_T+1-(t^2\pi_T^2+2t\pi_T+1))] \\
&= 2[\pi_l^9(t^2X(3t^4)) + \pi_l^8(t^2X(pt^2+6t^4)) + \pi_l^7(t^2X(4t^4+18t^2+12) - Y) \\
&\quad + \pi_l^6(t^2X(t^4+12t^2+18+\frac{3}{t^2}) - 4Y + (3t^2+4) - 4t^2) \\
&\quad + \pi_l^5(t^2X(3t^2+12+\frac{6}{t^2}) - 6Y + 2(3t^2+4) - 8t + 1 - t^2) + \pi_l^4(3t^2+4-4+2-2t) + \pi_l^3(1-1)] \\
&\geq 0
\end{aligned}
$$

as $t^2X \geq Y, X \geq 1, Y \geq 1, t \geq 2$. The calculations for the other two cases are analogue. This shows that

$$\frac{\partial F}{\partial x}(\pi_l) < \frac{\partial F}{\partial x}(\pi_m).$$

In the second step, I show that

$$\frac{\partial F}{\partial x}(\pi_m + \varepsilon) > \frac{\partial F}{\partial x}(\pi_m) \quad \forall 0 < \varepsilon < \pi_T - \pi_m.$$

$$
\begin{aligned}
&\frac{\partial F}{\partial x}(\pi_m+\varepsilon)-\frac{\partial F}{\partial x}(\pi_m)\\
&=-\frac{X(2(\pi_m+\varepsilon)+1)}{(\pi_m+\varepsilon)^2(\pi_m+\varepsilon+1)^2}+\frac{Y}{(Z+\pi_m+\varepsilon)^2}+\frac{X(2\pi_m+1)}{\pi_m^2(\pi_m+1)^2}-\frac{Y}{(Z+\pi_m)^2}\\
&=\Big\{X(Z+\pi_m)^2(Z+\pi_m+\varepsilon)^2[(2\pi_m+1)(\pi_m+\varepsilon)^2(\pi_m+\varepsilon+1)^2-(2(\pi_m+\varepsilon)+1)\pi_m^2(\pi_m+1)^2]\\
&\quad +Y\pi_m^2(\pi_m+1)^2(\pi_m+\varepsilon)^2(\pi_m+\varepsilon+1)^2[(Z+\pi_m)^2-(Z+\pi_m+\varepsilon)^2]\Big\}\\
&\quad /\Big\{(\pi_m+\varepsilon)^2(\pi_m+\varepsilon+1)^2(Z+\pi_m+\varepsilon)^2\pi_m^2(\pi_m+1)^2(Z+\pi_m)^2\Big\}
\end{aligned}
$$

The numerator simplifies to

$$
\begin{aligned}
&X(Z+\pi_m)^2(Z+\pi_m+\varepsilon)^2[6\varepsilon\pi_m^4+(12\varepsilon^2+12\varepsilon)\pi_m^3+(8\varepsilon^3+18\varepsilon^2+8\varepsilon)\pi_m^2+(2\varepsilon^4+8\varepsilon^3+8\varepsilon^2+2\varepsilon)\pi_m+\varepsilon^2(\varepsilon+1)^2]\\
&-Y\pi_m^2(\pi_m+1)^2(\pi_m+\varepsilon)^2(\pi_m+\varepsilon+1)^2(2\varepsilon(Z+\pi_m)+\varepsilon^2)
\end{aligned}
$$

Using $Z = \pi_T^2, \pi_m = \frac{\pi_T}{t}$, this equals

$$
\begin{aligned}
&X\left[\pi_T^8 + \frac{4}{t}\pi_T^7 + \frac{2\varepsilon t^2+5}{t^2}\pi_T^6 + \frac{6\varepsilon t^2+4}{t^3}\pi_T^5 + \frac{\varepsilon^2 t^4 + 6\varepsilon t^2 + 1}{t^4}\pi_T^4 + \frac{2\varepsilon^2 t^2 + 2\varepsilon}{t^3}\pi_T^3 + \frac{\varepsilon^2}{t^2}\pi_T^2\right] \\
&\left(\frac{6\varepsilon}{t^4}\pi_T^4 + \frac{12\varepsilon^2+12\varepsilon}{t^3}\pi_T^3 + \frac{8\varepsilon^3+18\varepsilon^2+8\varepsilon}{t^2}\pi_T^2 + \frac{2\varepsilon^4+8\varepsilon^3+8\varepsilon^2+2\varepsilon}{t}\pi_T + \varepsilon^2(\varepsilon+1)^2\right) \\
&-Y\left[\frac{1}{t^8}\pi_T^8 + \frac{4\varepsilon+4}{t^7}\pi_T^7 + \frac{6\varepsilon^2+14\varepsilon+6}{t^6}\pi_T^6 + \frac{4\varepsilon^3+18\varepsilon^2+18\varepsilon+4}{t^5}\pi_T^5\right. \\
&\left.\frac{\varepsilon^4+10\varepsilon^3+19\varepsilon^2+10\varepsilon+1}{t^4}\pi_T^4 + \frac{2\varepsilon^4+8\varepsilon^3+8\varepsilon^2+2\varepsilon}{t^3}\pi_T^3 + \frac{\varepsilon^2(\varepsilon+1)^2}{t^2}\pi_T^2\right] \\
&\left(2\varepsilon\pi_T^2 + \frac{2\varepsilon}{t}\pi_T + \varepsilon^2\right)
\end{aligned}
$$

$$
\begin{aligned}
=X \Bigg[& \frac{6\varepsilon}{t^4}\pi_T^{12} + \left(\frac{24\varepsilon}{t^5} + \frac{12\varepsilon^2+12\varepsilon}{t^3}\right)\pi_T^{11} + \left(\frac{30\varepsilon}{t^6} + \frac{60\varepsilon^2+48\varepsilon}{t^4} + \frac{8\varepsilon^3+18\varepsilon^2+8\varepsilon}{t^2}\right)\pi_T^{10} \\
& + \left(\frac{24\varepsilon}{t^7} + \frac{96\varepsilon^2+60\varepsilon}{t^5} + \frac{56\varepsilon^3+96\varepsilon^2+32\varepsilon}{t^3} + \frac{2\varepsilon^4+8\varepsilon^3+8\varepsilon^2+2\varepsilon}{t}\right)\pi_T^{9} \\
& + \left(\frac{6\varepsilon}{t^8} + \frac{84\varepsilon^2+48\varepsilon}{t^6} + \frac{118\varepsilon^3+162\varepsilon^2+40\varepsilon}{t^4} + \frac{24\varepsilon^4+68\varepsilon^3+48\varepsilon^2+8\varepsilon}{t^2} + (\varepsilon^4+2\varepsilon^3+\varepsilon^2)\right)\pi_T^{8} \\
& + \left(\frac{24\varepsilon^2+12\varepsilon}{t^7} + \frac{116\varepsilon^3+144\varepsilon^2+32\varepsilon}{t^5} + \frac{70\varepsilon^4+160\varepsilon^3+88\varepsilon^2+10\varepsilon}{t^3} + \frac{4\varepsilon^5+20\varepsilon^4+24\varepsilon^3+8\varepsilon^2}{t}\right)\pi_T^{7} \\
& + \left(\frac{38\varepsilon^3+42\varepsilon^2+8\varepsilon}{t^6} + \frac{80\varepsilon^4+164\varepsilon^3+80\varepsilon^2+8\varepsilon}{t^4} + \frac{20\varepsilon^5+71\varepsilon^4+66\varepsilon^3+17\varepsilon^2}{t^2} + (2\varepsilon^5+4\varepsilon^4+2\varepsilon^3)\right)\pi_T^{6} \\
& + \left(\frac{30\varepsilon^4+56\varepsilon^3+24\varepsilon^2+2\varepsilon}{t^5} + \frac{28\varepsilon^5+78\varepsilon^4+72\varepsilon^3+16\varepsilon^2}{t^3} + \frac{2\varepsilon^6+14\varepsilon^5+20\varepsilon^4+8\varepsilon^3)}{t}\right)\pi_T^{5} \\
& + \left(\frac{12\varepsilon^5+35\varepsilon^4+26\varepsilon^3+5\varepsilon^2}{t^4} + \frac{4\varepsilon^6+22\varepsilon^5+28\varepsilon^4+10\varepsilon^3}{t^2} + (\varepsilon^6+2\varepsilon^5+\varepsilon^4)\right)\pi_T^{4} \\
& + \left(\frac{2\varepsilon^6+10\varepsilon^5+12\varepsilon^4+4\varepsilon^3}{t^3} + \frac{2\varepsilon^6+4\varepsilon^5+2\varepsilon^4}{t}\right)\pi_T^{3} \\
& + \frac{\varepsilon^6+2\varepsilon^5+\varepsilon^4}{t^2}\pi_T^{2}\Bigg]
\end{aligned}
$$

$$
\begin{aligned}
&-Y\left[\frac{2\varepsilon}{t^8}\pi_T^{10}+\left(\frac{2\varepsilon}{t^9}+\frac{8\varepsilon^2+8\varepsilon}{t^7}\right)\pi_T^9+\left(\frac{9\varepsilon^2+8\varepsilon}{t^8}+\frac{12\varepsilon^3+28\varepsilon^2+12\varepsilon}{t^6}\right)\pi_T^8\right.\\
&+\left(\frac{16\varepsilon^3+32\varepsilon^2+12\varepsilon}{t^7}+\frac{8\varepsilon^4+36\varepsilon^3+36\varepsilon^2+8\varepsilon}{t^5}\right)\pi_T^7\\
&+\left(\frac{14\varepsilon^4+50\varepsilon^3+42\varepsilon^2+8\varepsilon}{t^6}+\frac{2\varepsilon^5+20\varepsilon^4+38\varepsilon^3+20\varepsilon^2+2\varepsilon}{t^4}\right)\pi_T^6\\
&+\left(\frac{6\varepsilon^5+38\varepsilon^4+56\varepsilon^3+24\varepsilon^2+2\varepsilon}{t^5}+\frac{4\varepsilon^5+16\varepsilon^4+16\varepsilon^3+4\varepsilon^2}{t^3}\right)\pi_T^5\\
&+\left(\frac{\varepsilon^6+14\varepsilon^5+35\varepsilon^4+26\varepsilon^3+5\varepsilon^2}{t^4}+\frac{2\varepsilon^5+4\varepsilon^4+2\varepsilon^3}{t^2}\right)\pi_T^4\\
&\left.+\frac{2\varepsilon^6+10\varepsilon^5+12\varepsilon^4+4\varepsilon^3}{t^3}\pi_T^3+\frac{\varepsilon^6+2\varepsilon^5+\varepsilon^4}{t^2}\pi_T^2\right]
\end{aligned}
$$

For $X = (\pi_T + 1)^2, Y = (t\pi_T + 1)^2$, this equals

$$\Big[\frac{6\varepsilon}{t^4}\pi_T^{14} + \left(\frac{24\varepsilon}{t^5} + \frac{12\varepsilon}{t^4} + \frac{12\varepsilon^2 + 12\varepsilon}{t^3}\right)\pi_T^{13} + \left(\frac{28\varepsilon}{t^6} + \frac{48\varepsilon}{t^5} + \frac{60\varepsilon^2 + 54\varepsilon}{t^4} + \frac{24\varepsilon^2 + 24\varepsilon}{t^3} + \frac{8\varepsilon^3 + 18\varepsilon^2 + 8\varepsilon}{t^2}\right)\pi_T^{12}$$
$$+ \left(\frac{18\varepsilon}{t^7} + \frac{60\varepsilon}{t^6} + \frac{88\varepsilon^2 + 76\varepsilon}{t^5} + \frac{120\varepsilon^2 + 96\varepsilon}{t^4} + \frac{56\varepsilon^3 + 108\varepsilon^2 + 44\varepsilon}{t^3} + \frac{16\varepsilon^3 + 36\varepsilon^2 + 16\varepsilon}{t^2} + \frac{2\varepsilon^4 + 8\varepsilon^3 + 8\varepsilon^2 + 2\varepsilon}{t}\right)\pi_T^{11}$$
$$+ \left(\frac{48\varepsilon}{t^7} + \frac{59\varepsilon^2 + 54\varepsilon}{t^6} + \frac{192\varepsilon^2 + 120\varepsilon}{t^5} + \frac{106\varepsilon^3 + 194\varepsilon^2 + 76\varepsilon}{t^4} + \frac{112\varepsilon^3 + 192\varepsilon^2 + 64\varepsilon}{t^3}\right.$$
$$\left. + \frac{24\varepsilon^4 + 76\varepsilon^3 + 66\varepsilon^2 + 16\varepsilon}{t^2} + \frac{4\varepsilon^4 + 16\varepsilon^3 + 16\varepsilon^2 + 4\varepsilon}{t} + (\varepsilon^4 + 2\varepsilon^3 + \varepsilon^2)\right)\pi_T^{10}$$
$$+ \left(\frac{-2\varepsilon}{t^9} + \frac{12\varepsilon}{t^8} + \frac{-2\varepsilon^2 + 12\varepsilon}{t^7} + \frac{168\varepsilon^2 + 96\varepsilon}{t^6} + \frac{76\varepsilon^3 + 152\varepsilon^2 + 56\varepsilon}{t^5} + \frac{236\varepsilon^3 + 324\varepsilon^2 + 80\varepsilon}{t^4}\right.$$
$$+ \frac{62\varepsilon^4 + 180\varepsilon^3 + 148\varepsilon^2 + 34\varepsilon}{t^3} + \frac{48\varepsilon^4 + 136\varepsilon^3 + 96\varepsilon^2 + 16\varepsilon}{t^2} + \frac{4\varepsilon^5 + 22\varepsilon^4 + 32\varepsilon^3 + 16\varepsilon^2 + 2\varepsilon}{t}$$
$$\left. + (2\varepsilon^4 + 4\varepsilon^3 + 2\varepsilon^2)\right)\pi_T^9$$
$$+ \left(\frac{-9\varepsilon^2 - 2\varepsilon}{t^8} + \frac{48\varepsilon^2 + 24\varepsilon}{t^7} + \frac{6\varepsilon^3 + 34\varepsilon^2 + 20\varepsilon}{t^6} + \frac{232\varepsilon^3 + 288\varepsilon^2 + 64\varepsilon}{t^5} + \frac{50\varepsilon^4 + 106\varepsilon^3 + 128\varepsilon^2 + 24\varepsilon}{t^4}\right.$$
$$+ \frac{140\varepsilon^4 + 320\varepsilon^3 + 176\varepsilon^2 + 20\varepsilon}{t^3} + \frac{18\varepsilon^5 + 75\varepsilon^4 + 96\varepsilon^3 + 45\varepsilon^2 + 6\varepsilon}{t^2} + \frac{8\varepsilon^5 + 40\varepsilon^4 + 48\varepsilon^3 + 16\varepsilon^2}{t}$$
$$\left. + (2\varepsilon^5 + 5\varepsilon^4 + 6\varepsilon^3 + \varepsilon^2)\right)\pi_T^8$$

$$
\begin{aligned}
&+\Bigg(\frac{-16\varepsilon^3-8\varepsilon^2}{t^7}+\frac{76\varepsilon^3+84\varepsilon^2+16\varepsilon}{t^6}+\frac{-6\varepsilon^4+36\varepsilon^3+48\varepsilon^2+10\varepsilon}{t^5}+\frac{160\varepsilon^4+328\varepsilon^3+160\varepsilon^2+16\varepsilon}{t^4}\\
&\quad+\frac{24\varepsilon^5+108\varepsilon^4+156\varepsilon^3+66\varepsilon^2+6\varepsilon}{t^3}+\frac{40\varepsilon^5+142\varepsilon^4+132\varepsilon^3+34\varepsilon^2}{t^2}\\
&\quad+\frac{2\varepsilon^6+14\varepsilon^5+24\varepsilon^4+16\varepsilon^3+4\varepsilon^2}{t}+(4\varepsilon^5+8\varepsilon^4+4\varepsilon^3)\Bigg)\pi_T^7\\
&+\Bigg(\frac{-14\varepsilon^4-12\varepsilon^3}{t^6}+\frac{60\varepsilon^4+112\varepsilon^3+48\varepsilon^2+4\varepsilon}{t^5}+\frac{-2\varepsilon^5+19\varepsilon^4+40\varepsilon^3+17\varepsilon^2+2\varepsilon}{t^4}\\
&\quad+\frac{56\varepsilon^5+156\varepsilon^4+144\varepsilon^3+32\varepsilon^2}{t^3}+\frac{3\varepsilon^6+20\varepsilon^5+32\varepsilon^4+18\varepsilon^3+4\varepsilon^2}{t^2}+\frac{4\varepsilon^6+28\varepsilon^5+40\varepsilon^4+16\varepsilon^3}{t}\\
&\quad+(\varepsilon^6+2\varepsilon^5+1\varepsilon^4)\Bigg)\pi_T^6\\
&+\Bigg(\frac{-6\varepsilon^5-8\varepsilon^4}{t^5}+\frac{24\varepsilon^5+70\varepsilon^4+52\varepsilon^3+10\varepsilon^2}{t^4}+\frac{6\varepsilon^5+4\varepsilon^4+8\varepsilon^3+2\varepsilon^2}{t^3}\\
&\quad+\frac{8\varepsilon^6+44\varepsilon^5+56\varepsilon^4+20\varepsilon^3}{t^2}+\frac{2\varepsilon^6+4\varepsilon^5+2\varepsilon^4}{t}+(2\varepsilon^6+4\varepsilon^5+2\varepsilon^4)\Bigg)\pi_T^5\\
&+\Bigg(\frac{-\varepsilon^6-2\varepsilon^5}{t^4}+\frac{4\varepsilon^6+20\varepsilon^5+24\varepsilon^4+8\varepsilon^3}{t^3}+\frac{\varepsilon^6+2\varepsilon^5+\varepsilon^4}{t^2}+\frac{4\varepsilon^6+8\varepsilon^5+4\varepsilon^4}{t}\Bigg)\pi_T^4\\
&+\frac{2\varepsilon^6+4\varepsilon^5+2\varepsilon^4}{t^2}\pi_T^3\Bigg]
\end{aligned}
$$

Using $t \geq 2$, this is larger than zero. The other cases of X and Y are analogue. Therefore

$$\frac{\partial F}{\partial x}(\pi_m + \varepsilon) > \frac{\partial F}{\partial x}(\pi_m) \quad \forall 0 < \varepsilon < \pi_T - \pi_m.$$

and

$$\frac{\partial F}{\partial x}(\pi_l) < \frac{\partial F}{\partial x}(\pi_h) \ \forall \pi_l < \frac{\pi_T}{t}, \pi_h > \frac{\pi_T}{t}.$$

$\square$

D.2 Parameter estimation

Table D.1: Mitigation cost parameter γ and damage cost parameter π for non-G20 countries. Values of γ and π in $\frac{EUR}{10^{15}*(tCO_2)^2}$.

Country	γ	π	Ratio $\frac{\pi}{\gamma}$
Albania	3,005,055	0.4	1.47E-07
Algeria	137,764	6.5	4.74E-05
Angola	49,048	5.9	1.21E-04
Armenia	1,950,603	0.7	3.67E-07
Azerbaijan	299,633	4.6	1.52E-05
Bahrain	1,483,125	0.7	4.45E-07
Bangladesh	79,901	18.9	2.36E-04
Belarus	114,457	5.2	4.54E-05
Benin	186,505	1.4	7.67E-06
Bolivia	632,482	0.8	1.26E-06
Bosnia and Herzegovina	464,742	0.6	1.21E-06
Botswana	227,080	2.9	1.29E-05
Brunei Darussalam	850,676	1.3	1.49E-06
Cambodia	1,830,733	1.5	8.43E-07
Cameroon	143,023	5.4	3.76E-05
Chile	124,054	7.5	6.03E-05
Colombia	143,750	9.6	6.65E-05

Congo	278,170	2.9	1.03E-05
Costa Rica	1,653,647	1.5	9.23E-07
Côte d'Ivoire	106,739	5.3	4.92E-05
Croatia	1,432,495	1.1	7.85E-07
Cuba	469,583	2.9	6.25E-06
Democratic Republic of Congo	232,638	3.5	1.52E-05
Dominican Republic	517,231	2.4	4.56E-06
Ecuador	314,463	1.5	4.78E-06
Egypt	28,234	66.3	2.35E-03
El Salvador	1,723,826	1.1	6.39E-07
Eritrea	1,702,809	0.3	1.98E-07
Ethiopia	168,895	8.2	4.85E-05
Gabon	381,259	2.7	7.11E-06
Georgia	1,114,272	1.1	1.02E-06
Ghana	86,581	3.7	4.25E-05
Guatemala	1,103,412	1.8	1.59E-06
Haiti	4,539,976	0.2	4.93E-08
Honduras	1,377,647	0.7	4.88E-07
Iceland	7,033,125	0.2	2.49E-08
Iran (Islamic Republic of)	50,191	29.6	5.90E-04
Iraq	1,193,223	1.2	9.97E-07
Israel	126,570	15.9	1.26E-04

Jordan	521,852	1.4	2.75E-06
Kazakhstan	28,124	8.0	2.85E-04
Kenya	65,134	7.7	1.19E-04
Kuwait	689,106	3.1	4.45E-06
Kyrgyzstan	1,081,827	0.5	4.29E-07
Lebanon	645,246	2.4	3.79E-06
Libyan Arab Jamahiriya	439,760	10.8	2.46E-05
Macedonia	1,227,376	0.3	2.72E-07
(the former Yugoslavian Republic of)			
Malaysia	38,895	24.3	6.26E-04
Moldova (Republic of)	1,094,593	0.5	4.28E-07
Mongolia	518,939	0.4	6.90E-07
Morocco	129,194	12.8	9.90E-05
Mozambique	240,725	4.0	1.65E-05
Namibia	341,143	2.4	6.99E-06
Nepal	1,044,121	2.0	1.92E-06
New Zealand	286,904	2.8	9.70E-06
Nicaragua	2,318,621	0.5	2.05E-07
Nigeria	11,476	41.1	3.58E-03
Norway	298,449	3.2	1.09E-05
Oman	628,547	1.8	2.87E-06
Pakistan	32,047	27.7	8.64E-04

Panama	988,384	1.3	1.36E-06
Paraguay	1,962,853	0.7	3.61E-07
Peru	234,885	5.8	2.47E-05
Philippines	92,187	21.7	2.35E-04
Qatar	610,857	2.2	3.55E-06
Senegal	125,930	3.1	2.50E-05
Singapore	126,212	17.2	1.37E-04
Sri Lanka	257,471	5.4	2.09E-05
Sudan	56,201	10.3	1.83E-04
Switzerland	496,576	4.7	9.53E-06
Syrian Arab Republic	214,914	2.8	1.32E-05
Tajikistan	2,448,286	0.4	1.75E-07
Tanzania (United Republic of)	101,043	9.4	9.32E-05
Thailand	38,497	31.7	8.23E-04
Togo	588,063	0.7	1.23E-06
Trinidad and Tobago	269,998	0.9	3.18E-06
Tunisia	331,179	6.4	1.94E-05
Turkmenistan	139,271	1.4	9.90E-06
Ukraine	24,124	6.5	2.70E-04
United Arab Emirates	311,136	6.3	2.02E-05
Uruguay	1,192,344	2.0	1.69E-06
Uzbekistan	79,010	5.7	7.23E-05

Venezuela (Bolivarian Republic of)	62,088	10.1	1.63E-04
Vietnam	63,874	10.4	1.63E-04
Yemen	2,461,837	1.1	4.53E-07
Zambia	226,632	3.0	1.33E-05
Zimbabwe	106,028	1.5	1.37E-05

Bibliography

J.-C. Altamirano-Cabrera, M. Finus, and R. Dellink. Do Abatement Quotas Lead To More Successful Climate Coalitions? *The Manchester School*, 76(1):104–129, 2008.

K. J. Arrow. *Aspects of the theory of risk-bearing.* Yrjö Jahnssonin Säätiö, Helsinki, 1965. URL `http://worldcatlibraries.org/wcpa/oclc/853074`.

K. J. Arrow, M. L. Cropper, C. Gollier, B. Groom, G. Heal, R. G. Newell, W. Nordhaus, R. S. Pindyck, W. A. Pizer, P. R. Portney, T. Sterner, R. S. Tol, and M. L. Weitzman. How Should Benefits and Costs Be Discounted in an Intergenerational Context? The Views of an Expert Panel. Resources for the future, 2012. URL `http://www.rff.org/files/sharepoint/WorkImages/Download/RFF-DP-12-53.pdf`.

G. B. Asheim, C. B. Froyn, J. Hovi, and F. C. Menz. Regional versus global cooperation for climate control. *Journal of Environmental Economics and Management*, 51(1):93–109, 2006.

B. E. Bagozzi. The multifaceted nature of global climate change negotiations. *The Review of International Organizations*, 2014.

S. Barrett. Self-Enforcing International Environmental Agreements. *Oxford Economic Papers*, 46:878–894, 1994.

S. Barrett. The strategy of trade sanctions in international environmental agreements. *Resource and Energy Economics*, 19(4):345–361, 1997.

S. Barrett. The theory of international environmental agreements. In Karl-Göran Mäler and Jeffrey R. Vincent, editor, *Handbook of Environmental Economics : Economywide and International Environmental Issues*, volume Volume 3, pages 1457–1516. Elsevier, 2005. ISBN 1574-0099.

S. Barrett. Climate treaties and approaching catastrophes. *Journal of Environmental Economics and Management*, 66(2):235–250, 2013.

H. Benchekroun and A. Ray Chaudhuri. Cleaner Technologies and the Stability of International Environmental Agreements. *Journal of Public Economic Theory*, page n/a, 2014.

H. Benchekroun and N. van Long. Do Increases in Risk Mitigate the Tragedy of the Commons? *Strategic Behavior and the Environment*, 4(1):1–14, 2013.

H. Benchekroun, W. MARROUCH, and A. Ray Chaudhuri. Adaptation Effectiveness and Free-Riding Incentives in International Environmental Agreements. *SSRN Electronic Journal*, 2011.

F. Biermann, P. Pattberg, and H. van Asselt. The Fragmentation of Global Governance Architectures: A Framework for Analysis. *Global Environmental Politics*, 9(4):14–40, 2009.

T. Bietenhader and Y. Okamoto. Core Stability of Minimum Coloring Games. *Mathematics of Operations Research*, 31(2):418–431, 2006.

D. Bodansky. U.S. Climate Policy After Kyoto: Elements for Success. Carnegie Endowment for International Peace, 2002.

O. Bondareva. Theory of the core in the n-person game. *Vestnik Leningrad University, Math.*, 13:141–142, 1962.

F. Bosello, B. Buchner, and C. Carraro. Equity, Development, and Climate Change Control. *Journal of the European Economic Association*, 1(2-3): 601–611, 2003.

V. Bosetti, C. Carraro, E. de Cian, E. Massetti, and M. Tavoni. Incentives and stability of international climate coalitions: An integrated assessment. *Energy Policy*, 55:44–56, 2013.

Y. Bramoullé and N. Treich. Can Uncertainty Alleviate the Commons Problem? *Journal of the European Economic Association*, 7(5):1042–1067, 2009.

T. Bréchet, F. Gerard, and H. Tulkens. Efficiency vs. stability in climate coalitions: a conceptual and computational appraisal. *Energy Journal*, 32 (1):49–76, 2011.

M. Breton, K. Fredj, and G. Zaccour. International Cooperation, Coalitions Stability and Free Riding in a Game of Pollution Control. *The Manchester School*, 74(1):103–122, 2006. URL http://onlinelibrary.wiley.com/doi/10.1111/j.1467-9957.2006.00485.x/pdf.

M. Burke, J. Dykema, D. B. Lobell, E. Miguel, and S. Satyanath. Incorporating Climate Uncertainty into Estimates of Climate Change Impacts. *Review of Economics and Statistics*, 97(2):461–471, 2015.

A. Caparrós and J.-C. Péreau. Multilateral versus sequential negotiations over climate change. GREThA, 2015. URL http://www.ipp.csic.es/sites/default/files/IPP/documento_trabajo/pdf/CSIC-IPP-WP-2015_09_Caparros.pdf.

A. Capelli. Potentialanalyse der Windenergie bis 2050 anhand einer Monte-Carlo-Simulation. Bachelor thesis, Hochschule Karlsruhe Technik und Wirtschaft, Karlsruhe, 2014. URL http://www.project-core.info/core-wAssets/docs/Capelli_BA.pdf.

C. Carraro and D. Siniscalco. Strategies for the international protection of the environment. *Journal of Public Economics*, 52(3):309–328, 1993.

C. Carraro, J. Eyckmans, and M. Finus. Optimal transfers and participation decisions in international environmental agreements. *The Review of International Organizations*, 1(4):379–396, 2006.

P. Chander. The gamma-core and coalition formation. *International Journal of Game Theory*, 35(4):539–556, 2007.

P. Chander and H. Tulkens. A Core-Theoretic Solution for the Design of Cooperative Agreements on Transfrontier Pollution. *International Tax and Public Finance*, 2:279–293, 1995.

P. Chander and H. Tulkens. The Core of an Economy with Multilateral Environmental Externalities. *International Journal of Game Theory*, 26:379–401, 1997.

P. Chander and M. Wooders. Subgame Perfect Cooperation In An Extensive Game. Vanderbilt University, Department of Economics, 2010.

M. S.-Y. Chwe. Farsighted Coalitional Stability. *Journal of Economic Theory*, 63:299–325, 1994.

L. Clarke, K. Jiang, K. Akimoto, M. Babiker, G. Blanford, K. Fisher-Vanden, J.-C. Hourcade, V. Krey, E. Kriegler, A. Löschel, D. McCollum, S. Paltsev, S. Rose, P. R. Shukla, M. Tavoni, van der Zwaan, Bob, and van Vuuren, Detlef P. Assessing Transformation Pathways. In O. Edenhofer, R. Pichs-Madruga, Y. Sokona, E. Farahani, S. Kadner, K. Seyboth, A. Adler, I. Baum, S. Brunner, P. Eickemeier, B. Kriemann, J. Savolainen, S. Schlömer, C. v. Stechow, and T. Zwickel, editors, *Climate Change 2014: Mitigation of Climate Change. Working group III Contribution to the Fifth Assessment Report of the Intergovernmental Panel on Climate Change*. Cambridge University Press, Cambridge, United Kingdom, and New York, NY, USA, 2015. ISBN 978-1-107-05821-7. URL `http://ipcc.ch/pdf/assessment-report/ar5/wg3/ipcc_wg3_ar5_chapter6.pdf`.

M. Collins, R. Knutti, J. M. Arblaster, J.-L. Dufresne, T. Fichefet, P. Friedlingstein, X. Gao, W. J. Gutowski, T. Johns, G. Krinner, M. E. Shongwe, C. Tebaldi, A. J. Weaver, and M. Wehner. Long-term Climate Change: Projections, Commitments and Irreversibility. In T. F. Stocker, D. Qin, G.-K. Plattner, M. Tignor, S. K. Allen, J. Boschung, A. Nauels, Y. Xia, V. Bex, and P. M. Midgley, editors, *Climate Change 2013 - The Physical Science Basis. Contribution of Working Group I to the Fifth Assessment Report of the Intergovernmental Panel on Climate Change*, pages 1029–1136. Cambridge University Press, Cambridge, 2013. ISBN 9781107415324.

S. Currarini and M. Marini. A Sequential Approach to the Characteristic Function and the Core in Games with Externalities. In M. R. Sertel and S. Koray, editors, *Advances in Economic Design*, Studies in Economic Design, pages 233–249. Springer Berlin Heidelberg, Berlin, Heidelberg, 2003. ISBN 3662056119. URL http://mpra.ub.uni-muenchen.de/1689/.

C. D'Aspremont, A. Jacquemin, J. J. Gabszewicz, and J. A. Weymark. On the Stability of Collusive Price Leadership. *The Canadian Journal of Economics / Revue canadienne d'Economique*, 16(1):17–25, 1983. URL http://www.jstor.org/stable/134972.

A. de Zeeuw. Dynamic effects on the stability of international environmental agreements. *Journal of Environmental Economics and Management*, 55 (2):163–174, 2008.

R. Dellink. Drivers of stability of climate coalitions in the STACO model. *Climate Change Economics*, 02(02):105–128, 2011.

R. Dellink and M. Finus. Uncertainty and climate treaties: Does ignorance pay? *Resource and Energy Economics*, 34(4):565–584, 2012.

R. Dellink, M. Finus, and N. Olieman. The stability likelihood of an international climate agreement. *Environmental and Resource Economics*, 39 (4):357–377, 2008.

X. Deng, T. Ibaraki, H. Nagamochi, and W. Zang. Totally balanced combinatorial optimization games. *Mathematical Programming*, 87(3):441–452, 2000.

S. Dessai. The climate regime from The Hague to Marrakech: Saving or sinking the Kyoto Protocol? Tyndall Centre for Climate Change Research, 2001. URL `http://www.tyndall.ac.uk/content/climate-regime-hague-marrakech-saving-or-sinking-kyoto-protocol`.

E. Diamantoudi and E. S. Sartzetakis. International Environmental Agreements - The Role Of Foresight. Université catholique de Louvain, Center for Operations Research and Econometrics (CORE), 2002.

E. Diamantoudi and E. S. Sartzetakis. Stable International Environmental Agreements: An Analytical Approach. *Journal of Public Economic Theory*, 8(2):247–263, 2006.

T. Driessen, D. Hou, and A. Lardon. Stackelberg oligopoly TU-games: characterization of the core and 1-concavity of the dual game. University of St. Etienne, France, 2011.

M. Drupp, M. Freeman, B. Groom, and F. Nesje. Discounting disentangled: an expert survey on the determinants of the long-term social discount rate. Grantham Research Institute on Climate Change and the Environment, 2015. URL `http://www.lse.ac.uk/GranthamInstitute/wp-content/uploads/2015/06/Working-Paper-172-Drupp-et-al.pdf`.

V. Duscha, J. Kersting, S. Peterson, J. Schleich, and M. Weitzel. Technological development of low-carbon power technology and the stability of international climate cooperation, 2016. URL `http://www.project-`

core.info/core-wAssets/docs/Technological-development-stability.pdf.

R. Eckersley. Moving Forward in the Climate Negotiations: Multilateralism or Minilateralism? *Global Environmental Politics*, 12(2):24–42, 2012.

T. Eichner and R. Pethig. Self-enforcing international environmental agreements and trade: taxes versus caps. *Oxford Economic Papers*, 67(4):897–917, 2015.

J. Eyckmans. On the farsighted stability of the Kyoto Protocol. Katholieke Universiteit Leuven, Centrum voor Economische Studiën, Energy, Transport and Environment, 2001.

J. Eyckmans and M. Finus. An Almost Ideal Sharing Scheme for Coalition Games with Externalities. Katholieke Universiteit Leuven, 2004. URL http://feb.kuleuven.be/drc/Economics/misc/ete_workingpapers/ete-wp-2004-14.pdf.

J. Eyckmans and H. Tulkens. Simulating coalitionally stable burden sharing agreements for the climate change problem. *Resource and Energy Economics*, 25:299–327, 2003.

M. Finus. *Game theory and international environmental cooperation.* New horizons in environmental economics. Edward Elgar, Cheltenman, U.K, Northampton, Mass, 2001. ISBN 9781840644081.

M. Finus. Stability and design of international environmental agreements: the case of transboundary pollution. In H. Folmer and T. Tietenberg, editors, *The international yearbook of environmental and resource economics 2003/2004*, New horizons in environmental economics, pages 82–158. Edward Elgar, Cheltenham, 2003. ISBN 9781843762133.

M. Finus and P. Pintassilgo. The role of uncertainty and learning for the success of international climate agreements. *Journal of Public Economics*, 103:29–43, 2013.

M. Finus and D. Rübbelke. Public Good Provision and Ancillary Benefits: The Case of Climate Agreements. *Environmental and Resource Economics*, 56(2):211–226, 2013.

M. Finus and B. Rundshagen. Membership rules and stability of coalition structures in positive externality games. *Social Choice and Welfare*, 32 (3):389–406, 2009. URL `http://link.springer.com/content/pdf/10.1007%2Fs00355-008-0330-z.pdf`.

M. Finus, J.-C. Altamirano-Cabrera, and E. C. van Ierland. The Effect of Membership Rules and Voting Schemes on the Success of International Climate Agreements. *Public Choice*, 125(1/2):95–127, 2005. URL `http://www.jstor.org/stable/30026656?origin=JSTOR-pdf`.

F. N. Fritsch and R. E. Carlson. Monotone Piecewise Cubic Interpolation. *SIAM Journal on Numerical Analysis*, 17(2):238–246, 1980.

A. Gerber and P. C. Wichardt. Providing public goods in the absence of strong institutions. *Journal of Public Economics*, 93(3–4):429–439, 2009.

M. Germain, P. Toint, H. Tulkens, and A. de Zeeuw. Transfers to sustain dynamic core-theoretic cooperation in international stock pollutant control. *Journal of Economic Dynamics and Control*, 28(1):79–99, 2003.

C. Gollier and J. K. Hammitt. The Long-Run Discount Rate Controversy. *Annual Review of Resource Economics*, 6(1):273–295, 2014.

S. Grant and J. Quiggin. Climate change and the precautionary principle. In J. Quiggin, D. Adamson, and D. Quiggin, editors, *Carbon pricing: early experiences and future prospects*, pages 167–178. Edward Elgar Publishing, 2014. ISBN 9781782547747.

M. Grasso and T. Roberts. A compromise to break the climate impasse. *Nature Climate Change*, 4(7):543–549, 2014.

A. Hagen and K. Eisenack. International environmental agreements with asymmetric countries: climate clubs vs. global cooperation, 2015. URL `http://www.feem.it/userfiles/attach/20156221022324NDL2015-058.pdf`.

G. Hardin. The Tragedy of the Commons. *Science*, 162(3859):1243–1248, 1968. URL `http://science.sciencemag.org/content/sci/162/3859/1243.full.pdf`.

B. Harstad. Climate Contracts: A Game of Emissions, Investments, Negotiations, and Renegotiations. *The Review of Economic Studies*, 79(4): 1527–1557, 2012. URL `http://restud.oxfordjournals.org/content/79/4/1527.full`.

S. Hart and M. Kurz. Endogenous Formation of Coalitions. *Econometrica*, 51(4):1047–1064, 1983.

C. Helm. On the existence of a cooperative solution for a coalitional game with externalities. *International Journal of Game Theory*, 30:141–146, 2001.

C. Helm and R. C. Schmidt. Climate cooperation with technology investments and border carbon adjustment. *European Economic Review*, 75: 112–130, 2015.

M. Hjerpe and N. Nasiritousi. Views on alternative forums for effectively tackling climate change. *Nature Climate Change*, 5(9):864–867, 2015.

M. Hoel and K. Schneider. Incentives to participate in an international environmental agreement. *Environmental and Resource Economics*, 9:153–170, 1997.

F. Hong and L. Karp. International Environmental Agreements with Endogenous or Exogenous Risk. *Journal of the Association of Environmental and Resource Economists*, 1(3):365–394, 2014.

J. Hovi, H. Ward, and F. Grundig. Hope or Despair? Formal Models of Climate Cooperation. *Environmental and Resource Economics*, 62(4):665–688, 2015.

J. Hovi, D. F. Sprinz, H. Sælen, and A. Underdal. Climate change mitigation: a role for climate clubs? *Palgrave Communications*, 2, 2016.

International Energy Agency. Climate Policy Uncertainty and Investment Risk, 2007. URL `https://www.iea.org/publications/freepublications/publication/Climate_Policy_Uncertainty.pdf`.

International Energy Agency. *World Energy Outlook 2008*. OECD Publishing, Paris, 2008. ISBN 9789264045613.

International Energy Agency. *World Energy Outlook 2013*. OECD Publishing, Paris, 2013. ISBN 978-92-64-20130-9.

International Energy Agency. Technology Roadmap - Solar Photovoltaic Energy: 2014 edition, 2014a. URL `http://www.iea.org/media/freepublications/technologyroadmaps/solar/TechnologyRoadmapSolarPhotovoltaicEnergy_2014edition.pdf`.

International Energy Agency. *World Energy Outlook 2014*. OECD Publishing, Paris, 2014b. ISBN 978-92-64-20804-9.

International Energy Agency. Energy and Climate Change - World Energy Outlook Special Report, 2015. URL `https://www.iea.org/publications/freepublications/publication/WEO2015SpecialReportonEnergyandClimateChange.pdf`.

IPCC. Summary for Policymakers. In T. F. Stocker, D. Qin, G.-K. Plattner, M. Tignor, S. K. Allen, J. Boschung, A. Nauels, Y. Xia, V. Bex, and P. M. Midgley, editors, *Climate Change 2013 - The Physical Science Basis. Contribution of Working Group I to the Fifth Assessment Report of the Intergovernmental Panel on Climate Change*. Cambridge University Press, Cambridge, 2013. ISBN 9781107415324.

IPCC. Summary for Policymakers. In C. B. Field, V. R. Barros, D. J. Dokken, K. J. Mach, M. D. Mastrandrea, T. E. Bilir, M. Chatterjee, K. L. Ebi, Y. O. Estrada, R. C. Genova, B. Girma, E. S. Kissel, A. N. Levy, S. MacCracken, P. R. Mastrandrea, and L. L. White, editors, *Climate Change 2014: Impacts, Adaptation, and Vulnerability. Part A: Global and Sectoral Aspects. Contribution of Working Group II to the Fifth Assessment Report of the Intergovernmental Panel on Climate Change*, pages 1–32. Cambridge University Press, Cambridge, United Kingdom, and New York, NY, USA, 2014a. URL `https://ipcc-wg2.gov/AR5/images/uploads/WG2AR5_SPM_FINAL.pdf`.

IPCC. Summary for Policymakers. In O. Edenhofer, R. Pichs-Madruga, Y. Sokona, E. Farahani, S. Kadner, K. Seyboth, A. Adler, I. Baum, S. Brunner, P. Eickemeier, B. Kriemann, J. Savolainen, S. Schlömer, C. von Stechow, T. Zwickel, and J. C. Minx, editors, *Climate Change 2014: Mitigation of Climate Change. Contribution of Working Group III to the Fifth Assessment Report of the Intergovernmental Panel on Climate Change*. Cambridge University Press, Cambridge, United Kingdom, and New York, NY, USA, 2014b.

N. Jaspers and R. Falkner. International Trade, the Environment, and Climate Change. In R. Falkner, editor, *The handbook of global climate and environment policy*, pages 412–427. John Wiley & Sons Inc, Chichester, West Sussex, Malden, MA, 2013. ISBN 978-0-470-67324-9.

S. G. Johnson. The NLopt nonlinear-optimization package, 2014. URL http://ab-initio.mit.edu/nlopt.

A. J. Jordan, D. Huitema, M. Hildén, H. van Asselt, T. J. Rayner, J. J. Schoenefeld, J. Tosun, J. Forster, and E. L. Boasson. Emergence of polycentric climate governance and its future prospects. *Nature Climate Change*, 2015.

L. Karp and L. Simon. Participation games and international environmental agreements: A non-parametric model. *Journal of Environmental Economics and Management*, 65(2):326–344, 2013.

J. Kersting. Cooperation of climate clubs, 2015. URL http://www.project-core.info/core-wAssets/docs/Kersting_2015_Cooperation-of-climate-clubs.pdf.

J. Kersting. Stability of global climate cooperation under uncertainty. *Strategic Behavior and the Environment*, Forthcoming.

J. Kersting, V. Duscha, and M. Weitzel. Cooperation on Climate Change under Economic Linkages: How the Inclusion of Macroeconomic Effects Affects Stability of a Global Climate Coalition. *The Energy Journal*, 38 (4), 2017.

E. King. Tempers fray as Russia blocks UN climate talks. *Climate Home*, 2013, 07/06/2013. URL http://www.climatechangenews.com/2013/06/07/tempers-fray-as-russia-blocks-un-climate-talks/.

A. Kitous, P. Criqui, E. Bellevrat, and B. Chateau. Transformation Patterns of the Worldwide Energy System - Scenarios for the Century with the POLES Model. *The Energy Journal*, 31(01), 2010.

B. S. Koelbl, M. A. van Den Broek, B. J. van Ruijven, A. Faaij, and van Vuuren, D. P. Uncertainty in the deployment of Carbon Capture and Storage

(CCS): A sensitivity analysis to techno-economic parameter uncertainty. *International Journal of Greenhouse Gas Control*, 27:81–102, 2014.

C. Kolstad and A. Ulph. Uncertainty, Learning and Heterogeneity in International Environmental Agreements. *Environmental and Resource Economics*, 50(3):389–403, 2011.

U. Kornek, K. Lessmann, and H. Tulkens. Transferable and non transferable utility implementations of coalitional stability in integrated assessment models. Center for Operation Research and Econometrics (CORE) - Université Catholique de Louvain, 2014. URL `http://www.uclouvain.be/cps/ucl/doc/core/documents/coredp2014_35web.pdf`.

V. Krey and K. Riahi. Implications of delayed participation and technology failure for the feasibility, costs, and likelihood of staying below temperature targets—Greenhouse gas mitigation scenarios for the 21st century. *Energy Economics*, 31:S94–S106, 2009.

E. Kriegler, J. P. Weyant, G. J. Blanford, V. Krey, L. Clarke, J. Edmonds, A. Fawcett, G. Luderer, K. Riahi, R. Richels, S. K. Rose, M. Tavoni, and van Vuuren, Detlef P. The role of technology for achieving climate policy objectives: Overview of the EMF 27 study on global technology and climate policy strategies. *Climatic Change*, 123(3-4):353–367, 2014.

S. Kucherenko and Y. Sytsko. Application of Deterministic Low-Discrepancy Sequences in Global Optimization. *Computational Optimization and Applications*, 30(3):297–318, 2005.

M. Lämmle. Assessment of the global potential for CO2 mitigation of carbon capture and storage (CCS) until 2050. Diploma thesis, Karlsruhe Institute of Technology, Karlsruhe, 2012. URL `http://www.project-core.info/core-wAssets/docs/Diplomarbeit-Manuel-Laemmle-Final.pdf`.

I. Lazkano, W. MARROUCH, and B. Nkuiya. Adaptation to climate change: How does heterogeneity in adaptation costs affect climate coalitions? *Environment and Development Economics*, pages 1–27, 2016.

M. Leimbach, N. Bauer, L. Baumstark, and O. Edenhofer. Mitigation Costs in a Globalized World: Climate Policy Analysis with REMIND-R. *Environmental Modeling & Assessment*, 15(3):155–173, 2010.

K. Lessmann and O. Edenhofer. Research cooperation and international standards in a model of coalition stability. *Resource and Energy Economics*, 33(1):36–54, 2011.

K. Lessmann, R. Marschinski, and O. Edenhofer. The effects of tariffs on coalition formation in a dynamic global warming game. *Economic Modelling*, 26(3):641–649, 2009.

K. Lessmann, U. Kornek, V. Bosetti, R. Dellink, J. Emmerling, J. Eyckmans, M. Nagashima, H.-P. Weikard, and Z. Yang. The Stability and Effectiveness of Climate Coalitions: A comparative analysis of multiple integrated assessment models. *Environmental and Resource Economics*, 62(4):811–836, 2015. URL https://lirias.kuleuven.be/bitstream/123456789/487973/1/Lessmann-etal-2015_postprint.pdf.

S. Lewandowsky, J. S. Risbey, M. Smithson, B. R. Newell, and J. Hunter. Scientific uncertainty and climate change: Part I. Uncertainty and unabated emissions. *Climatic Change*, 124(1-2):21–37, 2014.

Like-Minded Developing Countries in Climate Change. Submission on Elements of the 2015 Agreed Outcome, 2014. URL http://unfccc.int/files/documentation/submissions_from_parties/adp/application/pdf/adp_lmdc_ws1_20140309.pdf.

M. Lüken, O. Edenhofer, B. Knopf, M. Leimbach, G. Luderer, and N. Bauer. The role of technological availability for the distributive impacts of climate change mitigation policy. *Energy Policy*, 39(10):6030–6039, 2011.

D. McEvoy. Enforcing compliance with international environmental agreements using a deposit-refund system. *International Environmental Agreements: Politics, Law and Economics*, 13(4):481–496, 2013. URL http://dx.doi.org/10.1007/s10784-013-9209-2.

M. Meinshausen, S. J. Smith, K. Calvin, J. S. Daniel, Kainuma, M. L. T., J.-F. Lamarque, K. Matsumoto, S. A. Montzka, Raper, S. C. B., K. Riahi, A. Thomson, Velders, G. J. M., and D. van Vuuren. The RCP greenhouse gas concentrations and their extensions from 1765 to 2300. *Climatic Change*, 109(1-2):213–241, 2011.

R. Morel and I. Shishlov. Ex-post evaluation of the Kyoto Protocol: Four key lessons for the 2015 Paris Agreement. cdc climat research, 2014. URL http://www.cdcclimat.com/IMG/pdf/14-05_climate_report_no44_-_analysis_of_the_kp-2.pdf.

J. Morris, S. Paltsev, and J. Reilly. Marginal Abatement Costs and Marginal Welfare Costs for Greenhouse Gas Emissions Reductions: Results from the EPPA Model. *Environmental Modeling & Assessment*, 17(4):325–336, 2012.

S.-I. Na and H. S. Shin. International environmental agreements under uncertainty. *Oxford Economic Papers*, 50:173–185, 1998.

M. Nagashima, R. Dellink, E. van Ierland, and H.-P. Weikard. Stability of international climate coalitions — A comparison of transfer schemes. *Ecological Economics*, 68(5):1476–1487, 2009.

M. Naím. Minilateralism, 2009. URL http://www.foreignpolicy.com/articles/2009/06/18/minilateralism.

B. Narayanan, A. Aguiar, and R. McDougall. Global Trade, Assistance, and Production: The GTAP 8 Data Base. Center for Global Trade Analysis, Purdue University, 2012. URL https://www.gtap.agecon.purdue.edu/databases/v8/v8_doco.asp.

W. Nordhaus. Climate Clubs: Overcoming Free-riding in International Climate Policy. *American Economic Review*, 105(4):1339–1370, 2015.

W. D. Nordhaus. Economic aspects of global warming in a post-Copenhagen environment. *Proceedings of the National Academy of Sciences*, 107(26): 11721–11726, 2010.

OECD. *OECD Environmental Outlook to 2050: The Consequences of Inaction*. OECD environmental outlook. OECD Publishing, Paris, 2012. ISBN 9789264122161.

D. Osmani and R. Tol. Toward Farsightedly Stable International Environmental Agreements. *Journal of Public Economic Theory*, 11(3):455–492, 2009.

B. Peleg and P. Sudhölter. *Introduction to the Theory of Cooperative Games*. Theory and decision library: Game theory, mathematical programming, and operations research. Springer, 2007. ISBN 9783540729440.

S. Peterson and M. Weitzel. Reaching a climate agreement: Compensating for energy market effects of climate policy. *Climate Policy*, pages 1–17, 2015.

M. Powell. The BOBYQA algorithm for bound constrained optimization without derivatives. Department of Applied Mathematics and Theoretical Physics, 2009. URL `http://www.damtp.cam.ac.uk/user/na/NA_papers/NA2009_06.pdf`.

J. W. Pratt. Risk Aversion in the Small and in the Large. *Econometrica*, 32 (1/2):122–136, 1964.

D. Ray and R. Vohra. Coalitional Power and Public Goods. *Journal of Political Economy*, 109(6):1355–1384, 2001.

L. Renz. Abschätzung des CO2-Emissionsminderungspotentials der Photovoltaik bis 2050. Diploma thesis, Karlsruhe Institute of Technology, Karlsruhe, 2012. URL http://www.project-core.info/core-wAssets/docs/Diplomarbeit-Lea-Renz-final.pdf.

M. Rogna. Cooperative Game Theory Applied to IEAs: A Comparison of Solution Concepts. *Journal of Economic Surveys*, 2016. URL http://onlinelibrary.wiley.com/doi/10.1111/joes.12157/full.

R. C. Schmidt. Dynamic cooperation with tipping points in the climate system, 2015. URL http://repec.bdpems.de/repec/bdp/wpaper/pdf/WP_2015-18.pdf.

L. S. Shapley. On balanced sets and cores. *Naval Research Logistics Quarterly*, 14(4):453–460, 1967.

L. S. Shapley and M. Shubik. On Market Games. *Journal of Economic Theory*, 1:9–25, 1969.

Z. Shaw. G20 Leaders' Conclusions on Climate Change, 2008-2010. G20 Research Group, 2011. URL http://www.g20.utoronto.ca/analysis/conclusions/climatechange-1.pdf.

R. Smead, R. L. Sandler, P. Forber, and J. Basl. A bargaining game analysis of international climate negotiations. *Nature Climate Change*, 4(6):442–445, 2014.

J. Suijs, P. Borm, A. D. Wargenaere, and S. Tijs. Cooperative game with stochastic payoffs. *European Journal of Operational Research*, 113:193–205, 1999.

J. Timmer, P. Borm, and S. Tijs. Convexity in stochastic cooperative situations. *International Game Theory Review*, 07(01):25–42, 2005.

H. Tulkens. Cooperation versus Free-Riding in International Environmental Affairs: Two Approaches. In N. D. Hanley and H. Folmer, editors, *Game theory and the environment*, pages 30–44. Elgar, Cheltenham, UK, 1998. ISBN 978 1 85898 415 5.

H. Tulkens. Internal vs. core stability in the environmental externality game: A reconciliation, 2014. URL http://hdl.handle.net/2078.1/152573.

UNFCCC. Draft rules of procedure: FCCC/CP/1996/2, 1996. URL http://unfccc.int/resource/docs/cop2/02.pdf.

UNFCCC. Kyoto Protocol, 1998. URL http://unfccc.int/resource/docs/convkp/kpeng.pdf.

UNFCCC. Decision 1/CP.13 - Bali Action Plan, 2007. URL http://unfccc.int/resource/docs/2007/cop13/eng/06a01.pdf#page=3.

UNFCCC. Decision 2/CP.15 - Copenhagen Accord, 2009. URL http://unfccc.int/resource/docs/2009/cop15/eng/11a01.pdf.

UNFCCC. Decision 1/CP.17 - Establishment of an Ad Hoc Working Group on the Durban Platform for Enhanced Action, 2011. URL http://unfccc.int/resource/docs/2011/cop17/eng/09a01.pdf.

UNFCCC. Warsaw International Mechanism for Loss and Damage associated with Climate Change Impacts, 2013. URL http://unfccc.int/adaptation/workstreams/loss_and_damage/items/8134.php.

UNFCCC. Paris Agreement, 2015a. URL http://unfccc.int/files/meetings/paris_nov_2015/application/pdf/paris_agreement_english_.pdf.

UNFCCC. Decision 1/CP.21 - Adoption of the Paris Agreement, 2015b. URL http://unfccc.int/resource/docs/2015/cop21/eng/10a01.pdf.

UNFCCC. INDC Portal, 2016a. URL http://unfccc.int/focus/indc_portal/items/8766.php.

UNFCCC. Aggregate effect of the intended nationally determined contributions: an update, 2016b. URL http://unfccc.int/resource/docs/2016/cop22/eng/02.pdf.

UNFCCC. Parties to the Convention and Observer States, 2016c. URL http://unfccc.int/parties_and_observers/parties/items/2352.php.

United Nations. Framework Convention on Climate Change: UNFCCC, 1992. URL http://unfccc.int/files/essential_background/background_publications_htmlpdf/application/pdf/conveng.pdf.

United Nations, Department of Economic and Social Affairs, Population Devision. World Population to 2300, 2004. URL http://www.un.org/esa/population/publications/longrange2/WorldPop2300final.pdf.

United Nations, Department of Economic and Social Affairs, Population Devision. World Population Prospects: The 2012 Revision, 2012. URL http://esa.un.org/wpp/.

U.S. Energy Information Administration. Japan - International energy data and analysis, 2015. URL https://www.eia.gov/beta/international/analysis_includes/countries_long/Japan/japan.pdf.

D. Victor. Plan B for Copenhagen. *Nature*, 461(7262):342–344, 2009.

A. Vihma. Climate of Consensus: Managing Decision Making in the UN Climate Change Negotiations. *Review of European, Comparative & International Environmental Law*, 24(1):58–68, 2015. URL http://onlinelibrary.wiley.com/doi/10.1111/reel.12093/full.

C. von Hirschhausen, J. Herold, and P.-Y. Oei. How a Low Carbon Innovation Can Fail–Tales from a Lost Decade for Carbon Capture, Transport, and Sequestration (CCTS). *Economics of Energy & Environmental Policy*, 1(2), 2012.

J. Watson, F. Kern, and N. Markusson. Resolving or managing uncertainties for carbon capture and storage: Lessons from historical analogues. *Technological Forecasting and Social Change*, 81:192–204, 2014.

L. Weischer, J. Morgan, and M. Patel. Climate Clubs: Can Small Groups of Countries make a Big Difference in Addressing Climate Change? *Review of European Community & International Environmental Law*, 21(3):177–192, 2012.

M. Weitzel. Including renewable electricity generation and CCS into the DART model, 2010. URL `https://www.ifw-members.ifw-kiel.de/publications/including-renewable-electricity-generation-and-ccs-into-the-dart-model/DART-renewables-ccs.pdf`.

M. Weitzel. The role of uncertainty in future costs of key CO2 abatement technologies: A sensitivity analysis with a global computable general equilibrium model. *Mitigation and Adaptation Strategies for Global Change*, 2015.

M. Weitzel. Who gains from technological advancement? The role of policy design when cost development for key abatement technologies is uncertain. *Environmental Economics and Policy Studies*, 2016.

M. Weitzel, M. Hübler, and S. Peterson. Fair, optimal or detrimental? Environmental vs. strategic use of border carbon adjustment. *Energy Economics*, 34:198–207, 2012.

White House. Text of a Letter from the President to Senators Hagel, Helms, Craig, and Roberts, 2001. URL `http://georgewbush-whitehouse.archives.gov/news/releases/2001/03/20010314.html`.

O. Widerberg and P. Pattberg. International Cooperative Initiatives in Global Climate Governance: Raising the Ambition Level or Delegitimizing the UNFCCC? *Global Policy*, 6(1):45–56, 2015.

O. Widerberg and D. E. Stenson. Climate clubs and the UNFCCC: Complement, bypass or conflict? Forum for Reforms, Entrepreneurship and Sustainability, 2013.

World Bank. World Development Indicators 2014, 2014. URL `https://openknowledge.worldbank.org/handle/10986/18237`.